Revolutionary War Veterans
Chenango County, New York
Volume I
A–B
001 – 154

"CHENANGO PIONEERS"
WOODCARVING BY THE AUTHOR

Nelson B. Tiffany

SPONSORED BY
CHENANGO COUNTY HISTORICAL SOCIETY
IN COOPERATION WITH
CHENANGO COUNTY HISTORIAN
45 REXFORD STREET
NORWICH, NEW YORK 13815
PHONE (607) 334-9227

IN CELEBRATION OF
CHENANGO COUNTY'S BICENTENNIAL
1798–1998

HERITAGE BOOKS
2012

HERITAGE BOOKS
AN IMPRINT OF HERITAGE BOOKS, INC.

Books, CDs, and more—Worldwide

For our listing of thousands of titles see our website at
www.HeritageBooks.com

Published 2012 by
HERITAGE BOOKS, INC.
Publishing Division
100 Railroad Ave. #104
Westminster, Maryland 21157

Copyright © 1998 Nelson B. Tiffany
Chenango County Historical Society

Other Heritage Books by the author:

Revolutionary War Veterans, Chenango County, New York, Volume I: A–B
Revolutionary War Veterans, Chenango County, New York, Volume II: C–H
Revolutionary War Veterans, Chenango County, New York, Volume III: I–R
Revolutionary War Veterans, Chenango County, New York, Volume IV: S–Z

All rights reserved. No part of this book may be reproduced or transmitted in any form or by any means, electronic or mechanical, including photocopying, recording or by any information storage and retrieval system without written permission from the author, except for the inclusion of brief quotations in a review.

International Standard Book Numbers
Paperbound: 978-0-7884-0913-4
Clothbound: 978-0-7884-9181-8

REVOLUTIONARY WAR VETERANS
CHENANGO COUNTY-NEW YORK

TABLE OF CONTENTS

ACKNOWLEDGEMENTS	A
INTRODUCTION	B
CHENANGO COUNTY FORMATION	C
VETERANS PICTURES	D
CHENANGO COUNTY BURIAL GROUNDS	E
PENSION LEGISLATION	F
REVOLUTIONARY WAR BATTLES	G
CHENANGO COUNTY VETERANS	H
OTHER POSSIBLE VETERANS	I
VETERAN PAGE DESCRIPTION	J
VETERANS RECORDS	
FAMILY NAME INDEX	INDEX

REVOLUTIONARY WAR VETERANS
CHENANGO COUNTY-NEW YORK

ACKNOWLEDGEMENTS

NELSON B. TIFFANY
author
Member of the Chenango County Historical Society;
Retiree of Norwich Eaton Pharmaceuticals, Inc.,
a Procter & Gamble Company; Genealogist;

Has deep Chenango County ancestral roots as evidenced by having ten of his grandfathers included in this publication as Revolutionary War Veterans.

MRS. MAE SMITH
Chenango County Historian
Emeritus

The Chenango County Historian's office gave its total support. Mrs. Smith was responsible for initiating the project and she along with her Historical Research Assistant, Mrs Dale Green, aided during the gathering process.

ACKNOWLEDGEMENTS

D.A.R. FILES

Initial veteran identification and data collection was through the use of information collected by a group of dedicated Chenango County D.A.R. members. Over the passage of years their files had become part of the records contained in the Chenango County Historian's Office. All subsequent information collected for this book was added to the DAR data and stored in a folder for each veteran.

CEMETERY RECORDS

Nearly all known burial grounds in Chenango County have had tombstone readings taken over the past 50 to 60 years. Considerable work was done by the Chenango County DAR group in the 1930's. Thomas Lloyd, a local historian, spent the better part of eleven years in the mapping of abandoned Chenango County cemeteries. Various other people have also contributed to the recordings.

PENSION RECORDS

Access to pension records was achieved through the use of microfilm located at the Onondaga County Public Library in Syracuse, New York. In order to maximize the use of time on these trips, the writer was usually accompanied by two others. Several different people were involved and among those making the trips were Mrs. Dale Green, Mrs. Sarah (Sally) Blenis, Mrs. Mae Smith, Mrs. Carol Cruttenden and Ms. Sandy Davies.

FAMILY FOLDERS

Thanks to the many individuals who have contributed to the extensive family files located in The Chenango County Historian's Office and The Otis A. Thompson History Room of The Guernsey Memorial Library in Norwich, New York.

HISTORIANS

Thanks to various Chenango County town historians for their very valuable data contributions. Numerous town and county historians throughout New York State aided in finding burial locations for the veterans and their wives. Special thanks to The Cortland Historical Society who provided access to the publication "Genealogical Abstracts of Revolutionary War Pension Files"

REVOLUTIONARY WAR VETERANS
CHENANGO COUNTY-NEW YORK

ACKNOWLEDGEMENTS

INDIVIDUALS

The support and help of my wife, Patricia Bryant Tiffany, cannot be overstated. She spent many, many hours in libraries, cemetery trips, and data checking. Others of note are Shirley Hoag Edwards who spent hours on editing, Frank White for cemetery trips, and Sally Child Chirlin who was involved in computer file conversion.

GENEALOGY SOURCE LOCATIONS USED

Chenango County Historian's Office, Norwich, New York
The Otis A. Thompson History Room of The Guernsey Memorial Library, Norwich, New York
Chenango County Surrogate Court Office, Norwich, New York
Church of Jesus Christ of Latter Day Saints Norwich, New York Branch
Onondaga County Public Library, Syracuse, New York
New York State Historical Association Library, Cooperstown, New York
New York State Library, Albany, New York
Cortland County Historical Society, Cortland, New York

GENERAL PUBLICATIONS

DAR Patriot Index, National Society, Daughters Of The American Revolution - 1967
DAR Patriot Index Volume II, National Society, Daughters of the American Revolution - 1980
History of Chenango County by James H. Smith - 1880
Index of Revolutionary War Pension Applications, National Genealogical Society - 1976
Year Book of the Society of Sons of the Revolution in the State of New York - 1899
Abstract of Graves of Revolutionary War Patriots, by Patricia Law Hatcher - 1987
Genealogical Abstracts of Revolutionary War Pension Files, by Virgil D. White - 1990

GRANTS

Procter & Gamble Company Volunteer Support grant
Production and monetary support from The Chenango County Historical Society

REVOLUTIONARY WAR VETERANS
CHENANGO COUNTY-NEW YORK

INTRODUCTION

The official date given The American Revolutionary War is from April 19, 1775 to November 3, 1783, about 8 1/2 years.

In October 1987 Mrs. Mae Smith, Chenango County Historian approached me regarding the possibility of researching the Revolutionary War Veterans who came to Chenango County during its pioneer period. The first step was the submission of sample documents on October 13, 1987, covering three of the Veterans involved. The general layout was accepted and over time evolved to it's present form.

Initial information was taken from files which had been generated by the Daughters of The American Revolution organization at an earlier time and subsequently housed at The Chenango County Historical Society's office. The next step was the generation of a list of possible Veterans based on Chenango County Cemetery readings. The possible list, the DAR Patriot listing and The Revolutionary Pension files were checked for possible matches. Following this, a new publication covering a pension file extraction of genealogy and residency data, was found to be available. This step added about 180 more Veterans to the base. As the Veterans were identified various sources were used to build on the family information. These sources included Surrogate records, family genealogy folders, family genealogies, cemetery records, historical publications and various historians and individuals. A search for the burial place of the Veterans and their wives was undertaken in order to identify their final resting place and record tombstone readings.

Thousands of man hours have been utilized in this project. Gratification has been felt many times through the satisfaction of individual inquiries and knowing that the recording of the data can resist its loss as time goes ever onward.

The accuracy of the information contained herein is as accurate as the source it is generated from. All the above sources were utilized and are considered acceptable in varying degrees. It is understood that some genealogies, printed or hand written, can be in error but it is believed that the error rate contained herein to be of a minimal nature.

INTRODUCTION

Perhaps the material contained within this book can be an inspiration for the generation of a national computer file that would contain a similar data base for all the known Revolutionary War Veterans. It could be built, updated and accessed through any computer. What a memorial to all those who served!

It is requested that any additional information or corrections related to these Chenango County Veterans be reported to The CHENANGO COUNTY HISTORICAL SOCIETY so this document can be an even more valuable resource.

CHENANGO COUNTY FORMATION

Until after the close of the Revolutionary War, in 1783, the area which now includes the current boundaries of Chenango County was considered the Indian domain.

In a series of treaties dated October 22, 1784, June 28, 1785, and September 22, 1788 the Indian title to the land, later to be Chenango County, was assumed by the State of New York.

On February 25, 1789, the Legislature passed an act directing the Surveyor-General, Simeon Dewitt, to lay out and survey the lands acquired by the treaties. The land was divided into townships containing as near as possible 25,000 acres. The townships were broken into 100, 250 acre blocks, which became the basis for descriptions in all deeds in the early times.

After the completion of the survey, which was done in 1789 and 1790, an act was passed on March 22, 1791, amending an act previously passed for the disposition of the newly acquired lands. The commissioners of the land office under certain requirements set out to sell the land. The sales took place, but owing to the brief notice and the imperfect means of travel and communication they were lightly attended. The lands fell into the hands of jobbers and wealthy capitalists, who were in attendance upon legislative action, and always alert for lucrative investments. These people immediately advanced the price for small purchasers to twenty shillings per acre.

The earliest Chenango County settlers, mainly Vermont Sufferers, came into the southeast corner of the county in 1784 because this part of the area was acquired by an earlier Indian treaty. Subsequently the next settler was Avery Power who moved to Indian land which was to become part of the town of Norwich. He arrived in 1788 and built a cabin which became a shelter for the surveyors who came later. The immigration really took off after the initial land sale in 1791.

CHENANGO COUNTY FORMATION

Chenango County was actually formed on March 15, 1798 from parts of Tioga and Herkimer Counties. It had ten townships and it covered an area nearly twice as large as it is today. The original towns were Cazenovia, Sangerfield, Hamilton, DeRuyter, Sherburne, Brookfield, Norwich, Greene, Oxford, and Jericho.

Boundary and town changes since 1798 are as follows:

1803- Sullivan was formed from Cazenovia
1804- Sangersfield was annexed to Oneida County
1805- Columbus was formed from Brookfield
1806- Madison County was formed from Chenango County
1806- German was formed from DeRuyter
1806- Stonington was formed from Norwich
1806- Plymouth was formed from Norwich
1806 Preston was formed from Norwich
1806- Coventry was formed from Greene
1807- Columbus was enlarged from Norwich
1807- New Berlin was formed from Norwich
1808- Smithville was formed from Greene
1808- Stonington was renamed Pharsalia
1813- Eastern was formed from Oxford
1814- Jericho was renamed Bainbridge
1816- McDonough was formed from Preston
1817- Otselic was formed from German
1817- Eastern was renamed Guilford
1821- New Berlin was renamed Lancaster
1822- Lancaster was renamed New Berlin
1823- Lincklaen was formed from German
1827- Pitcher was formed from Lincklaen and German
1833- Pitcher was enlarged from Lincklaen
1840- Chenango Forks was annexed to Broome County
1843- Coventry was enlarged from Oxford and Greene
1849- North Norwich was formed from Norwich
1853- Sherburne was enlarged from New Berlin
1857- Afton was formed from Bainbridge

At this point Chenango County had assumed its present size and shape.
The Veterans included in this book were selected based on the residency within the present boundaries.

CHENANGO COUNTY FORMATION

NEW YORK STATE MAP WITH CHENANGO COUNTY POSITION

REVOLUTIONARY WAR VETERANS
CHENANGO COUNTY—NEW YORK
CHENANGO COUNTY FORMATION

MAP BY WHITMAN STUDIOS

REVOLUTIONARY WAR VETERANS
CHENANGO COUNTY-NEW YORK

VETERANS PICTURES

ANSON CAREY
Private from Connecticut
resided in Oxford

NEWCOMB RAYMOND
Private from Connecticut
Resided in Sherburne

JOSEPH RHODES
Ensign from Long Island
resided in Guilford

WILLIAM SMITH
Colonel from New York
buried in Sherburne

CHENANGO COUNTY BURIAL GROUNDS

EVERGREEN CEMETERY (White's Store)
Norwich, New York

This cemetery has the most known burials (20) of Revolutionary War veterans in the County. The date of organization for this location was January 18, 1805. It was called The Rhode Island Settlement in pioneer days and is the oldest active cemetery in the County. On May 23, 1995 this site was formally placed on the National Register of Historic Places.

CEMETERY - Literally a sleeping place; it was the name applied by early Christians to the places set apart for the burial of their dead.

The very early Chenango County settlers established burial places on their farms or near their homes. As churches were established, many had associated property which became a burial place for its members. Most of the current active cemeteries are the outgrowth of these initial conditions.

Over three hundred burial locations have been identified within the County. With the passage of time many of the gravestones have deteriorated and burial sites have grown over, making them harder to find and explore.

A list of all Chenango County burials for individuals who may have been participants in the American Revolution was developed. Burial Listings for all known locations by various people over the years were utilized. Anyone born before 1769 was considered for research. Visits to each location were made for the purpose of determining tombstone location and recording the readings. A few undocumented burials were found.

REVOLUTIONARY WAR VETERANS
CHENANGO COUNTY-NEW YORK

PENSION LEGISLATION

During and after the Revolutionary War, three principal types of pensions were provided by the United States for servicemen and their dependents. "Disability" or "invalid pensions" were awarded to servicemen for physical disabilities incurred in the line of duty; "service pensions" to veterans who served for specified periods of time; and "widows pensions" to women whose husbands had been killed in the war or were veterans who had served for specified periods of time.

Applications for the pensions were made to the court in the county of the applicant's current residence. Some of the men were very old and/or ill and could not always remember all details of their service, or even their life. If possible, they gave the year of enlistment, names of their officers, skirmishes and battles. Proof of service was required and often the applicant would name a number of men who fought with him. Under some pension laws the value of his property was required and names of his then dependents. Evidence of marriage was required in the case of a pension for a widow. Often Bible records were filed as proof. Applications for bounty land are also filed with the pension records.

The pension legislation of June 7, 1832 was a key which unlocked the ability of all surviving soldiers or their widows to file for pensions. This released a flood of applications which then became a basis for proof of service and various other facts about he and his family. It is very difficult to determine involvement in the War for those that died before this point in time. Many times the name can be found in listings of soldiers for a given State but the absense of age or family connections does not prove the name belongs to the one being checked.

The original surviving records are in The National Archives in Washington, D.C. Most of the papers filed prior to 1818 were supposedly destroyed by the burning of the War Department building in 1800 and 1814.

REVOLUTIONARY WAR VETERANS
CHENANGO COUNTY-NEW YORK

PENSION LEGISLATION

The following pension legislation was enacted:

Aug 26, 1776 – Half pay for officers and enlisted men who were disabled in the service of the United States and who were incapable of earning a living. This was to continue for the duration of the disability.

May 15, 1778 – Half pay for seven years after the conclusion of the war to all military officers who remained in the continental service to the end of the war. Enlisted men who continued to serve for the duration of the conflict were to receive $80.

Aug 24, 1780 – Half pay for seven years to widows and orphans of officers who met the requirements of the May 15, 1778 resolution.

Oct 21, 1780 – The May 15, 1778 resolution was amended to provide half pay for life to officers after the war.

Mar 22, 1783 – The Oct 15, 1778 resolution was amended to provide full pay for five years.

Sep 29, 1789 – Invalid pensions previously paid by the States, pursuant to resolutions of the Continental Congress, should be continued and paid for one year by the newly established Federal Government. Subsequent legislation often extended the time limit.

Mar 23, 1792 – Permitted veterans not already receiving invalid pensions under resolutions of the Continental Congress to apply for them directly to the Federal Government.

Apr 10, 1806 – The scope of earlier invalid-pension laws was extended to make veterans of State troops and militia eligible for Federal pensions.

Mar 18, 1818 – Covered officers and enlisted men who were in "reduced circumstances" Nine months of service or service to the end of the war was required.

May 01, 1820 – Required all pensioners then on the roll to file a schedule of property in their possession. As a result, many were dropped from the rolls.

PENSION LEGISLATION

Mar 01, 1823 - Restored pensions to many people who had been removed under the terms of the 1820 legislation, but who subsequently proved their need for aid.

May 15, 1828 - Granted full pay for life to surviving officers and enlisted men who were eligible for benefits under the legislation of May 15, 1778.

Jun 07, 1832 - Every officer or enlisted man who had served at least two years in the Continental Line or State troops, volunteers or militia, was eligible for a pension of full pay for life. Naval and marine officers and enlisted men were also included. Veterans who had served less than two years, but not less than six months, were eligible for pensions of less than full pay. Money due from the last payment until the date of death of a pensioner could be collected by his widow or his children.

Jul 04, 1836 - Provided for widows of soldiers, if she was married to him before the close of the soldier's service.

Jul 07, 1838 - Provided for five year pensions to widows of soldiers, if the marriage took place prior to Jan 1, 1794.

Mar 03, 1843 - Continued the 1838 Act.

Jun 17, 1844 - Continued the 1838 Act.

Feb 02, 1848 - Continued the 1838 Act.

Jul 29, 1848 - Provided life pensions to widows of veterans who were married before Jan 2, 1800.

Feb 03, 1853 - Continued the 1838 Act and all restrictions pertaining to the date of marriage were removed.

Jun 03, 1858 - All pensions were continued for life.

Mar 09, 1878 - Widows of soldiers who had served as few as 14 days or were in any engagement, were declared eligible for life pensions.

REVOLUTIONARY WAR VETERANS
CHENANGO COUNTY-NEW YORK

BATTLES-SKIRMISHES ETC.

This list is included so it can be referenced for dates as a Revolutionary War veteran is identified with a battle or skirmish.

Amboy	New Jersey	Mar 08, 1777
Amelia Island	Florida	May 18, 1777
Anderson, Fort	Georgia	Jul 23, 1780
Anne, Fort	New York	Jul 08, 1777
Augusta	Georgia	Jan 29, 1777
		Sep 14, 1780 - Sep 18, 1780
		Apr 16, 1781 - Jun 05, 1781
Balfour, Fort	S. Carolina	Apr 12, 1781
Barren Hill	Pennsylvania	May 20, 1778
Beaufort	South Carolina	Feb 03, 1779
Bedford	New York	Jul 02, 1779
Breed's Hill	Massachusetts	Jun 17, 1775
Bemus Heights	New York	Sep 19, 1777
Bennington	Vermont	Aug 16, 1777
Bergen	New Jersey	Jul 19, 1780
Biggin's Bridge	South Carolina	Apr 14, 1780
Black River	South Carolina	Oct 25, 1780
Black Storks	South Carolina	Nov 20, 1780
Block House	New Jersey	Jul 21, 1780
Blue Licks	Kentucky	Aug 19, 1782
Bordentown	New Jersey	May 08, 1778
Boston (siege)	Massachusetts	Jun 17, 1775 - Mar 07, 1776
Bound Brook	New Jersey	Apr 13, 1777
Brandywine	Delaware	Sep 11, 1777
Brattonville	South Carolina	Jul 12, 1780
Brewton Hill	Georgia	Dec 29, 1778
Brier Creek	Georgia	Mar 03, 1779
Bristol	Pennsylvania	Apr 17, 1778
Bristol	Rhode Island	Oct 07, 1775
Broad River	South Carolina	Nov 12, 1780
Brookland	Long Island	Aug 28, 1776
Brooklyn	New York	Aug 27, 1776
Bruce's Cross Rds	North Carolina	Feb 12, 1781
Brunswick	New Jersey	Dec 01, 1776
		Oct 26, 1779
Bulltown Swamp Savannah	Georgia	Nov 19, 1778
Bull's Ferry	New Jersey	Jul 21, 1780
Bunker Hill	Massachusetts	Jun 17, 1775
Bushwick	Long Island	Aug 27, 1776
Butt's Hill	Rhode Island	Aug 29, 1778

REVOLUTIONARY WAR VETERANS
CHENANGO COUNTY-NEW YORK

BATTLES-SKIRMISHES ETC.

Camden	South Carolina	Aug 16, 1780	
		Apr 25, 1781	
		May 10, 1781	
Cane Brake	South Carolina	Dec 22, 1775	
Cane Creek	North Carolina	Sep 12, 1780	
		Sep 13, 1781	
Car's Fort	Georgia	Feb 10, 1779	
Catawba Ford	South Carolina	Aug 18, 1780	
Caughnawaga	New York	May 22, 1780	
Cedars, The	Canada	May 19, 1776	
Cedar Springs	North Carolina	Jul 13, 1780	
Cedar Springs	South Carolina	Aug 08, 1780	
Chadd's Ford	Delaware	Sep 11, 1777	
Chambly	Canada	Oct 19, 1775	
		Jun 16, 1776	
Charles City Court House	Virginia	Jan 08, 1781	
Charleston (Siege)	South Carolina	Mar 29, 1780 - May 12, 1780	
(Sortie)		Apr 24, 1780	
(Occupied by the British)		May 12, 1780 - Dec 14, 1782	
Charleston Neck	South Carolina	May 11, 1779	
Charlestown	Massachusetts	Jan 08, 1776	
Charlotte	North Carolina	Sep 26, 1780	
Chatterton's Hill	New York	Oct 28, 1776	
Chemung	New York	Aug 29, 1779	
Cherokee Ford	South Carolina	Feb 14, 1779	
Cherry Valley	New York	Nov 10, 1778	
Chesapeake Bay		Jul 08, 1776 - Jul 10, 1776	
Chestnut Creek	New Jersey	Oct 06, 1778	
Chestnut Hill	Pennsylvania	Dec 06, 1777	
Clapp's Mill	North Carolina	Mar 02, 1781	
Clinton, Fort	New York	Oct 06, 1777	
Cobleskill	New York	Jun 01, 1778	
Cock Hill, Fort	New York	Nov 16, 1776	
Combahee Ferry	South Carolina	Aug 27, 1782	
Concord	Massachusetts	Apr 19, 1775	
Connecticut Farms	New Jersey	Jun 07, 1780 - Jun 23, 1780	
Coram	Long Island	Nov 21, 1780	
Cornwallis, Fort	Georgia	Sep 14, 1780	
		Jun 05, 1781	
Cowan's Ford	North Carolina	Feb 01, 1781	
Cowpens	South Carolina	Jan 17, 1781	
Crompo Hill	Connecticut	Apr 28, 1777	
Crooked Billet	Pennsylvania	May 01, 1778	

REVOLUTIONARY WAR VETERANS
CHENANGO COUNTY-NEW YORK

BATTLES-SKIRMISHES ETC.

Croton River	New York	May 14, 1781
Crown Point	New York	May 12, 1775
		Oct 14, 1776
		Jun 16, 1777
Cumberland, Fort	Nova Scotia	Nov 20, 1776
Currytown	New York	Jul 09, 1781
Danbury Raid	Connecticut	Apr 25, 1777 - Apr 27, 1777
Diamond Island	New York	Sep 23, 1777
Dorchester Neck	Massachusetts	Feb 14, 1776
Dreadnought, Fort	Georgia	May 21, 1781
Dutch Island	Rhode Island	Aug 02, 1777
Earl's Ford	North Carolina	Jul 15, 1780
East Chester	New York	Jan 18, 1780
Ebenezer	Georgia	Jun 23, 1782
Edge Hill	Pennsylvania	Dec 07, 1777
Egg Harbor	New Jersey	Oct 15, 1778
Elizabethtown	New Jersey	Jan 25, 1780
		Jun 06, 1780
Elmira	New York	Aug 29, 1779
Esopus	New York	Oct 13, 1777
Essenecca Town	South Carolina	Aug 01, 1776
Eutaw Springs	South Carolina	Sep 08, 1781
Fairfield	Connecticut	Jul 08, 1779
Falmouth	Maine	Oct 18, 1775
Fayette, Fort	New York	Jun 01, 1779
Fish Dam Ford	South Carolina	Nov 09, 1780
Fishing Creek	South Carolina	Aug 18, 1780
Flatbush	New York	Aug 22, 1776 - Aug 23, 1776
Fogland Ferry	Rhode Island	Jan 10, 1777
Fort Plain	New York	Aug 02, 1780
Four Corners	New York	Feb 03, 1780
Freehold Court House	New Jersey	Jun 28, 1778
Freeman's Farm	New York	Sep 19, 1777
Galpin, Fort	Georgia	May 21, 1781
Geneseo	New York	Sep 14, 1779
George, Fort	New York	Nov 16, 1776
		Oct 11, 1780
George, Fort	Long Island	Nov 21, 1780
German Flats	New York	Oct 29, 1780
Germantown	Pennsylvania	Oct 04, 1777
Gloucester	Massachusetts	Aug 13, 1775
Granby, Fort	South Carolina	May 15, 1781
Grape Island	Massachusetts	May 21, 1775
Great Bridge	Virginia	Dec 09, 1775
Great Savannah	South Carolina	Aug 20, 1780
Green Springs	South Carolina	Aug 01, 1780

BATTLES-SKIRMISHES ETC.

```
Green Springs       Virginia          Jul 06, 1781
Greenwich           Connecticut       Jun 19, 1779
Grierson, Fort      Georgia           Sep 14, 1780
                                      May 24, 1781
Griswold, Fort      Connecticut       Sep 06, 1781
Groton Hill         Connecticut       Sep 06, 1781
Guilford            North Carolina    Mar 15, 1781
Gum Swamp           South Carolina    Aug 16, 1780
Gwyn's Island       Chesapeake Bay    Jul 08, 1776 -
                                      Jul 10, 1776
Hampton             Virginia          Oct 26, 1775
Hancock's Bridge    New Jersey        Mar 21, 1778
Hanging Rock        South Carolina    Aug 06, 1780
Harlem Cove         New York          Nov 16, 1776
Harlem Heights      New York          Oct 16, 1776
Harlem Plains       New York          Sep 16, 1776
Haw River           North Carolina    Feb 25, 1781
Henry, Fort         Virginia          Sep 01, 1777
                                      Sep 26, 1778 -
                                      Sep 28, 1778
Hickory Hill        Georgia           Jun 28, 1779
Highlands           New York          Mar 24, 1777
Hillsborough        North Carolina    Apr 25, 1781 -
                                      Sep 12, 1781
Hobkirk's Hill      South Carolina    Apr 25, 1781
Hogg Island         Massachusetts     May 27, 1775
Horse Neck          Connecticut       Feb 26, 1779
                                      Dec 09, 1780
Hubbardton          Vermont           Jul 07, 1777
Hutchinson's Is.    Georgia           Mar 07, 1776
Independence of United States
 acknowledged by Great Britain        Nov 30, 1782
Indian Field        New York          Aug 31, 1778
Iron Hill           Delaware          Sep 03, 1777
Isle Aux Noix       Canada            Jun 24, 1776
Jamaica             Long Island       Aug 28, 1776
James Island        South Carolina    Jul    , 1782
Jamestown Ford      Virginia          Jul 06, 1781
Jefferd's Neck      New York          Nov 07, 1779
Jersey City         New Jersey        Jul 18, 1779
Jerseyfield         New York          Oct 30, 1781
John's Island       South Carolina    Nov 04, 1782
Johnson, Fort       South Carolina    Sep 14, 1775
Johnson Hall        New York          Oct 24, 1781
Johnstown           New York          May 22, 1780
                                      Oct 24, 1781
Kanassorga          New York          Oct 23, 1780
Kettle Creek        Georgia           Feb 14, 1779
Keyser, Fort        New York          Oct 19, 1780
```

REVOLUTIONARY WAR VETERANS
CHENANGO COUNTY-NEW YORK

BATTLES-SKIRMISHES ETC.

King's Bridge	New York	Jan 17, 1777	
		Jul 03, 1781	
King's Mountain	North Carolina	Oct 07, 1781	
Kingston	New York	Oct 13, 1777	
Klock's Field	New York	Oct 21, 1780	
Lake Champlain		Oct 11, 1776 -	
			Oct 13, 1776
Lake George	New York	Sep 18, 1777	
Lanneau's Ferry	South Carolina	May 06, 1780	
Lee, Fort	New Jersey	Nov 18, 1776	
Lexington	Massachusetts	Apr 19, 1775	
Lindley's Mill	North Carolina	Sep 13, 1781	
Lloyd's Neck	New York	Sep 05, 1779	
Long Cane	South Carolina	Dec 04, 1780	
Long Island	New York	Aug 27, 1776	
		Dec 10, 1777	
Marmaroneck	New York	Oct 21, 1776	
Manhattanville	New York	Nov 16, 1776	
Martha's Vineyard	Massachusetts	May 05, 1775	
McIntosh, Fort	Georgia	Feb 02, 1777 -	
			Feb 04, 1777
Medway Church	Georgia	Nov 24, 1778	
Mercer, Fort	New Jersey	Oct 22, 1777	
Middleburg	New York	Oct 15, 1780	
Middletown	New Jersey	Apr 27, 1779	
		Jun 12, 1780	
Mifflin, Fort	Pennsylvania	Oct 23, 1777	
		Nov 10, 1777 -	
			Nov 15, 1777
Millstone	New Jersey	Jan 22, 1777	
		Jun 17, 1777	
Mincock Island	New Jersey	Oct 15, 1778	
Minisink	New York	Jul 22, 1779	
Mohawk Valley	New York	Aug 02, 1780	
Monk's Corner	South Carolina	Apr 14, 1780	
		Oct 16, 1781	
Monmouth	New Jersey	Jun 28, 1778	
Montgomery, Fort	New York	Oct 06, 1777	
Montreal	Canada	Sep 25, 1775	
		Nov 12, 1775	
Montressor's Is.	New York	Sep 24, 1776	
Moore's Creek Br.	North Carolina	Feb 27, 1776	
Morris, Fort	Georgia	Jan 09, 1779	
Morrisania	New York	Aug 05, 1779	
		Jan 22, 1781	
		Mar 04, 1782	
Moses Kill	New York	Aug 02, 1777	
Motte, Fort	South Carolina	May 12, 1781	
Moultrie, Fort	South Carolina	May 07, 1780	

BATTLES-SKIRMISHES ETC.

Mount Washington	New York	Nov 08, 1776
Musgrove's Mills	S Carolina	Aug 18, 1780
Nelson, Fort	Virginia	May 09, 1779
Nelson's Ferry	South Carolina	May 14, 1781
Newark	New Jersey	Jan 25, 1780
New Bridge	New Jersey	Apr 15, 1780
New Haven	Connecticut	Jul 05, 1779
New London	Connecticut	Sep 06, 1781
New Rochelle	New York	Oct 18, 1776
Newtown	New York	Aug 29, 1779
New York City (attacked)	New York	Aug 29, 1775---
Occupied by British		Sep 15, 1776 - Nov 25, 1783
Ninety-Six	South Carolina	May 22, 1781 - Jun 19, 1781
Noddle's Island	Massachusetts	May 27, 1775
Nook's Hill	Massachusetts	Mar 08, 1776
Norfolk	Virginia	Jan 01, 1776 May 09, 1779
Norwalk	Connecticut	Jul 12, 1779
Ogechee Road	Georgia	May 21, 1782
Onandagas	New York	Apr 20, 1779
Orangeburg	South Carolina	May 11, 1781
Oriskany	New York	Aug 06, 1777
Osborne's	Virginia	Apr 27, 1781
Pacolett River	North Carolina	Jul 14, 1780
Paoli	Pennsylvania	Sep 20, 1777
Paramus	New Jersey	Mar 22, 1780 Apr 16, 1780
Parker's Ferry	South Carolina	Aug 30, 1781
Paulus Hook	New Jersey	Aug 19, 1779
Peace, treaty of (concluded)		Sep 03, 1783
Peekskill	New York	Mar 22, 1777
Pelham Manor	New York	Oct 18, 1776
Petersburg	Virginia	Apr 25, 1781
Philadelphia (occupied)	Pennsylvania	Sep 26, 1777 - Jun 18, 1778
Phipps' Farm	Massachusetts	Nov 09, 1775
Piscataway	New Jersey	May 08, 1777
Plain, Fort	New York	Aug 02, 1780
Plains of Abraham	Canada	May 06, 1776
Port Royal Island	South Carolina	Feb 03, 1779
Poundridge	New York	Jul 02, 1779
Princeton	New Jersey	Jan 03, 1777
Punk Hill	New Jersey	Mar 08, 1777
Quaker Hill	Rhode Island	Aug 29, 1778

REVOLUTIONARY WAR VETERANS
CHENANGO COUNTY-NEW YORK

BATTLES-SKIRMISHES ETC.

Quebec (siege)	Canada	Dec 08, 1775 -	Dec 31, 1775
Quinby's Bridge	South Carolina	Jul 17, 1781	
Quinton's Bridge	New Jersey	Mar 18, 1778	
Rahway Meadow	New Jersey	Jun 26, 1781	
Ramsour's Mill	North Carolina	Jun 20, 1780	
Rayburn Creek	South Carolina	Jul 15, 1776	
Red Bank	New Jersey	Oct 22, 1777	
Rhode Island		Aug 29, 1778	
Richmond	Virginia	Jan 05, 1781	
Ridgefield	Connecticut	Apr 27, 1777	
Rocky Mount	South Carolina	Jul 30, 1780	
Roxbury	Massachusetts	Jul 08, 1775	
Rugley's Mills	South Carolina	Dec 04, 1780	
Sag Harbor	New York	May 23, 1777	
Saratoga	New York	Oct 07, 1777 -	Oct 17, 1777
Savannah (occup)	Georgia	Dec 29, 1778 -	Jul 11, 1782
Savannah (siege)	Georgia	Sep 23, 1779 -	Oct 18, 1779
Schoharie	New York	Oct 17, 1780	
Schuyler, Fort	New York	Aug 04, 1777 -	Aug 22, 1777
Shallow Ford	North Carolina	Feb 06, 1781	
Sharon (near)	Georgia	May 24, 1782	
Short Hills	New Jersey	Jun 26, 1777	
Silver Bluff	South Carolina	May 21, 1781	
Skenesborough	New York	Jul 07, 1777	
Smith's Point	New York	Nov 23, 1780	
Somerset Court Hs	New Jersey	Jan 20, 1777	
Spencer's Hill	Georgia	Nov 19, 1778	
Spencer's Tavern	Virginia	Jun 26, 1781	
Springfield	New Jersey	Dec 17, 1776	
		Jun 23, 1780	
Sorrel River	Canada	Jul 24, 1776	
Stanwix, Fort	New York	Aug 04, 1777 -	Aug 22, 1777
Staten Island	New York	Aug 21, 1777 -	Aug 22, 1777
St George, Fort	Long Island	Nov 23, 1780	
Stillwater	New York	Sep 19, 1777	
		Oct 07, 1777	
St John, Fort	Canada	May 14, 1775	
St John's	Canada	Sep 18, 1775	
		Nov 03, 1775	
Stone Arabia	New York	Oct 19, 1780	
Stonington	Connecticut	Sep 30, 1775	
Stono Ferry	South Carolina	Jun 20, 1779	

REVOLUTIONARY WAR VETERANS
CHENANGO COUNTY-NEW YORK

BATTLES-SKIRMISHES ETC.

Stony Point	New York	Jun 01, 1779	
		Jul 16, 1779	
Sullivan, Fort	South Carolina	Jun 28, 1776 -	
		Jun 29, 1776	
Sullivan's Island	South Carolina	Jun 28, 1776 -	
		Jun 29, 1776	
		May 08, 1780	
Sunbury	Georgia	Jan 06, 1779 -	
		Jan 09, 1779	
Tappan	New York	Sep 28, 1778	
Tarcote Swamp	South Carolina	Oct 25, 1780	
Tarrytown	New York	Aug 30, 1779	
		Jul 15, 1781	
Threadwell's Neck	New York	Oct 10, 1781	
Three Rivers	Canada	Jun 08, 1776	
Throg's Neck	New York	Oct 12, 1776	
Ticonderoga	New York	May 10, 1775	
		Jul 06, 1777	
Tiger River	South Carolina	Nov 20, 1780	
Tiverton	Rhode Island	May 31, 1778	
Tom's River	New Jersey	Jul 19, 1780	
Torrence's Tavern	North Carolina	Feb 01, 1781	
Trenton	New Jersey	Dec 26, 1776	
		Jan 02, 1777	
Tryon, Fort	New York	Nov 16, 1776	
Valcour Island	New York	Oct 11, 1776	
Valley Grove	Long Island	Aug 26, 1776	
Vandreuil	Canada	May 26, 1776	
Verplanck's Point	New York	Jun 01, 1779	
Vincennes	Indiana	Jul 05, 1778	
		Dec 17, 1778	
		Feb 23, 1779	
Wahab's Plantation	South Carolina	Sep 21, 1780	
Ward's House	New York	Mar 16, 1777	
Warwarsing	New York	Aug 22, 1781	
Washington, Fort	New York	Nov 16, 1776	
Wateree, Ford	South Carolina	Aug 15, 1780	
Watson, Fort	South Carolina	Apr 15, 1781 -	
		Apr 23, 1781	
Waxhaws	South Carolina	May 29, 1780	
Weehawken	New Jersey	Aug 19, 1779	
West Canada Creek	New York	Oct 30, 1781	
West Chester	New York	Sep 16, 1778	
West Chester Cnty	New York	Mar 16, 1777	
West Farms	New York	Jan 25, 1777	
West Greenwich	Connecticut	Mar 26, 1779	
West Haven	Connecticut	Sep 01, 1781	
Wetzell's Mills	North Carolina	Mar 06, 1781	

REVOLUTIONARY WAR VETERANS
CHENANGO COUNTY-NEW YORK

BATTLES-SKIRMISHES ETC.

Wheeling	Virginia	Sep 01, 1777
		Sep 26, 1778 - Sep 28, 1778
White House	Georgia	Sep 15, 1780
Whitemarsh	Pennsylvania	Dec 05, 1777 - Dec 08, 1777
White Plains	New York	Oct 28, 1776
Williamson's Plt.	South Carolina	Jul 12, 1780
Wilmington	North Carolina	Feb 01, 1781
Wofford's Iron Works	South Carolina	Aug 08, 1780
Woodbridge	New Jersey	Apr 19, 1777
Wyoming	Pennsylvania	Jul 01, 1778 - Jul 04, 1778
Yorktown	Virginia	Sep 28, 1781 - Oct 19, 1781
Young's House	New York	Dec 25, 1778
		Feb 03, 1780

REVOLUTIONARY WAR VETERANS
CHENANGO COUNTY-NEW YORK

VETERANS LIST

PAGE	LAST	FIRST	BIRTH	DEATH	TOWN
001	Ackart	Peter	1755	1845	Oxford
002	Agard	Joseph	1746	1836	Smithville
003	Akeley	John	1758	1819	Norwich
					Oxford
004	Akin	John	1741	1825	Guilford
005	Albee	Eleazer	1756	1836	Norwich
006	Alden	John	1762	1843	Lincklaen
007	Aldrich	Joshua	1759	1849	Preston
					North Norwich
008	Aldrich	Stephen	1741	1808	Guilford
009	Allen	Apollos	1756	1807	Smyrna
					Sherburne
010	Allen	Azor	1762	1841	Greene
					Coventry
011	Allen	Hezekiah	1762		McDonough
					Columbus
012	Allen	Jacob	1755	1840	Lincklaen
013	Allen	Noah	1727	1802	Smyrna
014	Allen	Phinehas	1745	1830	Sherburne
015	Allis	Moses	1756	1842	Coventry
016	Ambler	John	1759	1835	New Berlin
017	Ames	John	1762	1844	Plymouth
018	Anderson	Alexander			Smyrna
019	Anderson	Samuel	1758	1834	New Berlin
020	Angell	Samuel	1742	1795	New Berlin
021	Arnold	Caleb	1757	1838	Norwich
022	Arnold	Jabez	1755	1839	New Berlin
023	Ashby	Zebulon	1754		Guilford
024	Atherton	Cornelius	1737	1809	Afton
025	Atkins	Joseph	1743	1820	Smyrna
026	Atwater	Jonathan	1765	1849	Coventry
027	Avery	Abraham	1754	1844	Preston
028	Avery	John	1755	1836	Preston
029	Avery	Uriah	1760	1843	Norwich
030	Aylesworth	Arthur	1755	1834	Guilford
031	Aylesworth	Peleg	1749	1824	New Berlin
032	Babcock	Christopher	1734	1815	Smyrna
033	Babcock	Daniel		1827	German
034	Babcock	Elisha	1762		New Berlin
035	Babcock	Jonathan	1764	1849	Lincklaen

REVOLUTIONARY WAR VETERANS
CHENANGO COUNTY-NEW YORK

VETERANS LIST

	- NAME -		- YEAR -		
PAGE	LAST	FIRST	BIRTH	DEATH	TOWN
036	Babcock	Roger	1758	1836	New Berlin
037	Bacon	Thomas	1749	1821	Bainbridge
038	Badger	Nathaniel	1752	1830	Coventry
039	Bagg	Daniel	1757	1829	New Berlin
040	Bailey	Jeremiah	1761	1798	New Berlin
041	Bailey	Timothy	1754	1834	Lincklaen
042	Baker	Abraham	1752	1834	New Berlin
043	Baker	Joseph	1755	1850	Guilford
044	Balcom	Henry	1740	1812	Oxford
045	Baldwin	Samuel	1758	1834	Pitcher
046	Baldwin	Samuel	1756	1842	Oxford
047	Baldwin	Stephen	1761	1835	Pitcher
048	Ballard	Moses	1756	1833	Smyrna
049	Ballou	Jeremiah	1749	1838	Columbus
050	Banks	Samuel	1755	1826	Bainbridge
051	Barden	Abraham	1765		Greene
052	Barker	John	1744	1836	Greene
053	Barker	Samuel	1758	1838	Greene
054	Barnes	Jonathan	1760	1829	Guilford
055	Barnett	Simon	1743	1837	Greene
056	Bartle	Henry	1763	1833	Oxford
057	Bartle	John	1729	1808	Oxford
058	Barton	Jonathan	1759	1831	New Berlin
					Bainbridge
059	Bartoo	Silas	1742	1831	Greene
060	Basford	James	1762	1845	Bainbridge
061	Bates	Jonathan	1755	1827	Bainbridge
062	Beadle	Benjamin	1741	1810	Sherburne
063	Beal	Azariah	1753	1811	Preston
064	Beatman	William	1741	1810	Afton
065	Beckley	Daniel	1758	1843	Greene
066	Beckwith	Joseph	1761	1853	Preston
					Smyrna
067	Beebe	Amon	1750	1830	Guilford
068	Beebe	David	1759	1832	Coventry
069	Beebe	Joseph	1746	1833	Columbus
070	Beecher	Amos	1749	1832	Greene
071	Benedict	Abijah	1765	1843	Coventry
072	Benedict	Benjamin	1740	1823	Coventry
073	Benedict	Noah	1763	1849	Coventry

REVOLUTIONARY WAR VETERANS
CHENANGO COUNTY-NEW YORK

VETERANS LIST

PAGE	LAST - NAME -	FIRST	BIRTH - YEAR -	DEATH	TOWN
074	Benjamin	Darius	1758	1850	Lincklaen
075	Bennett	Amos	1758	1840	Norwich
076	Bennett	Caleb	1758	1830	Bainbridge
077	Bennett	James		1819	Oxford
078	Bennett	Jared	1764	1845	Smyrna
079	Bennett	John	1759	1842	Greene
080	Bennett	Nathan	1750	1845	Greene
081	Bennett	Wolcott	1757	1831	Lincklaen
082	Berry	Peleg	1746	1796	Preston
083	Besancon	Peter	1762	1855	Norwich
084	Betts	Zopher	1761	1842	Oxford
085	Birdsall	Benjamin	1743	1828	Greene
086	Birge	John	1755	1838	Coventry
087	Bishop	John	1759	1842	Otselic
088	Bixby	Samuel	1740	1825	Bainbridge
089	Blackman	Elijah	1740	1825	Oxford
090	Blackman	Enoch	1760	1844	Lincklaen
091	Blackman	Samuel	1762	1857	Columbus Sherburne
092	Blair	David	1749	1829	Plymouth
093	Blanchard	Jedidiah	1762	1836	Oxford
094	Blanchard	John	1769	1847	Pitcher
095	Blount	Elisha	1763	1835	Lincklaen
096	Bonesteel	David F	1758	1848	Smithville German
097	Borden	Joshua	1756	1825	Norwich
098	Boss	Jabez	1759	1828	Smyrna Sherburne
099	Bosworth	Timothy	1758	1837	Pharsalia
100	Bowers	John	1757	1831	Plymouth
101	Breed	Jabez	1758	1818	McDonough
102	Breed	Joseph	1761	1850	Lincklaen
103	Breed	Joseph	1763	1828	Pharsalia
104	Brewer	Elisha	1766	1857	Lincklaen
105	Brewer	John	1764	1846	Plymouth
106	Brewster	Nathan	1758		New Berlin
107	Bridgeman	Orlando	1743	1813	Bainbridge
108	Briggs	George	1734	1816	Smyrna
109	Brigham	Origin	1757	1816	Norwich
110	Brockett	Hezekiah	1759	1851	Oxford

REVOLUTIONARY WAR VETERANS
CHENANGO COUNTY-NEW YORK

VETERANS LIST

PAGE	LAST	FIRST	BIRTH	DEATH	TOWN
111	Brookins	Artemas	1757	1824	Norwich
112	Brooks	Levi	1757	1829	Norwich
113	Brooks	Thomas	1761	1822	Plymouth
114	Brown	Adonijah	1766	1847	Guilford
115	Brown	Barnabus	1762	1855	New Berlin
116	Brown	Baron	1750	1829	Sherburne
117	Brown	Christopher	1759	1807	Norwich
118	Brown	Elisha	1758	1832	Norwich
119	Brown	Elisha	1731	1813	
120	Brown	Jesse	1739	1813	Norwich
121	Brown	John	1758	1847	Norwich
122	Brown	John	1755	1809	Norwich
123	Brown	Jonathan	1757	1830	Otselic
124	Brown	Jonathan	1748	1841	Sherburne
125	Brown	Josiah	1748		Norwich
126	Brown	Nathan	1765	1847	Pharsalia
127	Brown	Reuben	1748	1830	Oxford
128	Brown	Samuel	1737	1812	New Berlin
129	Brown	Thomas	1733	1814	New Berlin
130	Brundage	Martin	1763	1832	Pitcher
131	Brush	William	1750	1830	Norwich
132	Buck	Thomas	1763	1841	Greene
133	Buckingham	Reuben	1745	1828	Otselic
134	Bugbee	George	1762		Columbus
135	Burdick	Caleb	1753	1822	McDonough Guilford
136	Burdick	Elijah	1758	1833	Pharsalia
137	Burdick	Gideon	1762	1846	
138	Burdick	Hazzard	1759	1841	Norwich Preston
139	Burdick	Luke	1749	1825	Lincklaen
140	Burlingame	Nathan	1762	1856	Bainbridge
141	Burlingame	Silas	1739	1829	New Berlin
142	Burlingham	Jeremiah	1753	1826	Norwich
143	Burritt	Blackleach	1740	1794	Sherburne
144	Burrows	Hubbard	1763	1832	Coventry
145	Burrows	Nathan	1744	1808	Coventry
146	Burzett	Charles	1762		German
147	Bush	Abial	1739		Oxford
148	Bush	Charles	1766		Bainbridge

REVOLUTIONARY WAR VETERANS
CHENANGO COUNTY-NEW YORK

VETERANS LIST

PAGE	LAST - NAME - FIRST		BIRTH - YEAR - DEATH		TOWN
149	Bush	Elnathan	1728	1791	Bainbridge
150	Bush	Jonathan	1747	1816	Guilford Oxford
151	Butler	Allen	1754	1839	Greene
152	Button	Elias	1748	1830	Pharsalia
153	Button	Joseph	1760	1845	Columbus
154	Button	Zebulon	1753		Coventry
155	Cables	Zebulon	1735	1838	Afton
156	Calkins	Matthew	1764	1844	New Berlin
157	Campbell	Jacob	1762	1845	Columbus
158	Campbell	John	1761	1846	Bainbridge
159	Carey	Anson	1762	1842	Oxford
160	Carey	Joseph	1760	1841	Otselic
161	Carhartt	John	1752	1836	Oxford
162	Carpenter	Benjamin	1767	1836	Afton
163	Carpenter	Cyril	1758	1832	Preston
164	Carpenter	Nathan	1757	1814	Norwich
165	Carson	Samuel	1749		Oxford
166	Carter	Heman	1764	1846	Greene
167	Carter	Stephen	1741	1824	Columbus
168	Case	Roger	1745	1827	Smyrna
169	Catlin	Elisha	1759	1826	Lincklaen
170	Chamberlain	Wyatt	1758	1826	Guilford
171	Chamberlin	Judah	1761	1847	Oxford
172	Champlain	Silas	1748	1828	Preston
173	Champlin	George	1756	1844	Lincklaen
174	Champlin	Jonathan	1755	1842	Pharsalia Pitcher
175	Chandler	Jonathan	1762	1844	Pitcher
176	Chandler	Matthew	1764	1852	German
177	Chapel	John	1756	1822	Pitcher
178	Chapin	Joel	1761	1845	Bainbridge
179	Chapman	Constant	1761	1847	Smithville
180	Chase	Jerameel	1760	1837	Pharsalia New Berlin
181	Chubb	Joseph	1754		Preston
182	Church	Caleb	1754	1842	Columbus
183	Church	Eleazer	1759		Bainbridge
184	Church	James	1765	1855	Columbus Sherburne

REVOLUTIONARY WAR VETERANS
CHENANGO COUNTY-NEW YORK

VETERANS LIST

PAGE	LAST	FIRST	BIRTH	DEATH	TOWN
185	Church	John	1755	1824	Norwich
					Pharsalia
186	Church	Nathaniel	1748	1844	North Norwich
187	Churchill	William	1767	1859	Afton
188	Clark	Cornelius	1746	1810	Sherburne
189	Clark	Gershom	1755	1840	Guilford
190	Clark	Israel	1757	1827	Norwich
191	Clark	Moses	1747	1833	Guilford
192	Clark	Roswell	1744	1820	Norwich
193	Clark	Solomon	1750	1825	Bainbridge
194	Clark	William	1754	1840	Preston
195	Cleveland	Benjamin	1755	1803	German
196	Cleveland	Joseph	1749	1844	Guilford
197	Clute	Frederick	1760		Sherburne
198	Coates	Christopher	1762	1838	Otselic
199	Cobb	Abel	1763		Smyrna
200	Coe	Asher	1757	1832	Bainbridge
201	Coggleshall	James	1759	1807	Pharsalia
202	Cole	Amos	1759	1852	Sherburne
203	Cole	Thomas	1733	1825	Norwich
204	Colegrove	Jonathan	1745	1812	Norwich
205	Coley	William	1758	1843	Otselic
206	Collins	Benjamin			
207	Connick	William	1761	1840	German
208	Converse	Thomas	1738	1809	Columbus
209	Cook	David	1731	1816	Norwich
					Plymouth
210	Cook	Gideon	1745	1813	Norwich
211	Cook	Joseph	1751		North Norwich
212	Cook	Solomon	1761	1823	Pitcher
					Lincklaen
213	Cook	William			Greene
214	Cooley	James	1760	1823	Oxford
215	Cooley	Mathewson			Pharsalia
216	Cornell	Ebenezer	1738	1785	Guilford
217	Cornell	Enos	1768	1843	Afton
218	Cornell	Samuel	1742	1804	Afton
219	Coston	Ebenezer	1765	1814	Sherburne
220	Covel	James	1742		Sherburne
221	Covell	Jacob	1762	1845	Plymouth

REVOLUTIONARY WAR VETERANS
CHENANGO COUNTY-NEW YORK

VETERANS LIST

PAGE	- NAME - LAST	FIRST	BIRTH	- YEAR - DEATH	TOWN
222	Covey	Joseph	1759	1839	Guilford
223	Covil	David	1755	1820	Norwich
224	Cowden	James	1746	1838	Norwich
					Plymouth
225	Cowles	Timothy	1746	1831	Smithville
226	Coy	Elisha	1763	1843	Guilford
227	Coye	Nehemiah	1757	1837	Lincklaen
					German
228	Crandall	Azel	1755		Greene
229	Crandall	Elisha	1765		Smithville
					Lincklaen
230	Crandall	Ezekiel	1746	1838	New Berlin
231	Crandall	George	1739	1832	Smithville
232	Crandall	Joseph	1746	1820	Coventry
233	Crandall	Laban	1765	1815	German
					New Berlin
					Smithville
234	Crandall	Sylvester	1752	1845	Plymouth
235	Crane	Elijah	1763	1834	Bainbridge
236	Crane	Jonathan	1757	1820	Plymouth
237	Cranston	Peleg	1757	1822	New Berlin
238	Crego	Abraham	1757	1843	Sherburne
239	Crocker	Job	1748	1831	Pitcher
240	Cross	William	1747	1834	Otselic
241	Crumb	Phineas	1750		Plymouth
242	Curtis	James	1762	1835	Sherburne
243	Curtis	James	1746	1818	McDonough
244	Curtis	Joel	1764	1847	Greene
245	Curtis	Solomon	1755	1838	Oxford
246	Cutting	Eliphalet	1767	1843	Plymouth
247	Daily	William	1759	1833	Smithville
					Bainbridge
					Greene
248	Daniels	Nathan	1760	1845	Preston
					North Norwich
249	Dann	Jonathan	1752		North Norwich
250	Darling	David	1761	1839	Norwich
251	Darling	Joseph	1746	1824	Lincklaen
252	Davenport	Richard	1762	1845	Smithville
253	Davidson	James	1745		Bainbridge

REVOLUTIONARY WAR VETERANS
CHENANGO COUNTY-NEW YORK

VETERANS LIST

PAGE	- NAME - LAST	FIRST	- YEAR - BIRTH	DEATH	TOWN
254	Davis	John	1760	1832	Norwich
255	Davis	William	1759	1826	Coventry
256	Delong	Daniel	1761		German
257	Deming	Jeremiah	1762	1822	Oxford
258	Deming	John	1761	1837	Guilford
259	Denison	George	1753	1835	Preston Guilford
260	Denison	James P	1761	1850	Columbus
261	Deshon	Daniel	1754	1826	Preston
262	Dewey	John	1762	1839	Sherburne
263	Dexter	Thomas	1746		Bainbridge
264	Dickerman	John	1765	1848	Guilford
265	Dixon	David	1756	1820	Sherburne
266	Dixon	Joseph	1754	1839	Sherburne Smyrna
267	Dodge	Amos	1759	1852	Bainbridge
268	Dodge	John	1751	1830	Oxford
269	Dodge	Reuben	1756	1813	Oxford
270	Dorn	Abraham	1755	1838	Lincklaen
271	Doty	Moses	1758	1823	Norwich
272	Driskill	William	1755	1834	Greene
273	Dudley	Roswell	1761		Preston
274	Dunbar	Nehemiah	1765	1833	McDonough
275	Dunn	Timothy	1757	1842	Smyrna
276	Durand	Eleazer	1754	1833	New Berlin
277	Dutton	Stephen	1754	1800	Afton
278	Eastwood	Daniel	1751	1837	Norwich
279	Eastwood	John	1761	1837	Norwich
280	Eaton	Ebenezer	1760	1839	Sherburne
281	Eaton	Ebenezer	1734	1815	Sherburne
282	Eccleston	David	1755	1843	Preston
283	Eddy	Olney	1750	1835	Plymouth
284	Eddy	Willard	1760	1854	Norwich Sherburne
285	Edgerton	Jedediah	1753	1838	
286	Edgerton	Roger	1761	1844	Coventry
287	Edmunds	Benjamin	1751	1828	Norwich
288	Edwards	Paul	1749	1831	Pitcher
289	Egleston	Thomas	1740	1822	Sherburne
290	Elliott	Joseph		1844	Bainbridge

REVOLUTIONARY WAR VETERANS
CHENANGO COUNTY-NEW YORK

VETERANS LIST

PAGE	- NAME - LAST	FIRST	- YEAR - BIRTH	DEATH	TOWN
291	Elsworth	John	1756	1844	Bainbridge
292	Enos	Joab	1745		Oxford Norwich
293	Evans	David	1761	1839	Plymouth
294	Evans	Henry	1734	1792	Bainbridge
295	Everitt	Daniel	1764		Greene
296	Everitt	Oliver	1764	1845	McDonough
297	Everts	Edward	1752	1837	Greene
298	Fairchild	Abel	1763	1840	Lincklaen
299	Fairchild	Amos	1763	1838	Bainbridge
300	Fairchild	Benjamin	1758	1831	Pitcher
301	Fairchild	Joseph	1757	1842	Coventry
302	Fanning	Asa	1766	1838	Preston
303	Farnham	Levi	1748	1776	Oxford
304	Farnsworth	Moses	1756	1837	Greene
305	Fenton	Elijah	1762	1850	Pitcher
306	Fenton	Solomon	1749	1831	Oxford
307	Ferris	Israel	1751	1844	North Norwich
308	Field	Israel	1741		Bainbridge
309	Finch	Nathaniel	1740		Pitcher
310	Finch	Silvanus	1762	1844	Pitcher
311	Fish	Ephraim	1760	1838	McDonough
312	Fisher	Timothy	1760	1833	New Berlin
313	Fitch	Ephraim	1736	1832	Oxford
314	Fitch	John	1758	1824	Oxford
315	Fitch	Jonathan	1745	1821	Bainbridge
316	Fletcher	John	1757		Columbus
317	Fletcher	John	1762	1847	Columbus
318	Foot	Joseph	1760	1861	Coventry
319	Foote	Daniel	1755	1820	New Berlin
320	Foote	Isaac	1746	1842	Smyrna
321	Fowler	John			Coventry
322	Fowler	Samuel	1765	1846	Sherburne
323	Fox	Samuel	1763	1832	Sherburne
324	Francis	Thomas	1759		Norwich
325	Fredenburg	Elias	1749		Bainbridge
326	Freeman	Daniel	1759		Greene
327	Frink	Nathan	1767	1839	Pharsalia
328	Frink	Prentice	1764	1848	Pharsalia
329	Fry	Rhodes	1754	1829	Columbus

VETERANS LIST

PAGE	LAST	FIRST	BIRTH	DEATH	TOWN
330	Gallop	Robert	1760	1858	Plymouth
					Norwich
					Greene
331	Gardner	Elijah	1735		Plymouth
332	Gardner	Elisha	1742		Oxford
333	Gardner	Seth	1760	1826	Plymouth
334	Gardner	Townsend	1763	1840	Plymouth
335	Gartsee	John	1755	1831	Plymouth
336	German	Silas	1733	1824	North Norwich
337	Gibson	John	1736	1803	Norwich
338	Gibson	John		1850	Norwich
339	Gilmore	John	1748		Sherburne
340	Gleason	Jason	1763	1838	Norwich
341	Goff	David	1761	1849	Guilford
342	Goff	Richard	1763	1842	New Berlin
					Oxford
343	Goodenough	David	1735	1814	Coventry
344	Goodrich	David	1754	1850	New Berlin
345	Gould	Benjamin	1753	1824	Coventry
346	Gould	Simeon	1759	1828	
347	Grant	Isaac	1760	1841	Smithville
348	Graves	James	1764	1845	Greene
					Oxford
349	Graves	Matthew	1735	1824	Norwich
350	Gray	Elijah	1764	1847	Sherburne
351	Gray	Jeduthan	1756	1830	Greene
352	Gray	John	1739	1822	Sherburne
353	Gray	John	1769	1859	Sherburne
354	Gray	Joseph	1732	1796	Greene
355	Gray	Nathaniel	1736	1810	Sherburne
356	Green	Duty	1761	1842	Bainbridge
357	Green	Gideon	1763		Bainbridge
358	Green	Isaac	1764	1833	Columbus
359	Green	Joseph	1758		Norwich
					Columbus
360	Greene	Edward	1757	1824	Norwich
361	Greenleaf	Israel	1734	1822	Columbus
362	Gregory	Joseph	1758	1849	Oxford
					Guilford
363	Gregory	Solomon			Smyrna

REVOLUTIONARY WAR VETERANS
CHENANGO COUNTY-NEW YORK

VETERANS LIST

PAGE	LAST	FIRST	BIRTH	DEATH	TOWN
364	Griffin	Joshua	1755	1831	New Berlin
365	Griffing	Samuel	1764	1836	Norwich Oxford
366	Griffeth	Samuel	1755	1838	Bainbridge
367	Griswold	Miles	1739	1804	Guilford
368	Guile	Benjamin	1749	1813	New Berlin
369	Guthrie	James	1732	1804	Sherburne
370	Guthrie	Joseph	1760	1845	Sherburne
371	Hackett	Abel	1760		Oxford
372	Hackett	Edward	1748	1834	Oxford
373	Hackett	Joseph	1721		Oxford
374	Hackett	Josiah	1758	1845	Oxford
375	Hadley	Jane (Fisk)	1733	1819	Preston
376	Hadlock	Thomas	1759	1851	Norwich
377	Haight	Samuel	1738	1806	North Norwich Sherburne
378	Hakes	Richard	1741	1815	Pitcher
379	Hall	John	1757	1832	Preston
380	Hallett	Solomon	1759	1841	Bainbridge
381	Hamilton	Jesse	1754	1814	Oxford
382	Hamilton	Silas	1736	1816	Guilford
383	Hancock	Nathan	1762	1832	Oxford
384	Harden	Nathan			Columbus
385	Harrington	John	1758	1842	Guilford Oxford
386	Harris	David	1764	1835	Guilford
387	Hart	Thomas	1757	1847	Sherburne
388	Hartwell	Oliver	1739	1835	North Norwich
389	Harvey	John	1762	1848	Preston
390	Haskell	Josiah	1767	1829	Sherburne
391	Hatch	Joel	1764	1855	Sherburne
392	Hatch	John	1761	1839	Oxford
393	Hatch	Timothy	1758	1847	Sherburne
394	Hawkins	Robert	1729	1828	Coventry
395	Hawks	William	1767	1851	Otselic Columbus
396	Hayden	Daniel	1757		McDonough
397	Hayes	James	1740	1823	Norwich
398	Hayes	John	1766	1830	Greene
399	Hayes	Nathaniel	1764	1838	Greene

REVOLUTIONARY WAR VETERANS
CHENANGO COUNTY-NEW YORK

VETERANS LIST

PAGE	LAST	FIRST	BIRTH	DEATH	TOWN
400	Hayward	Ebenezer	1760		
401	Hazzard	Stewart	1745	1833	Oxford
402	Herrick	Robert	1754	1817	New Berlin McDonough
403	Hickcox	Gideon	1752	1824	Pitcher
404	Hicks	John	1761	1842	German Norwich
405	Higgins	Thomas	1755	1842	Sherburne
406	Hill	Barnard	1761	1832	New Berlin
407	Hill	Ebenezer	1756		Columbus
408	Hinckley	Jared	1758	1828	Oxford
409	Hinman	Jonas	1752	1833	Bainbridge Pitcher
410	Hitchcock	Eli	1754	1833	Norwich
411	Hodge	David	1754	1831	Coventry
412	Hoffman	Herman	1765		Oxford Bainbridge
413	Holcomb	Abraham	1753	1844	Plymouth
414	Holcomb	Luthur	1752	1839	Afton
415	Holcomb	Return	1742	1832	Coventry Greene
416	Holcomb	Zephaniah	1750	1822	Norwich
417	Holden	Ebenezer	1764	1845	New Berlin
418	Hollenbeck	Abraham	1760	1844	Oxford
419	Hollenbeck	Ephraim	1758		Oxford
420	Holmes	Edward	1762	1837	Greene Sherburne
421	Holmes	Jedediah	1763	1840	New Berlin
422	Holmes	John	1760	1849	Oxford
423	Holmes	Joshua	1752	1827	New Berlin
424	Holmes	Orsamus	1757	1835	Sherburne
425	Holt	Joseph			Greene
426	Holt	Jotham	1765	1839	Pitcher
427	Hopkins	Frederick	1768	1855	Oxford
428	Horton	Josiah	1747	1821	Sherburne
429	Hotchkiss	Jeremiah	1759	1842	Smithville
430	Houk	Tobias	1760	1836	Guilford
431	Hovey	Benjamin	1758	1811	Oxford
432	Howard	Thomas	1742	1837	Columbus
433	Howard	Thomas	1760	1836	Sherburne

REVOLUTIONARY WAR VETERANS
CHENANGO COUNTY-NEW YORK

VETERANS LIST

PAGE	LAST	FIRST	BIRTH	DEATH	TOWN
434	Howard	William	1747	1813	Columbus Sherburne
435	Howe	Joseph	1754	1830	Oxford
436	Hoyt	Silas	1763	1848	Guilford
437	Hoyt	William	1758	1838	Greene
438	Hubbard	David	1755	1825	Bainbridge
439	Hudson	Daniel	1750	1815	
440	Humphrey	Thomas	1737	1818	Bainbridge
441	Hungerford	James	1761	1832	Coventry
442	Hunt	George	1756	1833	New Berlin Norwich
443	Huntley	Jehiel	1747	1833	Oxford
444	Huntley	Reuben	1750	1847	Sherburne New Berlin
445	Huston	James	1758		Norwich
446	Hyde	Daniel	1756	1831	Afton
447	Ingersoll	Oliver	1752	1826	Guilford
448	Ingersoll	Phillip	1744	1835	Bainbridge
449	Ingham	Isaac	1755	1828	Sherburne
450	Isham	Isaac	1751	1819	New Berlin
451	Ives	Abraham	1746	1814	Guilford
452	Jacobs	Cornelius	1754	1811	Oxford
453	Jacobs	Israel	1744	1832	Oxford
454	James	Paul	1755	1843	Smyrna
455	Jennings	Joseph	1756	1831	Afton
456	Jennison	Joseph	1756	1839	Norwich
457	Jewell	Aaron	1742	1829	Guilford
458	Jewell	Elisha	1757	1842	Oxford Guilford
459	Jewell	Penuell	1767	1822	Guilford
460	Johnson	Abel		1798	Preston
461	Johnson	Daniel	1760	1840	Guilford
462	Johnson	Jesse	1747	1824	Plymouth
463	Johnston	John	1753	1829	Afton
464	Johnston	Samuel	1763	1830	Afton
465	Johnston	William	1751	1843	Afton
466	Jones	Asa	1740	1832	Greene
467	Jones	Benjamin	1757	1840	Coventry
468	Jones	Ebenezer	1763	1835	Oxford
469	Jones	Elkanah	1761	1849	Norwich

REVOLUTIONARY WAR VETERANS
CHENANGO COUNTY-NEW YORK

VETERANS LIST

PAGE	LAST	FIRST	BIRTH	DEATH	TOWN
470	Jones	Isaac	1756	1840	Columbus
471	Jones	Samuel	1761	1840	Lincklaen
472	Jones	William	1759	1850	Smyrna
473	Jones	Zimri	1764		Greene
474	Judd	John	1761	1825	
475	Judson	John B	1759	1829	Oxford
476	Juliand	Joseph	1749	1821	Greene
477	Justice	Walcott	1763	1848	Lincklaen
478	Keith	Peter	1760	1843	Norwich
479	Kellogg	Nathaniel	1757	1846	Greene Oxford
480	Kelsey	Heth	1755	1850	Coventry Bainbridge
481	Kelsey	Stephen	1736	1807	North Norwich Smyrna
482	Kendrick	Heth`	1764	1843	Bainbridge
483	Ketchum	Benjamin	1769	1848	McDonough
484	Keys	Ebenezer	1756	1836	Pitcher Lincklaen
485	King	George	1755		New Berlin
486	King	George H	1762	1848	Norwich
487	King	Isaac	1751		Sherburne
488	King	John	1753	1841	North Norwich
489	King	William	1759		Bainbridge
490	Kingsley	Martin	1756		Columbus
491	Kinney	Nathaniel	1753	1829	Columbus
492	Kirby	Reuben	1760	1827	Bainbridge
493	Kirkland	Joshua	1756		Norwich
494	Knapp	Daniel	1763	1842	Sherburne
495	Knapp	Daniel	1753	1836	Oxford
496	Knapp	Hezekiah	1744	1822	Guilford
497	Knapp	Joshua	1762	1829	Sherburne
498	Knapp	William	1764	1846	Bainbridge
499	Knowlton	Ephraim	1756		Smithville
500	Lamphier	Benjamin	1761	1848	Pitcher
501	Landers	Ebenezer	1758	1846	Bainbridge
502	Landers	Isaiah	1769	1844	Afton
503	Landers	Joseph	1763	1845	Bainbridge
504	Latham	Joseph	1755	1837	Guilford
505	Lathrop	Josiah	1757	1854	Sherburne

REVOLUTIONARY WAR VETERANS
CHENANGO COUNTY-NEW YORK

VETERANS LIST

PAGE	LAST	FIRST	BIRTH	DEATH	TOWN
506	Lawton	John	1759	1838	Pitcher
507	Lawton	John	1757	1836	Smithville
508	Lee	Samuel	1754	1823	Plymouth
509	Leonard	Timothy	1757	1830	Smyrna
510	Lewis	Benjamin	1760	1838	German
511	Lewis	Beriah	1750	1837	Norwich
512	Lewis	Samuel	1744	1818	Preston
513	Lewis	William	1760	1835	Pharsalia
514	Lillie	Joseph	1757	1820	Bainbridge
515	Livermore	Abraham	1749	1826	German
516	Livermore	Isaac	1752	1838	Smithville
517	Long	Matthew	1757	1822	Afton
518	Loomis	Abijah	1743	1820	Greene
519	Loomis	Benaiah	1752	1838	Oxford Smithville
520	Loomis	Simon	1758	1842	Oxford
521	Loomis	Thomas	1756	1842	New Berlin
522	Lord	Joseph	1757	1839	Pharsalia
523	Luce	Ebenezer	1750	1830	Bainbridge
524	Lumereaux	Joseph	1760	1840	
525	Luther	Martin	1760	1837	Afton
526	Lynde	John	1745	1816	Sherburne
527	Lyon	Alexander	1765		Oxford
528	Lyon	Moses	1762	1844	Bainbridge
529	Lyon	Samuel	1754	1828	Oxford
530	Man	Abel	1750		Smyrna
531	Manning	Robert	1746	1781	Coventry
532	Marble	Sampson		1783	Smyrna
533	Mason	James	1759	1820	Preston
534	Mather	Joseph	1756	1848	Sherburne
535	Mathews	Ebenezer	1758	1848	German
536	Mathewson	John	1750	1815	New Berlin
537	Matteson	James	1757	1833	Smithville
538	May	Samuel	1739	1810	Guilford
539	Maynard	John	1754	1833	Smithville
540	McCall	John	1756	1823	Preston
541	McCullough	Alexander	1744	1830	Norwich
542	McCullough	James	1749	1828	Norwich
543	McFarland	John	1766	1843	Oxford
544	McNitt	John	1759	1843	Norwich

REVOLUTIONARY WAR VETERANS
CHENANGO COUNTY-NEW YORK

VETERANS LIST

PAGE	LAST	FIRST	BIRTH	DEATH	TOWN
545	Mead	Amos	1760	1827	North Norwich
546	Mead	John	1753	1820	Norwich
547	Mead	Jonathan	1727	1800	North Norwich
548	Mead	Michael	1744		German
549	Mead	Samuel	1756	1830	Guilford Bainbridge
550	Mead	Stephen		1830	Oxford
551	Mead	William	1749	1833	Preston
552	Meaker	Ephraim	1754	1831	New Berlin
553	Medbury	Isaac	1724	1797	New Berlin
554	Medbury	Isaac	1761		New Berlin
555	Medbury	Joseph	1758	1839	New Berlin
556	Melendy	Samuel	1741	1813	Afton
557	Merchant	Gurdon	1760	1837	Columbus
558	Merriam	Ichabod	1755	1838	Smithville
559	Merrill	Thomas	1759	1847	Sherburne Plymouth
560	Mersereau	John	1757	1841	Guilford
561	Mersereau	Joshua	1728	1804	Guilford
562	Mersereau	Joshua	1761	1857	Guilford
563	Messenger	Isaac	1746	1839	Lincklaen
564	Messenger	Joseph	1741		Lincklaen
565	Metcalf	Luke	1764	1836	Oxford
566	Miles	Burrage	1766	1848	Coventry
567	Miles	Isaac	1763	1843	Coventry
568	Mills	Aaron	1754	1835	Sherburne
569	Mills	Samuel	1754	1837	Guilford
570	Miner	Ephriam	1758	1827	Pharsalia
571	Miner	Sylvester	1756	1832	Preston
572	Minor	Phillip	1760	1828	Guilford
573	Monroe	Isaac	1745	1825	Greene Plymouth
574	Monroe	Leonard	1757	1827	Norwich
575	Monroe	Samuel	1720	1777	Norwich
576	Monroe	William	1761	1838	Norwich Plymouth
577	Moore	Roderick	1761	1841	Bainbridge
578	Morgan	Benjamin		1810	Bainbridge
579	Morgan	Joseph	1754	1829	Bainbridge
580	Morgan	Roswell	1764	1838	Guilford

REVOLUTIONARY WAR VETERANS
CHENANGO COUNTY-NEW YORK

VETERANS LIST

	- NAME -		- YEAR -		
PAGE	LAST	FIRST	BIRTH	DEATH	TOWN
581	Morley	Demick	1750	1834	Smyrna
582	Morton	Joel	1754	1849	Norwich
583	Moss	Joseph	1742	1819	New Berlin
584	Mowers	Conrad	1758		Smyrna
585	Mudge	Aaron	1748	1827	Guilford
586	Mudge	Abraham	1753	1833	Bainbridge Sherburne
587	Mudge	Jared	1757	1841	Guilford
588	Mudge	John	1755	1839	Sherburne
589	Munroe	Lemuel	1759	1818	New Berlin
590	Munson	Wilmot	1755	1845	Oxford
591	Murray	Elihu	1753	1835	Guilford Oxford
592	Nash	John	1747	1834	Guilford
593	Newall	Thomas	1765	1822	Bainbridge
594	Newton	Thaddeus	1745	1812	Afton
595	Newton	Winslow	1756	1835	Plymouth
596	Nichols	James	1742	1816	Afton
597	Nichols	Paul	1753	1831	Afton
598	Nichols	Samuel	1766	1852	Bainbridge
599	Nicholson	William	1758	1831	Preston
600	Noble	Lyman	1758	1840	Greene
601	Northrup	Joel	1753	1801	Sherburne
602	Northrup	Stephen	1758	1841	Sherburne
603	Norton	Abel	1757		Greene
604	Norton	Seba	1760	1835	Norwich
605	Norton	Stephen	1756		Norwich
606	Norton	William	1766		McDonough
607	Noyes	Gersham	1764	1832	Preston
608	Nurse	Caleb	1760		Bainbridge
609	Odle	Warren	1752	1823	Otselic German
610	Olney	Emor	1741	1830	Columbus
611	Olney	Esek	1755	1841	Columbus
612	Ostrander	Moses		1814	New Berlin
613	Owen	Alvan	1764	1850	Guilford
614	Owen	Alvan	1737	1820	Guilford
615	Owen	William	1741	1827	
616	Packard	Oliver	1761	1838	Coventry
617	Paddleford	Phillip	1753	1830	Greene

REVOLUTIONARY WAR VETERANS
CHENANGO COUNTY-NEW YORK

VETERANS LIST

PAGE	- NAME -		- YEAR -		
	LAST	FIRST	BIRTH	DEATH	TOWN
618	Padget	James	1746	1830	Oxford
619	Page	Jeremiah	1740	1814	Columbus
620	Page	Joseph	1761	1834	Columbus
621	Palmer	Elijah	1766	1834	Columbus
622	Palmer	John	1757	1843	Columbus
623	Palmer	Josiah	1745	1831	Columbus
624	Palmer	Nehemiah	1738	1830	Columbus
625	Palmer	Nehemiah	1764	1836	Columbus
626	Palmer	Noah	1756	1840	Sherburne
627	Palmer	Stephen	1760	1845	Greene
628	Parker	John	1752	1823	Norwich
629	Parker	Jotham	1754	1815	Coventry
630	Parker	Samuel	1750	1835	Greene
631	Partridge	Ozias	1763	1836	Otselic
632	Payne	Rufus	1757	1837	Sherburne Otselic
633	Peck	Azel	1764	1834	Columbus
634	Peck	John	1742	1819	North Norwich Sherburne
635	Peck	William	1763	1840	North Norwich
636	Pendleton	Nathan	1754	1841	Norwich
637	Pendleton	Simeon	1756	1822	New Berlin
638	Percival	John	1754	1837	Smyrna
639	Perlee	Edmund	1752	1822	North Norwich
640	Perry	David	1759	1836	Sherburne Lincklaen
641	Perry	Ebenezer		1787	Oxford
642	Perry	Jonathan	1762		Pharsalia
643	Phelps	Joel	1759	1836	Guilford
644	Phelps	Jonathan	1764	1857	Smithville
645	Phelps	Levi	1749	1829	Plymouth
646	Phelps	Oliver	1765	1848	Guilford
647	Phetteplace	Samuel	1735	1813	Norwich
648	Philley	Rememberance	1753	1837	McDonough Guilford
649	Phillips	Aaron	1758	1831	Norwich Guilford New Berlin
650	Phillips	Isaac	1762	1858	Greene
651	Phillips	James	1753	1836	New Berlin

REVOLUTIONARY WAR VETERANS
CHENANGO COUNTY-NEW YORK

VETERANS LIST

PAGE	LAST - NAME -	FIRST	BIRTH - YEAR -	DEATH	TOWN
652	Phillips	Joseph	1751	1834	
653	Phillips	Luke	1759	1838	Oxford
654	Phillips	Sylvester	1758	1841	Guilford
655	Pier	Levi	1754	1826	Oxford
656	Pierce	Daniel		1823	
657	Pierce	Joseph	1757	1835	Smithville
658	Pike	Jesse	1756	1799	North Norwich
659	Pike	Joseph	1760	1842	Coventry
660	Plumb	Joseph	1762		North Norwich
661	Plymate	Benoni	1755		New Berlin
662	Pollard	David	1745	1830	Afton
663	Pond	Phinehas	1758	1846	Smithville
664	Porter	Ezekiel	1762	1840	Smithville
665	Porter	Samuel	1755	1837	Coventry
666	Porter	Truman	1763	1838	Coventry
667	Powers	Avery	1748	1813	Norwich
668	Pratt	Levi	1766	1846	Afton
669	Pratt	Solomon	1752	1838	New Berlin
670	Prentis	Joseph	1733	1804	Plymouth
671	Prentis	Samuel	1764	1854	Plymouth
672	Preston	Isaac	1748	1785	Oxford
673	Preston	Samuel	1763	1836	Columbus
674	Prince	Edward	1755	1837	Bainbridge
675	Pritchard	George	1747	1826	Smyrna Otselic
676	Provost	Thomas	1756		Greene
677	Pulford	Joseph	1759	1838	Lincklaen
678	Punderson	John	1747	1836	McDonough
679	Purdy	Abner	1752	1821	North Norwich
680	Purdy	Ebenezer	1707	1806	North Norwich
681	Purdy	James	1750	1828	Plymouth
682	Purdy	Jeremiah	1761	1842	Sherburne
683	Purdy	Josiah	1760	1849	Sherburne
684	Purdy	Stephen	1754	1812	North Norwich
685	Race	Phillip	1748	1820	Greene
686	Ramsdell	James	1758	1821	Plymouth
687	Randall	Jedediah	1758	1844	Norwich
688	Randall	Thomas	1741	1831	Norwich

VETERANS LIST

PAGE	LAST	FIRST	BIRTH	DEATH	TOWN
689	Ransom	Elisha	1746	1818	North Norwich
					Plymouth
					Norwich
690	Rathbone	Moses	1754	1823	Greene
691	Rathbun	Paris	1760	1824	Oxford
692	Ray	Benjamin	1756	1834	Preston
693	Raymond	Abraham	1757	1830	Sherburne
694	Raymond	Newcomb	1763	1852	Sherburne
695	Redfield	Levi	1745	1838	Bainbridge
696	Reed	Garret	1752	1842	Sherburne
					Columbus
697	Rexford	Joel	1750	1821	Sherburne
					Smyrna
698	Reynolds	Isaac	1758	1846	Afton
699	Reynolds	Jacob	1757	1837	Norwich
					Guilford
700	Rhodes	Joseph	1758	1830	Guilford
701	Rice	Abner	1753	1822	Guilford
702	Rice	Chauncey	1756		Norwich
703	Richmond	David	1748	1818	Guilford
704	Robbins	Joseph	1756	1827	Smithville
705	Robertson	Ebenezer	1759	1850	German
					Guilford
706	Robinson	Samuel	1752	1815	Oxford
707	Roby	Silas	1754	1833	Smithville
708	Root	Ebenezer	1760	1842	Guilford
					Bainbridge
					Oxford
709	Root	Moses	1745	1818	Pitcher
710	Root	Nicholas	1743	1813	Coventry
711	Root	William	1759	1848	Greene
712	Rosa	Abraham	1760	1844	Greene
713	Rose	Joseph	1760	1840	Sherburne
714	Ross	Andrew	1741	1819	Oxford
715	Rouse	Casper	1734	1811	Norwich
716	Rowland	Benjamin	1754	1831	Sherburne
717	Rowlandson	Reuben	1757	1830	Columbus
					Sherburne
718	Rowley	Seth	1757	1833	Norwich
					New Berlin

REVOLUTIONARY WAR VETERANS
CHENANGO COUNTY-NEW YORK

VETERANS LIST

PAGE	LAST	FIRST	BIRTH	DEATH	TOWN
719	Rundel	Joseph	1762	1855	Oxford
720	Sabin	Ziba	1749	1825	Plymouth
721	Sage	Daniel	1756	1852	New Berlin
722	Sanford	Jonathan	1757	1836	Coventry
723	Saunders	Joseph	1764		Bainbridge
724	Sayles	Richard	1752	1822	Norwich
725	Scarritt	James	1761	1839	Smyrna
726	Scoville	Bela	1758	1818	Sherburne
727	Scoville	Timothy	1762	1845	Smithville Greene
728	Scribner	Daniel	1744	1813	New Berlin
729	Secor	John	1764	1846	Norwich Guilford
730	Seeley	Eli	1764	1850	Bainbridge
731	Serls	Amos	1754		
732	Sexton	Elijah	1754	1839	Smyrna
733	Sexton	George	1744	1815	Plymouth
734	Seymour	Zadock	1757	1845	Sherburne
735	Shapley	David	1760	1827	Oxford
736	Shapley	Utter	1754		Guilford
737	Shattuck	John	1752	1821	Norwich
738	Shattuck	Thomas	1752	1834	Smithville
739	Sheffield	Joseph	1759	1848	New Berlin
740	Sheldon	Benjamin	1751	1816	Norwich
741	Sheldon	Epaphras	1753	1829	Smithville
742	Sheldon	Ezekiel	1758	1846	Plymouth
743	Sheldon	Isaac	1755	1844	Sherburne
744	Shepard	Rufus	1766		Sherburne
745	Sherburne	James	1743	1824	Sherburne
746	Sherman	Bacheldor	1761	1828	New Berlin
747	Sherwood	Asa	1762	1834	Guilford
748	Shippey	Thomas	1747	1823	Norwich
749	Shute	William	1750	1841	Oxford
750	Simmons	John	1761	1843	New Berlin
751	Simmons	William	1765	1849	Oxford
752	Simonds	Joshua	1734	1824	New Berlin
753	Simonds	Joshua	1767	1838	New Berlin
754	Simons	Ensley	1745	1832	Smithville Oxford
755	Simons	Joseph	1757	1842	Smyrna

VETERANS LIST

PAGE	LAST	FIRST	BIRTH	DEATH	TOWN
756	Skinner	Luther	1753	1827	Otselic
757	Skinner	Stephen	1753	1842	Sherburne
758	Slater	Joseph	1745	1828	Preston
759	Sloan	William	1755	1828	Norwich
760	Smiley	William	1753	1825	Preston Norwich
761	Smith	Ebenezer	1761	1823	Coventry
762	Smith	Eleazer	1727	1822	Oxford
763	Smith	Elisha	1757	1846	Norwich Guilford
764	Smith	Enoch	1760	1852	German Greene
765	Smith	Esquire	1768	1824	Norwich
766	Smith	Israel	1739	1811	Bainbridge
767	Smith	Jehial	1761	1825	Coventry
768	Smith	John	1758	1852	Smithville McDonough
769	Smith	John	1760	1810	Sherburne
770	Smith	Justus	1761	1816	Sherburne
771	Smith	Obadiah		1818	
772	Smith	William	1755	1816	Sherburne
773	Somes	John	1761	1856	Afton
774	Soper	Timothy	1745	1845	Pitcher
775	Spaulding	Sampson	1745	1832	Columbus
776	Spear	Elkanah	1758		Norwich
777	Spencer	Nathaniel	1737	1807	Bainbridge
778	Spencer	Orange	1765	1843	Guilford
779	Spencer	William	1763	1842	Coventry Guilford
780	Sprauge	Ebenezer	1747	1837	Oxford
781	Sprauge	Samuel	1763		Oxford
782	Sprague	Silas	1762	1840	Greene
783	Stafford	Andrew	1755	1842	Sherburne
784	Stanley	Timothy	1755		Smyrna German
785	Starr	Samuel	1765	1844	Smyrna
786	Stebbins	Samuel	1758	1833	Sherburne

REVOLUTIONARY WAR VETERANS
CHENANGO COUNTY-NEW YORK

VETERANS LIST

PAGE	LAST - NAME -	FIRST	BIRTH - YEAR -	DEATH	TOWN
787	Stephens	James	1740	1836	McDonough
					Smithville
					Greene
					Oxford
788	Stevens	Abijah	1756	1844	Afton
789	Stewart	John	1744	1810	Oxford
					Smithville
790	Stewart	John	1763	1848	Columbus
791	Stockwell	Abel	1744	1805	Bainbridge
792	Stoddard	Frederick	1761		Norwich
793	Stone	Seth	1763	1826	Afton
794	Stone	William	1759	1840	Bainbridge
795	Stow	Samuel	1742	1835	Oxford
796	Stowell	Asa	1760	1826	Afton
797	Stowell	Hezekiah	1732	1793	Afton
798	Stowell	Israel	1765	1832	Afton
799	Straight	Daniel	1742	1817	
800	Straight	Joshua	1758	1826	Greene
801	Straight	William	1758	1841	Bainbridge
802	Sullivan	Charles		1822	Pitcher
803	Swartout	Moses	1761		German
804	Sweet	John	1754	1837	Smyrna
					Otselic
805	Taylor	Gad	1757	1841	Otselic
806	Taylor	George	1765	1860	Pitcher
807	Taylor	Martin	1764		Norwich
808	Taylor	Reuben	1759	1833	Norwich
809	Taylor	Samuel	1765	1827	Guilford
810	Taylor	Thomas	1744	1826	Oxford
811	Tenbroeck	John	1764	1854	Oxford
812	Terry	Ebenezer	1753	1854	Guilford
813	Terry	Elnathan	1758	1840	Norwich
814	Terwilliger	James	1759	1835	Greene
815	Terwilliger	Josiah	1756	1833	Guilford
816	Terwilliger	Simon	1753	1831	Greene
817	Thompson	Caleb	1758	1845	Norwich
					Sherburne
818	Thompson	Joel	1760	1843	Sherburne
819	Thorn	Henry	1759		Plymouth
820	Throop	Benjamin	1744	1822	Oxford

REVOLUTIONARY WAR VETERANS
CHENANGO COUNTY-NEW YORK

VETERANS LIST

PAGE	- NAME -		- YEAR -		
	LAST	FIRST	BIRTH	DEATH	TOWN
821	Throop	Dan	1768	1824	Oxford
822	Tiffany	Humphrey	1750	1831	New Berlin
					North Norwich
823	Tiffany	Philemon	1759	1841	Plymouth
824	Tillotson	Jacob	1761	1843	Columbus
					Sherburne
825	Tillotson	Joseph			Greene
826	Tobey	Joseph	1759	1830	Smyrna
827	Tracy	Ebenezer	1762	1835	Plymouth
828	Tracy	John	1755	1821	Columbus
829	Tracy	Uri	1764	1838	Oxford
830	Tremain	Daniel	1758	1853	Greene
831	Truair	Manuel	1759	1841	Sherburne
832	Tubbs	Ichabod	1759	1832	Greene
					Coventry
833	Tuthill	William	1760		Oxford
834	Tyler	Chauncey	1764	1854	McDonough
835	Tyler	Nathan	1752	1831	Norwich
					Columbus
836	Tyler	Nathaniel	1761	1795	Greene
837	Vanderhule	Abraham	1757	1837	Bainbridge
					Preston
838	VanGaasbeck	Thomas	1756	1841	Oxford
839	VanWagenen	Gerritt	1753	1835	Oxford
840	Vaughn	John	1736	1827	Sherburne
841	Vergeson	Daniel	1763	1844	Plymouth
842	Vickery	Elijah	1761	1821	Smithville
843	Vosburg	Peter	1756	1841	German
844	Wait	Asa	1747	1827	Norwich
845	Wait	John	1743	1801	Preston
846	Wait	Joseph	1750	1832	Norwich
847	Wakefield	Samuel	1753	1840	Pitcher
848	Wales	Nathan	1750	1825	Plymouth
849	Walker	Edward	1756	1842	Bainbridge
					Greene
850	Walker	James	1752	1841	Greene
					Oxford
851	Wallace	John	1756	1840	Oxford
					Greene
852	Wallis	Henry	1758	1840	Bainbridge

REVOLUTIONARY WAR VETERANS
CHENANGO COUNTY-NEW YORK

VETERANS LIST

PAGE	- NAME -		- YEAR -		
	LAST	FIRST	BIRTH	DEATH	TOWN
853	Walsworth	William	1755	1825	Preston
854	Warne	Richard	1740	1800	Greene
855	Warner	Amasa	1759		New Berlin
856	Warner	James	1767	1837	Smithville
857	Warner	Solomon	1761	1839	Bainbridge
858	Warren	Ichabod			McDonough
859	Warren	Moses	1755	1833	Columbus
860	Warriner	Willard	1753	1835	Sherburne
861	Warters	David	1748	1834	Guilford
862	Wasson	John	1764	1839	Norwich
863	Waterman	Darius	1760	1846	Pharsalia
864	Waters	Bigelow	1760	1833	Sherburne
865	Wattles	Charles	1758	1834	Norwich
866	Wattles	Nathaniel	1750	1798	Oxford
867	Weaver	Jonathan	1753	1813	Plymouth
868	Weaver	Joshua	1753	1811	Pharsalia
869	Weaver	Lodowick	1763	1848	Pharsalia
870	Webb	Andrew	1759	1834	Norwich
871	Wedge	David	1743	1813	Bainbridge
872	Welch	Ebenezer	1758	1823	Norwich
873	Welch	John	1745	1831	Norwich
874	Welch	John	1763	1841	Norwich
875	Welch	Thomas	1756		Oxford
876	Wells	Asa	1756	1841	Oxford
					Preston
877	Wells	Ephriam	1831	1799	Preston
878	Wells	Ephraim	1770	1854	Preston
879	Wells	Gurden	1757	1827	Lincklaen
880	Welton	Shubael	1761	1831	Guilford
881	Westcott	Amos	1761	1840	Oxford
					Norwich
882	Westcott	Thomas	1761		Oxford
883	Westgate	James	1757		Sherburne
					Smyrna
884	Wheeler	Ezekial	1748	1826	Guilford
885	Wheeler	Hezekiah	1750	1828	Oxford
886	Wheeler	Jesse	1762		Bainbridge
					Smyrna
887	Wheeler	Samuel	1758	1808	Greene
888	White	Ichabod	1761	1813	Norwich

REVOLUTIONARY WAR VETERANS
CHENANGO COUNTY-NEW YORK

VETERANS LIST

PAGE	LAST - NAME -	FIRST	BIRTH	- YEAR - DEATH	TOWN
889	White	Samuel	1765	1814	New Berlin
890	White	Theophilus	1755	1842	Guilford
891	White	William	1742	1827	Bainbridge
892	White	William	1759	1840	
893	White	William	1763	1850	Norwich
894	Whitford	Christopher	1758	1811	Sherburne
895	Whiting	Jesse	1763	1845	Bainbridge
896	Whitmarsh	Ezra	1760	1835	Greene
897	Whitmore	James	1761	1840	Greene Bainbridge
898	Widger	Eli	1756	1848	Preston
899	Wilbur	Record	1763	1862	Coventry
900	Wilcox	Job	1743	1808	Smithville
901	Wilder	Reuben	1761	1840	Greene
902	Willard	Simon	1751	1789	Greene
903	Williams	Henry	1762	1850	Columbus
904	Williams	McKane			Columbus
905	Willoughby	Bliss	1767	1849	Oxford Preston
906	Willson	Benjamin	1741	1809	Oxford
907	Winsor	Anan	1749	1820	Norwich
908	Winsor	Stephen	1744	1820	Guilford
909	Wood	Abner	1744	1821	Norwich
910	Wood	Charles	1750	1841	Bainbridge
911	Wood	Joshua	1766	1845	Plymouth
912	Woodcock	Nehemiah	1738	1816	
913	Woodruff	Samuel	1753	1823	Guilford
914	Woods	Elisha	1760	1841	Bainbridge
915	Woodward	Samuel	1763		Bainbridge
916	Wright	Silas	1752	1827	Afton
917	Wylie	James	1753	1842	Coventry
918	Wynkoop	William	1753	1827	
919	Yale	Job	1738	1799	Coventry
920	Yale	Uriah	1761	1833	Guilford
921	Yarrington	William	1760	1840	Plymouth
922	York	John	1716	1784	Norwich
923	Young	Joseph	1760	1842	Smyrna

REVOLUTIONARY WAR VETERANS
CHENANGO COUNTY-NEW YORK

POSSIBLE VETERANS

- NAME -		- YEAR -		
LAST	FIRST	BIRTH	DEATH	TOWN
Aldrich	Benjamin	1753	1831	Norwich
Aldrich	Gardner	1768	1853	Norwich
Aldrich	Timothy	1762	1837	Norwich
Alexander	Thomas	1751	1810	Greene
Allason	Aner	1751	1831	Coventry
Allcott	Benjamin	1764	1858	Columbus
Amsbry	Israel	1740	1825	Otselic
Andrews	Judah	1746	1830	Oxford
Avery	George	1763	1860	Oxford
Aylesworth	Andrew	1763	1840	Afton
Babcock	Jesse	1750	1831	Sherburne
Balcom	Francis	1767	1850	Oxford
Baldwin	Henry	1763	1831	Sherburne
Baldwin	Jonathan	1765	1845	Oxford
Ballou	Sylvanus	1767	1857	Norwich
Bamford	James	1763	1843	Plymouth
Barber	Asa	1757	1829	Lincklaen
Barker	William	1762	1855	McDonough
Barnes	Abel	1723		Columbus
Barnes	William W	1750	1834	Greene
Barnum	Noah	1758	1821	Columbus
Barstow	William	1762	1826	Guilford
Baxter	John	1754	1827	New Berlin
Beardslee	Samuel	1751	1830	Coventry
Beardslee	William	1768	1846	McDonough
Beattey	Alexander	1763	1835	New Berlin
Beech	Curtis	1753	1820	Pitcher
Beers	John	1768	1832	Sherburne
Bement	Judah	1730	1815	Plymouth
Benedict	Benjamin	1767	1850	Coventry
Bennett	Moses	1748	1832	Oxford
Benson	Ebenezer	1767	1833	Greene
Bent	Thomas	1740	1819	Sherburne
Bentley	Ebenezer	1762	1839	Lincklaen
Benton	Abraham	1763	1816	Afton
Benton	Nathaniel	1761	1845	Afton
Bidwell	Jacob	1727	1794	Coventry
Billings	John	1765	1828	Smyrna
Birdsall	Henry	1758	1837	Greene
Blakeslee	Clement	1763	1853	Coventry

POSSIBLE VETERANS

— NAME —   — YEAR —

LAST	FIRST	BIRTH	DEATH	TOWN
Bliven	John	1759	1825	Preston
Blood	Jared	1764	1835	Columbus
Bolster	Lott	1752		German
Borden	Jacob P	1753	1821	Smithville
Bradley	David	1753	1837	Greene
Bridgeman	Reuben	1764	1834	Afton
Briggs	Spencer	1764	1825	Columbus
Brown	Consider	1754	1833	Preston
Brown	Jerediah	1764	1813	Smithville
Brown	Joshua	1757	1808	New Berlin
Brown	Nehemiah	1740	1824	Pharsalia
Brown	Nehemiah	1768	1845	Pharsalia
Brown	Obadiah	1761	1828	Plymouth
Brown	Stephen	1764	1841	Preston
Brownell	Jonathan	1768	1859	Columbus
Browning	Benjamin	1752	1828	Norwich
Bryan	Richard	1747	1811	Sherburne
Burdick	Daniel	1746	1808	Lincklaen
Burdick	Kinyon	176-	1850	Pitcher
Burlingame	Joshua	1768	1852	Norwich
Burlison	James	1762	1842	Guilford
Burwell	Samuel	1765	1818	North Norwich
Butler	Benjamin	1764	1839	Oxford
Byram	George	1767	1831	Greene
Calkins	Asa	1757	1834	New Berlin
Calkins	Nathaniel	1766	1842	Columbus
Calkins	Nathaniel	1742	1823	Columbus
Camp	Simeon	1757	1817	New Berlin
Campbell	Ephraim	1745	1815	Columbus
Campbell	John		1808	Bainbridge
Canneff	Jeremiah	1754	1842	Greene
Carpenter	John	1750	1828	Smithville
Carrier	Asa	1766	1845	Columbus
Chandler	Henry	1754	1826	Bainbridge
Chappel	S.C.	1753	1838	Smithville
Church	John	1766	1825	Oxford
Church	John	1732	1808	Oxford
Church	Richard	1768	1813	Afton
Clark	Anthony	1760	1837	New Berlin
Clark	George	1761	1813	Columbus

REVOLUTIONARY WAR VETERANS
CHENANGO COUNTY-NEW YORK

POSSIBLE VETERANS

- NAME -		- YEAR -		
LAST	FIRST	BIRTH	DEATH	TOWN
Clark	Jared C	1758	1841	Columbus
Clark	Jonathan	1760	1827	Guilford
Clarke	Christopher	1744	1813	New Berlin
Cline	Frederick	1768	1815	Smithville
Clitz	John	1754	1831	Plymouth
Coe	Benjamin	1742	1834	Sherburne
Cole	Jacob	1705	1800	North Norwich
Colwell	Charles	1741	1822	Plymouth
Colwell	Robert	1765	1858	Plymouth
Cone	Joseph	1750	1814	New Berlin
Cook	Elijah	1750	1812	Norwich
Cook	Joseph	1750	1808	Plymouth
Corbin	John	1724	1818	Smithville
Cornell	Elemuel	1767	1848	Guilford
Coy	Simeon	1768	1832	Guilford
Crandall	Reuben	1763	1815	Smithville
Crosby	Elisha	1763	1818	Afton
Crosby	Samuel	1741	1823	Norwich
Curtis	Samuel	1764	1840	Oxford
Davis	Reuben	1766	1844	Sherburne
Decker	Cornelius	1765	1829	New Berlin
Denison	Daniel	1740	1818	Norwich
Denison	John	1767	1836	Guilford
Dermend	John	1751	1840	Guilford
DeZang	Frederick	1756	1838	Bainbridge
Dickenson	Daniel T	1767	1841	Guilford
Dodge	James	1740	1816	Preston
Dodge	Solomon	1768	1830	Oxford
Dorman	James	1755	1838	Guilford
Dow	Cyrus	1765	1842	Sherburne
Dungan	Thomas	1765	1849	North Norwich
Dyer	Oliver	1739	1823	New Berlin
Easton	Oliver	1765	1839	Afton
Eddy	John	1767	1820	Guilford
Egenton	John	1763	1807	Plymouth
Egleston	John	1744	1830	Greene
Elliott	Adin	1763	1837	Greene
Elliott	Joseph	1730	1800	Greene
Elliott	Thomas	1766	1851	Greene
Elsworth	George	1758	1829	Pitcher

REVOLUTIONARY WAR VETERANS
CHENANGO COUNTY-NEW YORK

POSSIBLE VETERANS

- NAME -		- YEAR -		
LAST	FIRST	BIRTH	DEATH	TOWN
Elsworth	Theophilus	1748	1838	Coventry
Enos	Ebenezer	1765	1808	Oxford
Fairchild	Daniel	1748	1804	Pitcher
Fairchild	David	1743	1805	Preston
Fisher	Daniel	1757	1820	North Norwich
Fisher	John	1738	1817	Oxford
Fitch	Uriah	1755	1808	Plymouth
Foster	Asa	1747	1813	Norwich
Foster	Nathan	1753		Norwich
Fox	Amasa	1767	1858	Sherburne
French	Manasseh	1751		Norwich
Frisbee	Luman	1760	1818	Pharsalia
Gardner	Levi	1768	1826	Plymouth
Gates	Simeon	1757	1829	Norwich
Genung	Gilbert	1760	1839	New Berlin
Gibbs	William	1764	1838	Guilford
Gibson	Allen	1762	1834	Lincklaen
Gibson	William	1762	1829	Norwich
Gilmore	James	1747	1824	Norwich
Gilmore	Lemuel	1756	1826	Coventry
Gleason	Luthur	1761	1819	Plymouth
Glover	James	1768		Preston
Goodrich	Hubbard	1766	1829	Otselic
Graham	James	1747	1837	Bainbridge
Grant	Joshua	1754	1824	New Berlin
Grant	Noah	1747	1801	Preston
Graves	Charles	1762	1842	Norwich
Graves	Israel	1760		Norwich
Gray	Amos	1753	1820	Greene
Griswold	Samuel	1762	1842	Coventry
Grover	Jonathan	1764	1845	Otselic
Grow	Jacob	1765	1818	North Norwich
Guthrie	William	1768	1813	Bainbridge
Hall	Alpheus	1765	1832	Smyrna
Hall	Benjamin	1763	1845	New Berlin
Hall	Samuel	1742	1810	Sherburne
Hamilton	John	1752	1825	Norwich
Hammond	Samuel	1757	1821	Norwich
Harmon	John	1754	1819	Afton
Harris	John	1744	1797	Norwich

REVOLUTIONARY WAR VETERANS
CHENANGO COUNTY-NEW YORK

POSSIBLE VETERANS

- NAME -		- YEAR -		
LAST	FIRST	BIRTH	DEATH	TOWN
Harris	Thomas	1747	1827	Sherburne
Harrison	Andrew	1758	1811	Smithville
Harrison	James	1767	1849	Smithville
Hart	David	1749	1830	Smithville
Hartwell	Ebenezer	1768	1857	North Norwich
Hayes	Nathaniel	1742	1807	Greene
Haynes	Samuel	1764	1844	Guilford
Hazzard	James	1764	1847	New Berlin
Hewitt	Dudley	1765		Preston
Hewitt	Gurdon	1767	1816	Preston
Hibbard	John	1760	1830	Sherburne
Hill	Caleb	1754	1814	New Berlin
Hinman	Amos	1765	1822	Coventry
Holdridge	Richard	1757	1824	Smithville
Holliday	John	1761	1833	Sherburne
Holt	Elijah	1768	1850	Columbus
Holt	John	1757	1825	Sherburne
Horton	Calvin	1764	1835	Coventry
Horton	Rueben	1765	1845	Greene
Howell	Jesse	1755	1835	Norwich
Hull	Samuel	1742	1830	Norwich
Hunt	Luthur	1761	1830	Oxford
Huntley	Stephen	1740	1825	Sherburne
Huntley	Sylvenus	1749	1825	Smithville
Huntley	Zenos	1759	1805	Columbus
Hutchinson	Aaron	1767	1833	Sherburne
Hutchinson	Jesse	176-		Sherburne
Hyde	Abel	1757	1839	Columbus
Inman	Jesse	1765	1855	Plymouth
Ives	Amasa	1763	1823	Coventry
Ives	Samuel	1766	1811	Guilford
Jackson	Comfort	1740	1834	Greene
Jackson	Isaac	1758	1850	Columbus
Jackson	Richard	1753	1821	North Norwich
Jacox	John	1765	1852	New Berlin
Jewell	Justus	1748	1834	Guilford
Johnson	Benjamin	1758	1822	Otselic
Johnson	Jesse	1768	1840	Greene
Johnson	Joel	1768	1806	Guilford
Jones	Simon	1750	1817	Coventry

REVOLUTIONARY WAR VETERANS
CHENANGO COUNTY-NEW YORK

POSSIBLE VETERANS

- NAME -		- YEAR -		
LAST	FIRST	BIRTH	DEATH	TOWN
Judd	Harvey	1763	1857	Coventry
Judson	Ezekial	1743	1821	New Berlin
Kendall	Phineas	1747	1838	Oxford
Kenyon	Jonathan	1752	1831	Pitcher
Kenyon	Joshua	1751	1814	Coventry
Ketchum	Stephen	1752	1810	Greene
Kimball	Enos	1762	1845	New Berlin
Kinney	Barnabus	1754	1834	New Berlin
Knapp	Colby	1768	1853	Guilford
Knapp	Jonas	1757	1829	Smithville
Lamphere	Jeffery	1765	1855	Pharsalia
Lane	Caleb	1766	1840	Greene
Lathrop	Eleazer	1766	1842	Sherburne
Lathrop	John	1762	1825	Sherburne
Lawton	Gideon	1766	1821	McDonough
Lawton	Noyes	1762	1834	McDonough
Lee	Ashel	1755	1817	Sherburne
Lee	Daniel	1745	1836	Sherburne
Lee	Joel	1742		Sherburne
Lee	Philamon	1746	1823	Guilford
Light	Henry	1764	1846	New Berlin
Lobdell	John	1767	1848	Sherburne
Locke	Nathaniel	1723		Oxford
Locke	Nathaniel	1766	1820	Oxford
Loomis	John	1765	1805	Bainbridge
Low	Thomas	1755	1819	Sherburne
Lowrey	George	1761	1838	Coventry
Lyon	Benjamin	1767	1854	Sherburne
Maine	Luthur	1766	1846	Oxford
Mandeville	John	1750	1819	Coventry
Mann	Israel	1750	1805	Norwich
Marks	Richard	1754	1829	Norwich
Marsh	Ely	1764	1839	Sherburne
Martin	Samuel	1763	1840	Coventry
Maynard	Jesse	1765	1843	McDonough
McCulloch	Alexander	1763	1808	Sherburne
McGeorge	Horatio	1755	1852	Oxford
McMaster	John	1758	1836	Sherburne
McMinn	John	1754	1846	Pharsalia
McNeil	John	1767	1832	Oxford

REVOLUTIONARY WAR VETERANS
CHENANGO COUNTY-NEW YORK

POSSIBLE VETERANS

- NAME -		- YEAR -		
LAST	FIRST	BIRTH	DEATH	TOWN
Mead	Jonathan	1765	1843	North Norwich
Medbury	Benjamin	1768	1841	New Berlin
Medbury	Nathaniel	1747	1813	New Berlin
Merritt	Ebenezer	1763	1850	Afton
Miles	John	1745	1818	Coventry
Miller	Andrew	1743	1812	Oxford
Miller	William	1761	1814	Guilford
Monroe	David	1739	1809	Norwich
Moore	Jonah	1764	1815	Oxford
Moore	Richard	1763	1830	Smithville
Morse	Hezekiah	1767	1827	Oxford
Mowry	George	1765	1823	Oxford
Mudge	Daniel	1745	1826	Guilford
Muir	John	1753	1823	Sherburne
Nichols	Ishmael	1766	1824	Smithville
Norris	Henry	1748	1835	Smithville
Noyes	John	1768	1830	Preston
Olds	Ezekiel	1765	1849	Oxford
Ostrom	Rudolph	1763	1839	Guilford
Packer	William	1763	1852	Preston
Paddelford	Jonathan	1745	1825	Sherburne
Palmer	Ashel	1755	1842	Sherburne
Palmer	Daniel	1749		Guilford
Parker	Amos	1749	1817	Coventry
Parker	Levi	1767	1846	Coventry
Parker	Nathan	1765	1855	Norwich
Parker	Stephen	1765	1809	Sherburne
Parker	William	1763	1855	German
Pearsall	Samuel	1765		Bainbridge
Pearsall	Thomas	1752	1826	Bainbridge
Pease	George	1766	1845	Smyrna
Peck	Gideon	1741		New Berlin
Peck	Joseph	1741	1817	Bainbridge
Pellet	Asa	1767	1838	Norwich
Pellet	Hezekiah	1758	1816	Norwich
Perry	Daniel	1756	1818	Bainbridge
Perry	Isaac	1762	1810	Greene
Pheips	William	1760	1844	New Berlin
Phillips	James	1751	1841	Coventry
Pierce	Samuel	1754	1825	Pitcher

REVOLUTIONARY WAR VETERANS
CHENANGO COUNTY - NEW YORK

POSSIBLE VETERANS

LAST	FIRST	BIRTH	DEATH	TOWN
Pike	Jarvis	1763	1829	North Norwich
Pike	Michael	1763	1832	McDonough
Potter	Abel	1726		Bainbridge
Pratt	Joshua	1742	1827	Sherburne
Prentis	Nathaniel	1766	1809	Plymouth
Prince	Jonathan	1753	1829	Greene
Purdy	Stephen	1727	1805	North Norwich
Randall	John	1754	1818	Norwich
Ransford	Hascall	1766	1839	Norwich
Ransford	William	1728	1814	Norwich
Ranson	Elisha	1746	1818	North Norwich
Rathbun	Gideon	1736		Columbus
Rathbun	Thomas	1736		Norwich
Record	Comfort	1766	1849	Sherburne
Redfield	Jared	1766	1814	Bainbridge
Reynolds	Nathan	1766	1850	Pitcher
Rice	Phinehas	1767	1844	Smyrna
Robbins	Job	1766	1860	Afton
Robinson	Noah	1766	1836	Sherburne
Robinson	William	1764	1838	North Norwich
Rogers	Davis	1754	1833	Preston
Rogers	Ethan	1768	1841	Preston
Rogers	Jesse	1743	1835	Oxford
Rogers	Stephen	1747	1817	Coventry
Roos	Gideon	1767	1830	Greene
Root	Joel	1767		Guilford
Root	Joshua	1741	1809	Oxford
Root	Thomas	1765	1853	Oxford
Rosseter	Elnathan	1739		New Berlin
Rundell	Jesse	1754	1802	North Norwich
Salisbury	Gilbert	1740	1824	Norwich
Salisbury	Hale	1764	1841	Greene
Sarle	Thomas	1752	1817	New Berlin
Saunders	John	1754	1812	Afton
Scott	Stephen	1762	1828	New Berlin
Seabury	Caleb	1766	1835	Norwich
Sears	Stephen	1763	1847	Columbus
Selleck	James	1762	1830	Smithville
Sharp	Conrad	1750	1825	Greene
Sherman	Elkanah	1761	1845	New Berlin

REVOLUTIONARY WAR VETERANS
CHENANGO COUNTY-NEW YORK

POSSIBLE VETERANS

- NAME -		- YEAR -		
LAST	FIRST	BIRTH	DEATH	TOWN
Sherwood	Isaac	1768	1841	Oxford
Sherwood	Levi	1764		Oxford
Simons	Joseph	1761	1840	Bainbridge
Skeel	Elial	1765	1841	Bainbridge
Skinner	Jacob	1766	1847	Norwich
Skinner	Joseph	1768	1854	Norwich
Slater	Isaac	1765	1847	Norwich
Smith	Benjamin	1761	1825	Sherburne
Smith	David	1763	1823	Preston
Smith	Jedediah	1767	1849	Bainbridge
Smith	John	1765	1858	Greene
Smith	Joseph	1763	1840	Guilford
Smith	Joseph	1764	1853	Pitcher
Smith	Nathan	1766	1850	Pitcher
Southworth	Edward	1763	1830	Pitcher
Spaulding	Sampson	1765	1845	Columbus
Spencer	Obadiah	1735	1806	Sherburne
Spicer	William	1767	1829	Sherburne
Spoor	John	1764	1832	Oxford
Stafford	Isaac	1763	1831	Preston
Stafford	Job	1767	1846	Norwich
Steere	Stephen	1736	1816	Norwich
Steere	William	1758	1822	McDonough
Stevens	John	1760	1847	Afton
Stillman	Samuel	1747	1834	Lincklaen
Stoddard	John	1763	1821	Coventry
Stoneman	Richard	1768	1822	New Berlin
Stover	William	1765	1841	Smyrna
Stowel	Elijah	1764		Afton
Sumners	Nathan	1744	1815	New Berlin
Talbot	Benjamin	1733	1814	North Norwich
Talbot	Richmond	1763	1825	New Berlin
Talcott	Hezekiah	1739	1824	Sherburne
Talcott	Joshua	1749	1804	Sherburne
Taylor	James	1766	1827	Columbus
Taylor	Simon	1756	1834	Plymouth
Terwilliger	Peter	1751	1813	Greene
Terwilliger	Solomon	1748	1826	Greene
Thompson	James	1744	1811	Sherburne
Thompson	John	1768	1831	Bainbridge

REVOLUTIONARY WAR VETERANS
CHENANGO COUNTY-NEW YORK

POSSIBLE VETERANS

- NAME -		- YEAR -		
LAST	FIRST	BIRTH	DEATH	TOWN
Thornton	Jonathan	1764	1847	Norwich
Thrasher	William	1751	1824	New Berlin
Tiffany	Abner	1768		Guilford
Tillotson	Jacob	1737	1804	Sherburne
Tillotson	John	1742	1819	Sherburne
Titus	James	1765	1821	North Norwich
Titus	Samuel	1739	1804	North Norwich
Tower	Shubel	1768	1858	Plymouth
Townsend	Benjamin	1767	1839	Greene
Treat	Samuel	1744	1814	Oxford
Tubs	Abner	1742	1827	Sherburne
Tucker	Daniel	1763	1845	Oxford
Turner	Daniel	1750		Norwich
Tuttle	Enos	1764	1838	Smyrna
Underwood	Elias	1748	1799	Columbus
Vail	Caleb	1726	1817	New Berlin
Vail	Job	1757	1825	New Berlin
Waldron	Nathaniel	1768	1831	Pharsalia
Warner	Daniel	1729		Otselic
Warner	Timothy	1766	1835	Otselic
Warren	Elisha	1765	1806	Coventry
Watson	Robert	1737	1836	Greene
Watson	Stephen	1761	1828	Greene
Weatherby	Daniel	1765	1814	Oxford
Webb	James	1758		McDonough
Webb	John	1756	1832	Oxford
Weed	Nothene	1732	1815	Greene
Weeks	Stephen	1766	1813	Guilford
Welch	David	1725		Norwich
West	William	1744	1810	North Norwich
Whaples	Jonathan	1763	1808	Norwich
Whitcomb	Cornelius	1748	1815	Guilford
Whitmarsh	Zachariah	1765	1849	Greene
Whitney	Ephraim	1740	1820	Sherburne
Whittenhall	William	1759	1848	McDonough
Wightman	Benjamin	1756	1824	New Berlin
Wilcox	Hopson	1739	1822	Smyrna
Wilcox	Robert	1763	1836	Smyrna
Wilcox	Whitman	1766	1856	Norwich
Wilkins	Colley	1767	1851	Coventry

REVOLUTIONARY WAR VETERANS
CHENANGO COUNTY-NEW YORK

POSSIBLE VETERANS

- NAME -		- YEAR -		
LAST	FIRST	BIRTH	DEATH	TOWN
Williams	Asa	1763	1845	New Berlin
Williamson	William	1757	1815	Greene
Wilson	John	1759	1843	Lincklaen
Wilson	Lemuel	1766	1855	New Berlin
Wood	Joseph	1743	1810	New Berlin
Wood	Noah	1768	1811	Smyrna
Wood	Thomas	1768	1813	Norwich
Wright	Enos	1763	1842	Coventry
Wylie	James	1722	1806	Coventry
Yale	Benjamin	1751	1853	Guilford
Yale	Ozias	1766	1853	Coventry

REVOLUTIONARY WAR VETERANS
CHENANGO COUNTY-NEW YORK

VETERAN PAGE DESCRIPTION

The data gathered for each veteran has been given a unique sequence number and placed in a common format in order to facilitate the analysis of the various information.

The following will explain the various data shown:

YEAR- When a year of birth is shown without being preceded by a month it was generated by calculation. This could have been from a pension file or a tombstone where an age may have been given.

PENSION FILE NUMBER- Found under the initial printing of the veterans name on the left hand side of the page. The five digit number represents the file number given to the pension application when it was filed. A prefix was assigned to each number to indicate as follows: S=soldier ; W=widow; R=initial rejection. An application by the Veteran Followed by a subsequent application by the widow is also given a "W". The "R" (rejected) does not mean the individual did not serve, but was rejected under the early legislation for lack of minimum service, or too many assets.

DAR PATRIOT INDEX- If found on the right hand side of the page under the initial printing of the Veterans name, means that the Veteran can be found in the Patriot Index published by The Daughters Of The American Revolution. Its absence means the Veteran was not found therein.

RESIDENT DATE- The years between which the Veteran lived in Chenango County.

TOWN- Town/s of residency in Chenango County. The accuracy of this indication can be challenged in certain instances. Town boundaries were changed. Please refer to "Chenango County Formation" (C 2 in this book). An example is one area of the County starting out as "Jericho". It was renamed "Bainbridge" in 1814. In 1857 "Afton" was formed from "Bainbridge". This means that pension files will contain the fact that a Veteran resided in Jericho or Bainbridge but in reality was in the area subsequently called Afton. If the pension file shows Bainbridge and the burial occurred in Afton, you will find both towns indicated. There are a few occasions where residency was described only as Chenango County and other checking has not identified the town.

VETERAN PAGE DESCRIPTION

OTHER MASTER DATA- As available the veterans birth date, birth place, father, mother, death date, death place, burial cemetery, and burial location is shown.

SERVICE- A large part of the service information was taken from the material contained in the Veterans pension applications. In many cases copies of letters answering inquires are part of the pension file. A summary of service and genealogy type data is contained therein, so these letters were used when they existed. Most of the time you will find more detail regarding the Veteran's service by examining all the material contained within the pension file. As battles or skirmishes are listed, the date can be determined by referring to section "G". The officers named in the service section are not included in the family index.

FAMILY INFORMATION- This section will contain the soldiers marriage, her parents, birth date, prior marriage, death date and burial place.

CHILDREN- All known children will be listed along with the known genealogy as follows: Birth date, place of birth, marriage date, to whom married, [spouse's birth date, parents, other marriage, death date and burial place], death date, place of death, and burial place. Other notes may appear such as service in a war or place of residency. Codes are as follows: B= birth, M= marriage, D= death, Bur= burial, Bp= baptism, Cem= cemetery.

OTHER INFORMATION- This will contain all other known information for the Veteran. This could be an occupation, residency, pension application dates etc.

Peter   ACKART   001   Peter   ACKART
            S. 31510 Sergeant   DAR Patriot Index

RESIDENT DATE: 1792 -
TOWN: Oxford
BIRTH DATE: Nov 9, 1755
BIRTH PLACE: Rhinebeck, New York   (Dutchess County)
FATHER: John David **Ackart**
MOTHER: Anna Eva **Fraleigh**
DEATH DATE: Mar 17, 1845
DEATH PLACE: Schaghticoke, New York
CEMETERY: Elmwood
LOCATION: Schaghticoke, New York (Rensselaer Co.)

TOMBSTONE INSCRIPTION:

Peter Ackart	Jemima
Peter Ackart	Wife of
Died	Peter Ackart
March 17. 1845.	Died
Aged 89 years	Nov. 28. 1839.
4 months & 8 days.	Aged 78 yrs. 1 mo.
	& 15 days.

SERVICE: While a resident of Schaghticoke, Albany County, New York, he enlisted and served with the New York Troops; from March 1776, for six months as a corporal in Captain Walter Groesbeck's and Hodge's Companies in Colonel's John Knickerbocker's, Christopher Yates' and Gansecort's Regiments; from sometime in June 1777, three months and twenty days as a corporal in Captain Walter Grosebeck's Company, Colonel John Knickerbocker's Regiment. He was in both the battles of Stillwater; in 1778, for three months and thirteen days as a sergeant in Captain Matthew DeGarmo's Company, Colonel John Knickerbocker's Regiment. In 1779 he served two or three short tours, totaling one month, as a sergeant in Captain Jacob Yates' Company, Colonel Peter Yates' Regiment. From March 1780, served three months as a sergeant in Captain Jacob Yates' Company, Colonel Peter Yates' Regiment. From sometime in 1781 until the close of the Revolution he served various times, amounting to three and one-half months in all, as a sergeant in Captain Jacob Yates' Company, Colonel Peter Yates' Regiment.

FAMILY INFORMATION: He married Jemima **Benway**. She was born Oct 13, 1761, died Nov 28, 1839 and is buried with her husband.

Peter ACKART   001   Peter   ACKART

Children:
Peter   B-Jan 27,1784 Schaqticoke,NY.
           M-Maria **Benway** (B-Sep 21,1789;
           D-Aug 24,1866). D-Apr 23,1861. Both bur
           Elmwood Cem, Schaghticoke, NY.
Margaret   B-Jan 02,1792 in Oxford, NY. M-1815
           Blockville, Harmony, NY to Reuben **Pier**
           (B-Oct,1791 Otsego City; Son of Rev War
           Vet Levi and Anna (**Dewey**) **Pier**;
           M2-_____; D-Meadville, PA).D-Nov 5,1836.
           Bur Blockville Cem, Harmony, NY.

OTHER INFORMATION: He was allowed pension on his application executed Aug 6, 1832, at which time he was a resident of Schaghticoke, New York.

Joseph AGARD   002   Joseph   AGARD
           S. 45179 Sergeant   DAR Patriot Index

RESIDENT DATE: 1798 - 1836
TOWN: Smithville
BIRTH DATE: Aug 17, 1746
BIRTH PLACE: Litchfield, Connecticut
FATHER: John **Agard**
MOTHER: Mary Mason **Hosford**
DEATH DATE: Aug 25, 1836
DEATH PLACE: Smithville Flats, New York
CEMETERY: Upper
LOCATION: Smithville, New York

TOMBSTONE INSCRIPTION:

    Joseph Agard
Sgt. Van Schaichs NY Bn
    Revolutionary War
Aug 17 1746   Aug 25 1836
    (separate stone)

Joseph Agard
Died
Aug. 25. 1836
Aged 90 ys.

Tabitha
Wife of
Joseph Agard
Died
Sept. 9. 1818
Parents of
Erastus Agard

Prior reading of a stone for Tabitha -
(currently not found)
"Tabitha Agard, wife of Joseph Agard, Esq., who was one of the first settlers in this town, A.D. 1798, who died Sept.9, 1818, aged 68 years. This woman after many years of the greatest toil in this howling wild,

Joseph AGARD   002   Joseph AGARD

in which she, together with her family suffered much by hunger and nakedness, was taken with a lingering illness, which lasted several years. She suffered great pain of body and depression of spirit. She knew in whom she believed and waited with patience the coming of the Lord. She was an obedient wife, a loving mother - and a keeper at home. She was a succorer of many in the settling in this country, both Indians and white men have often received food from her hands. She instructed her children to be always obedient to their father and to God. Every day she was attentive to prayer bowing knee to the Lord Jesus. Thus leaving a glorious example for all her sex to be obedient to their own husbands, teachers of good things, and chaste keepers at home. She had four sons that cleared this ground where she and all this great family of children lie."

SERVICE: He enlisted at Litchfield, Connecticut. about Dec 1, 1775 as a private in Captain Eleazer Curtis's Company. He marched with said Company to Albany, joined Captain Martin's Company, Colonel G. Van Schaick's New York Regiment, served in that organization, was on the expedition to Canada, and was discharged at Fort George, length of service ten months; part of the time he was a sergeant. He enlisted sometime in December 1776 and served two months as private in Captain Nathaniel Goodwin's Connecticut Company; in 1777 he volunteered on the expedition against Burgoyne, length of service and names of officers not known. He was present at Burgoyne's surrender at the battle of Saratoga.

FAMILY INFORMATION: Married to Tabitha **Leach**, a daughter of Richard Jr. and Rebecca (**Bugbee**) **Leach**. She was born Nov 20, 1750, died Sep 9, 1818 and is buried with her husband.

Children:
    Joseph   B-May 11,1776 Litchfield,CT. D-Sep 11,1798 at New York, NY of yellow fever.
    Tabitha (Roxa) B-May 17,1779 Litchfield,CT. M-1801 (first marriage in the town) to Enos Bishop **Bragg** (B-1780; D-Dec 25,1858; M2-Charlotte _____ [1784; Oct 19,1872]). D-Sep 29, 1814.
                All three Bur Upper Cem, Smithville,NY.
    John   B-Aug 21,1781 at Arlington,VT. M-Virginia **Ackley**. D-Oct 26,1835 in MI.

Joseph   AGARD   002   Joseph   AGARD

   George   B-Mar 2,1785 at Tamhannock, NY. M-Clarissa
               Young (B-1787; D-Feb 21,1869; Bur Upper
               Cem, Smithville, NY).
               D-May 14,1854 at Springville,NY.
   Erastus A B-Feb 11,1787 Litchfield,CT. M-Jan 5,1817
               Sarah Carpenter (B-1797; dau of Capt
               Samuel Carpenter; D-Jun 5,1863).
               D-Oct 1,1863 at Smithville Flats, NY.
               Both Bur Upper Cem, Smithville,NY.

OTHER INFORMATION: He applied for pension Apr 17, 1818, at which time he resided in Smithville, formerly Greene, Chenango County, New York. His claim was allowed. Noah Agard, soldier's brother, resided in Catherine, Tioga County, New York in 1830; he served in the same Company with Joseph during the war. Joseph purchased his land in February, 1798, coming in that year from Litchfield, Connecticut, in company with Major Epaphras Sheldon, from the same place, who had previously prospected the locality, and induced Agard to accompany him. Major Sheldon had been a man of property, and Agard had worked for him as a day laborer in Connecticut. They were the first settlers in the town. Joseph donated the land for the Upper Smithville Cemetery.

John   AKELEY   003   John   AKELEY
        W. 25340 Drummer

RESIDENT DATE: - 1819
TOWN: Norwich/Oxford
BIRTH DATE: Sep   1758
BIRTH PLACE:
FATHER:
MOTHER:
DEATH DATE: Apr 1, 1819
DEATH PLACE: Oxford, New York
CEMETERY:
LOCATION:

TOMBSTONE INSCRIPTION:

SERVICE: He enlisted about Jan 1, 1776, at Long Meadow, Massachusetts, served as a drummer in Captain Walker's Company, Colonel Stark's Regiment, was in the battle of Trenton and was discharged Jan 1, 1777; he enlisted about Feb 1, 1777, served as drum major in Captain Asa Coburn's Company, Colonel's Ichabod

John AKELEY   003   John AKELEY

Alden's and Brook's Massachusetts Regiments, was at the taking of Burgoyne and in the battle of Cherry Valley, where Colonel Alden was killed; length of service, three years. It is stated that he served also during 1781 and 1782 but no details are available.

FAMILY INFORMATION: He married Oct 29, 1781, at Suffield, Connecticut, Mariam **Ward**. He was then of Long Meadow, Massachusetts, and she of East Springfield, Massachusetts. She was born in 1764 and was buried at Rocky Hill, Connecticut.

Children:
   Polly   M-John **Flint** (B-1778).
   John

OTHER INFORMATION: He was allowed a pension on his application executed Mar 25, 1818 while residing in Norwich, Chenango County, New York. His widow, was allowed pension on her application executed Jan 9, 1839, while residing in Wethersfield, Connecticut, where she had resided since the death of her husband. In 1848, she was residing in Rocky Hill, Hartford County, Connecticut.

John AKIN   004   John AKIN
   -, ------ Private

RESIDENT DATE:
TOWN: Guilford
BIRTH DATE: 1741
BIRTH PLACE: Amenia, New York (Dutchess County)
FATHER:
MOTHER:
DEATH DATE: Jan 3, 1825
DEATH PLACE:
CEMETERY: Maplewood
LOCATION: Guilford, New York

TOMBSTONE INSCRIPTION: In
                              Memory of
                              John Akin
                              Who died
                              Jan 3d 1825
                              Ae 84 yrs

John AKIN   004   John AKIN

SERVICE: Served in the Third Regiment of the Dutchess County New York Militia. Listed as an enlisted man in "New York In The Revolution".

FAMILY INFORMATION: He married May 5, 1765 in Amenia, Dutchess County, New york to Mary/Polly **Ford**.

Children:
  Loton   M-1805 Unadilla,NY to Sarah **Mudge**.

OTHER INFORMATION: Probably a descendant of the **McAkin** family. Guilford resident Uriah **Yale** also served in his Regiment.

Eleazer ALBEE   005   Eleazer ALBEE
         S. 45189 Ensign

RESIDENT DATE: - 1836
TOWN: Norwich
BIRTH DATE: Jul 28, 1756
BIRTH PLACE: Mendon, Massachusetts (Worcester Co)
FATHER: Ebenezer **Albee**
MOTHER: Esther **Fish**
DEATH DATE: Jul 13, 1836
DEATH PLACE: New Berlin, New York
CEMETERY: Albee
LOCATION: New Berlin, New York

TOMBSTONE INSCRIPTION: Eleazer Albee
                              Died July 13, 1836
                                 Ae 80 yrs.
                               Ye that pass by
                       Behold the man of age must die

SERVICE: In April 1775, he enlisted for eight months as a private in Captain Andrew Peter's Company, Colonel Joseph Read's Massachusetts Regiment and was in the battle of Bunker Hill. A few days previous to the expiration of the eight months he reenlisted and served one year as sergeant in the same Company and Regiment and was in the battle of White Plains. He enlisted in December 1777, in Captain Warren's Company, Colonel Sprout's Massachusetts Regiment and after serving about a month he was commissioned ensign and continued to serve as such in said Corps for the remainder of three years, the term for which he had enlisted, and was in the battles of Monmouth and Rhode Island.

Eleazer ALBEE   005   **Eleazer ALBEE**

FAMILY INFORMATION: Married June 2, 1775 at Mendon, Massachusetts to Ruhamah **Washburn**, a daughter of Henry and Sarah (**Battles**) **Washburn**. She was born July 15, 1757 at Bridgewater, Plymouth, Massachusetts.

Children:
  Lois   B-Sep 02,1775 Mendon,MA. M-1792 Upton,MA
             Elisha **Hayward**.
  Eliba (Elihu) B-Jun 16,1780 Mendon,MA.
  Benjamin B-Aug 20,1781 Uxbridge,Worchester,MA.
          M-May 22,1803 Mendon,MA Lydia **Taft**
          (B-Aug 21,1781 Mendon,MA). Both D-1860/64
          Amboy,Oswego Co,NY.
  Ruth   B-May 31,1785.
  Philee (Phila) B-Jun 8,1788.
  Sally   B-Sep 20,1790.
  Ebenezer B-Oct 8,1795.
  Amila   B-Apr 3,1798.

OTHER INFORMATION: He was allowed pension on his application executed Jun 13, 1820 while living in Norwich, Chenango County, New York. His statement included the fact that his wife was living with one of her own children at Gates, Monroe County, New York.

John Adams ALDEN   006   **John Adams ALDEN**
       W. 20589 Private   DAR Patriot Index

RESIDENT DATE: - 1832
TOWN: Lincklaen
BIRTH DATE: July 11, 1762
BIRTH PLACE: Medway, Massachusetts (Norfolk County)
FATHER: John **Alden**
MOTHER:
DEATH DATE: April 13, 1843
DEATH PLACE: Lincklaen, New York
CEMETERY: Union Valley
LOCATION: Taylor, New York (Cortland County)

John Adams ALDEN   006   **John Adams ALDEN**

TOMBSTONE INSCRIPTION:
John A Alden.
Died
April 13, 1843,
Aged 80 years.
9 months &.
2 days.

Hannah
His wife
Died
Oct 9 1843
Aged 75 years
8 months &
12 days
Go home kind friends dry up your tears
we must lie here till Christ appears.

SERVICE: While residing at Medway, Massachusetts he enlisted and served as a private with the Massachusetts troops as follows: from about August 1, 1778, eighteen days in Captain Adam Peters' Company, Colonel Howes' Regiment and marched to Rhode Island; was in the battle there under General Sullivan; from about June 1, 1779 six months in Colonel Howes' regiment, again went to Rhode Island and acted as a guard at Providence; from July 1, 1780 six months in Captain Howell's Company, Colonel Greaton's Regiment; from September 1781 three months in Colonel Greaton's Regiment.

FAMILY INFORMATION: Married Hannah **Daniels**, a daughter of Joshua and Hannah **Daniels** on June 1, 1786 as shown in town records of Medway, Norfolk County, Massachusetts. He was then of Medway and she of Mendon, Massachusetts. Hannah was born February 27, 1768 in Mendon, Worcester County, Massachusetts, died October 9, 1843 and is buried with her husband.

Children:
Hannah 2nd	B-Oct. 28,	1787
Reuben	B-Oct. 15,	1789
Phinehas	B-Jun. 17	1791
Sally	B-Feb. 12,	1793
Luther	B-Jan. 11,	1795
Hannah 3rd	B-Mar. 27,	1797
Ira	B-Feb. 28,	1799
Mary	B-Nov. 25,	1800
John	B-Feb. 08,	1803
Lyman	B-Mar. 27,	1806

John Adams ALDEN   006   John Adams ALDEN

In 1846, the only surviving children were Phinehas **Alden** of Newfane, Windham County Vermont; Luther **Alden** of North Adams, Massachusetts; Ira **Alden** of Hoosick, New York; Lyman **Alden** of Solon, Cortland County, New York. These were children allowed the pension due their mother on an application made February 4, 1846.

OTHER INFORMATION: Allowed pension on his application executed August 24, 1832 while residing in Lincklaen, Chenango County, New York. After the Revolution he resided at Rutland, Massachusetts for a few years; then moved to Jamaica, Vermont; thence to Greenwich, Massachusetts; thence to Dover, Vermont where he resided for a number of years; thence to Lincklaen, New York.

Joshua ALDRICH   007   Joshua ALDRICH
          W. 23426 Private   DAR Patriot Index

RESIDENT DATE: 1804 - 1849
TOWN: Preston/ North Norwich
BIRTH DATE: September 28, 1759
BIRTH PLACE: Smithfield, Rhode Island
FATHER: Abram **Aldrich**
MOTHER: Ruth **Sheldon**
DEATH DATE: October 17, 1849
DEATH PLACE: Norwich, New York
CEMETERY: North Norwich
LOCATION: North Norwich, New York

TOMBSTONE INSCRIPTION: Joshua Aldrich   Ruth
                       died   Wife of
                       Oct 17, 1849   Joshua Aldrich
                       aged   Died
                       90 years   Jan 11, 1851
                                              Aged
                                              95 years

SERVICE: While a resident of Smithfield, Rhode Island, he enlisted in December 1776, and served two weeks, as a substitute for Samuel Aldrich, no relationship given, as a private in Captain Enoch Barnes' Company, Colonel Brown's Rhode Island Regiment. He enlisted Feb 4 or 5, 1777, and served one month as a private in Captain Enoch Barnes' or Captain John Carpenter's Rhode Island Company. He enlisted March 4 or 5, 1777, and served one year and ten days as a private in Captain James Parker's Company,

Joshua ALDRICH   007   Joshua ALDRICH

Colonel Archibald Crary's Rhode Island Regiment. He enlisted March 16 or 17, 1778, and served one year as a private in Captain James Parker's Company, Colonel Archibald Crary's Rhode Island Regiment.

FAMILY INFORMATION: Married about 1782 to Ruth **Evans** a daughter of David and Jemima (**Bishop**) **Evans**. She was born Apr 11, 1755 at Smithfield, Rhode Island, died Jan 11, 1851 at Norwich, New York and is buried with her husband.

Children: All born at Smithfield, Rhode Island.
Joseph   B-Jul 01,1783. M-?   D-Mar 27,1859.
         Bur Wattsburg,PA Cem.
Reuben   B-Oct 26,1784. M-Apr 14,1816 Amy **Stafford**
         (B-May 17,1798; Dau of Job and Amy
         [**Slater**] **Stafford**; D-Mar 6,1860).
         D-Jul 15,1866. Both bur Foster Cem,
         Norwich,NY.
Esek   B-Jul 06,1787. M-Anna _____. D-Aug 29,1855.
         Bur Aldrich Cem, Norwich,NY.
Nancy   B-Aug 27,1789. M-William **Brewer**.
         D-Feb 16,1878. Bur North Norwich Cem,
         North Norwich,NY.
Betsey   B-Aug 03,1792. M-Charles **Aldrich** (B-1794;
         Son of Gardner & Ann [**Colwell**] **Aldrich**;
         M2-Maria _____ [B-1811; D-Apr 19,1883]).
         D-Mar 17,1872 Plymouth,NY; Both bur South
         Plymouth Cem,Plymouth, NY). D-Nov 9,1833.
         Bur Colwell Cem,Plymouth,NY.
Polly   B-Oct 04,1794. (Unmarried). D-Apr 23,1885.
         Bur North Norwich Cem,North Norwich,NY.
Rhoda   B-Feb 15,1798 in RI. M-Jesse F **Brewer**
         (B-Jan 19,1800; Son of John and Mary
         [**Twist**] **Brewer**;D-May 22,1882).
         D-May 1,1884. Both bur South Plymouth Cem,
         Plymouth,NY.
Phoebe   B-Jun 04,1802. M-Cornelius **Kennedy**
         (D-Dec 1, 1878). D-Nov 27, 1874. Both bur
         North Norwich Cem,North Norwich,NY.

OTHER INFORMATION: He settled in the northeast part of Preston, Chenango County, New York, then moved to North Norwich when well advanced in age. He was allowed a pension on his application executed Oct 9, 1832, at which time he was a resident of Norwich, New York.

Stephen **ALDRICH**   008   Stephen **ALDRICH**
-. ----- Private   DAR Patriot Index

RESIDENT DATE: wife only ? to 1837
TOWN: Guilford
BIRTH DATE: March 15, 1741
BIRTH PLACE: Gloucester, Rhode Island
FATHER: John **Aldrich**
MOTHER: Johann **Saunders**
DEATH DATE: March 15, 1808
DEATH PLACE: Gloucester, Rhode Island
CEMETERY:
LOCATION:

TOMBSTONE INSCRIPTION: Mrs
                            Sarah wife of
                            Stephen Aldrich
                            Died Nov 20, 1837
                            Ae 92 yrs & 21 ds.
                         An emigrant from Rhode
                                Island

SERVICE: He was in a Militia Company commanded by Captain Abraham Tourtellot, included in Colonel Archibald Crary's Regiment from June 6, 1778 to March 16, 1778. In the Military papers, State Archives V.7, P.7 there is a certificate of money due him as a soldier in Colonel Olney's Regiment. His name appears in the military census of 1777 as of Gloucester, aged 16 and 50, "able to bear arms".

FAMILY INFORMATION: He married Jan 20, 1761 at Uxbridge, Worcester County, Massachusetts Mary **Brown**. He married second about 1766 to Sarah **Irons** who was born at Gloucester, Rhode Island to Samuel and Hannah (**Waterman**) **Irons** on October 24, 1745 and died at Guilford, New York on November 20, 1837. She is buried in the Gospel Hill cemetery, Guilford, New York.

    Children:
      Rhoba   M-Charles **Wright**
      Levina   M-Benjamin **Wright**
      Mary   M-Jorton **Sprague**
      Huldah   M-Gideon **Mowry**
      Charlotte B-Feb 15,1786 at Gloucester,RI. M-Caleb
                    Winsor. (B-1781; D-Jan 22,1847).
                    D-Mar 31,1861, Guilford,NY.
                    Both bur Gospel Hill Cem, Guilford,NY.
      Samuel   (died young)

OTHER INFORMATION:

Apollos ALLEN   009   Apollos ALLEN
                            DAR Patriot Index

RESIDENT DATE: 1798 - 1807
TOWN: Smyrna/Sherburne
BIRTH DATE: Dec. 14, 1756
BIRTH PLACE: Gill, Massachusetts
FATHER: Noah **Allen**
MOTHER: Ruth **Martindale**
DEATH DATE: September 18, 1807
DEATH PLACE: Smyrna, New York
CEMETERY: West Hill
LOCATION: Sherburne, New York

TOMBSTONE INSCRIPTION:
In
Memory of
Apollos Allen
Died Sept 18th
1807,
In the 52nd year
Of his
Age
But still in silent accents he doth say
prepare to mingle with your fellow clay

                    1   In   8
                         Memory of
                         Deborah W.
                           Wife of
                       Apollas Allen.
                       Died Nov 8th
                           1807
                       In the 50 year
                    1   of her age   9
              She sleeps in Jesus and is blessed,
                  How kind her slumbers are.

SERVICE: Served in Captain Agrippa Wells' Company, Colonel Asa Whitcomb's Regiment in 1775, also in Captain Taylor's Company, Colonel Nicholas Dyke's Regiment, also in Captain Timothy Child's Company, Colonel David Field's Regiment. In August 1777 he served 4 days on an alarm at Bennington.

FAMILY INFORMATION: Married Jan 24, 1780 in Greenfield, Franklin County, Massachusetts Deborah **Pardee** a daughter of Nathaniel and Rebecca (**Wheadon**) **Pardee** of Farmington, Connecticut. She was born in 1758, at Southington, Harford County, Connecticut, died Nov 8, 1807 at Smyrna, New York and is buried with her husband.

Apollos ALLEN   009   Apollos ALLEN

Children:
  Lovina   M-William **Ladd**. D-1805.
  Amanda   B-1785. M-_____ **Crosby**. D-Feb 11,1876 in
            Viraqua,WI.
  Marsena   B-Sep 08,1789 Gill,MA. M-Sep 19,1811 Hannah
            Gates **Percival** (dau of John and Ruth
            [**Crocker**] **Percival**; D-Jul 29,1861
            Rochester,NY). D-Jun 18,1861 Mount
            Morris,NY.
  Willard   B-1792. D-Apr 21,1807. Bur West Hill Cem,
            Sherburne,NY.
  Chester   B-Mar 03,1794 Gill,MA. M-Hannah **Blair**
            (B-1787; dau of David and Marium
            [**Boise**] **Blair**; D-Nov 21,1862 Smyrna,NY).
            D-Oct 1,1877 Smyrna,NY. Both bur Stover
            Cem, Smyrna,NY.
  (female) B-1797. M-_____ **Briggs**. M2-Oril **Corbin**.
            D-Feb 21,1873 in Traverse City,MI.
  Ruth   B-1799. M-Thomas **Sweet** (B-1796; D-1841).
            D-1873. Both bur West Hill Cem,
            Sherburne,NY.

OTHER INFORMATION: The family came from Massachusetts and settled on a large farm which now includes the village of Smyrna. The Allen home was on the upper side of the street near the little green at the head of Tannery Hill. In 1803 Apollos **Allen** and Jesse **Hutchinson** bought lot number 15 and the west half of lot 16.

Azor ALLEN   010   Azor ALLEN
      W. 20592 Private

RESIDENT DATE: 1832 - 1841
TOWN: Greene/Coventry
BIRTH DATE: Feb 11, 1762
BIRTH PLACE: Windham, Connecticut   (Windham County)
FATHER :   Joseph **Allen**
MOTHER: Rebeckah
DEATH DATE: March 22, 1841
DEATH PLACE:
CEMETERY:
LOCATION:

TOMBSTONE INSCRIPTION:

Azor ALLEN   010   Azor ALLEN

SERVICE: While residing in Windham, Connecticut, he enlisted and served as a private in the Connecticut troops as follows: from June 1779 two months in Captain Tinker's company, Colonel Storms' Regiment and was stationed at New London and Groton; from April 1780 nine months in Captain Nathaniel Wales' Company, Colonel Levi Wells' Regiment; from Sept. 1781 two months and again served at New London and Groton, names of officers not shown; after this he was frequently called out on short tours and on alarms, about two months in all. He stated that he was in no battle but was in several skirmishes.

FAMILY INFORMATION: Married in the spring of 1782 at Canterbury, Windham County, Connecticut to Anna **Adams**, a daughter of Abner and Abigail (**Hubbard**) **Adams**. She was born Jul 15, 1762 at Pomfret, Windham County, Connecticut, died Feb. 15, 1853 at Coventry, Chenango County, New York.

Children:
```
 (female)   B-May 31,1784 Windham,CT.
 Eliashib   B-Mar 28,1786 Windham,CT.
 Asher      B-Sep 13,1788 Canterbury,CT.
*Luther     B-Jun 07,1791 Canterbury,CT.
 Esther     B-Jun 07,1791 Canterbury,CT.
 Zeruah     B-            1801. In Coventry in 1853.
* lived in Greene NY 1845
```

OTHER INFORMATION: He was allowed pension on his application executed July 30, 1832 while residing in Greene, Chenango County, New York. After the Revolution he resided at Canterbury, Windham County, Connecticut; in New Lisbon, Otsego County, New York; in Coventry, Chenango County, New York; and in Greene, Chenango County, New York. His wife, Anna was allowed pension on September 26, 1845 at the age of 83 while residing in Greene, New York.

Hezekiah ALLEN   011   Hezekiah ALLEN
         S. 23093 Private   DAR Patriot Index

RESIDENT DATE: 1802 - 1814
TOWN: McDonough/Columbus
BIRTH DATE: Oct 30, 1762
BIRTH PLACE: Mansfield, Connecticut (Tolland County)
FATHER: Hezekiah **Allen**
MOTHER: Sarah **Cushman**
DEATH DATE:

Hezekiah ALLEN   011   Hezekiah ALLEN

DEATH PLACE:
CEMETERY: Willett
LOCATION: Willett, New York (Cortland County)

TOMBSTONE INSCRIPTION: (front peeled off)
        (large slate stone in eastern part of cemetery)
                (near other family stones)

SERVICE: He served in the Connecticut Line. He entered the service at Mansfield, Connecticut in June 1779, to serve as a fifer. Although he was enlisted as a fifer he served as a private or waiter to Lieutenant Joseph Hearn, of the second Company, under Captain James Dana in Lieutenant Colonel Wells fifth Regiment of Connecticut. He served 8 months and was discharged Feb 7, 1780. He volunteered in a number of alarms of several days each after his discharge. At one time, he volunteered and served 14 days, at the burning of New London and Fort Griswold.

FAMILY INFORMATION: He married Mar 24, 1784 at Mansfield, Tolland County, Connecticut to Elizabeth **Cummins**.

Children:
  Horace   Bp-Apr 24,1785 Mansfield,CT.
  Artemas   Bp-Jan 20,1787 Mansfield,CT.
  (male)   M-Nancy ____ (M2-William **Clark**). Resided
            Willett,NY.

OTHER INFORMATION: He lived in Mansfield for seven years after the war. The family then moved to Burlington, Otsego County, New York, and lived there twelve years; thence to Columbus, Chenango County, New York for twelve years; thence to Scipio, Cayuga County, New York for five to seven years; thence to McDonough, Chenango County, New York. He was allowed pension on his application dated Jun 29, 1832, while a resident of McDonough, Chenango County, New York. Residents of McDonough who were mentioned in his application were Michah **Covil** Esquire, John F **Niell** Esquire (Merchant), Martin **Dodge**, ____ **Rice**, Henry **Dodge**, ____ **Burns** (Innkeeper), and John **Nickerson** (Clergyman). He was in the 1810 census at Columbus, New York.

Jacob ALLEN   012   Jacob   ALLEN
       R. 24697 Private   DAR Patriot Index

RESIDENT DATE: 1820 - 1840
TOWN: Lincklaen
BIRTH DATE: Jan 20, 1755
BIRTH PLACE: Norton, Massachusetts
FATHER:
MOTHER:
DEATH DATE: Aug 21, 1840
DEATH PLACE: Lincklaen, New York
CEMETERY:
LOCATION:

TOMBSTONE INSCRIPTION: (Not found)

SERVICE: While residing on Long Island, near New York, he was in the battle of Long Island, and was taken prisoner at Fort Washington; the names of officers and length of this service are not shown. He enlisted in the spring of 1777, in Taunton, Massachusetts, and served as a private in Captain Cooper's Company, Colonel Bradford's Massachusetts Regiment, and afterwards in Captain Zebulon King's Company, Colonel Brooks' Massachusetts Regiment, he was in the battle of Saratoga at the taking of Burgoyne, and was in the battle of Monmouth continuing in the sevice until Jun 4, 1783, when he was discharged at New Windsor, New York.

FAMILY INFORMATION: He married second Jan 1, 1800, in Saratoga, New York, Armenia **Brown**. She was born in 1768 and died June 12, 1848, in Odessa, New York.

Children:
  Henry   B-1802.
  John   B-1804.
  Jacob   B-1806.
  Rhoda   B-1809.
  Earbinana   B-1812.
  Spafford   B-1812. Was residing in Fabius, Onondaga
              Co, NY in 1893.
  Helen   B-Oct 2 or 7, 1814 at Oneida Castle, NY.
              M-Apr 29, 1840 to Thomas H **Sloan**
              (D-Jul 18, 1882 in Wellsboro, PA).

OTHER INFORMATION: After the war, he lived "some three years" in Virginia; in 1800, he resided in Saratoga, New York, about the year 1811, moved to Sackets Harbor, New York, and in 1814 or 1815, resided in Oneida Castle, Oneida, New York, later in Sullivan,

Jacob **ALLEN**   012   Jacob **ALLEN**

Madison County, New York. He was allowed pension on his application executed Jul 4, 1818, at which time he resided in Sullivan, New York. In 1820, he resided in Lincklaen, Chenango County, New York. He is listed in the 1840 census of pensioners in Lincklean, Chenango County, New York.

Noah **ALLEN**   013   Noah **ALLEN**
        -. -------Lieutenant   DAR Patriot Index

RESIDENT DATE: 1797 - 1802
TOWN: Smyrna
BIRTH DATE: June 24, 1727
BIRTH PLACE: Greenfield, Massachusetts
FATHER: John **Allen**
MOTHER: Abigail **Severance**
DEATH DATE: February 17, 1802
DEATH PLACE: Smyrna, New York
CEMETERY: West Hill
LOCATION: Sherburne, New York

TOMBSTONE INSCRIPTION: In
                              Memory of
                              Noah Allen
                            Died Feb 17th
                                1802
                          In the 77th year
                               of his
                                age.

SERVICE: Led a company of minute men to Cambridge on the Lexington Alarm.

FAMILY INFORMATION: Married on October 16, 1752 at Westfield, Hampden County, Massachusetts to Ruth **Martindale** daughter of Edward and Ruth **Martindale**. She was born Oct 12, 1734 at Westfield, Hampden County, Massachusetts. Ruth returned to Guilford, Vermont after her husband's death where she lived to the age of 96.

  Children: (5 daughters and 3 sons)
   Experience B-Nov 10,1753 Greenfield,MA.
   Apollos   B-Dec 14,1756 Greenfield,MA. M-Deborah W
               Pardee of Farmington,CT. (B-1757;
               D-Nov 8,1807). Rev War Vet.
               D-Sep 18,1807. Both bur West Hill Cem,
               Sherburne,NY.
   Ruth   B-Apr 01,1759 Greenfield,MA.

Noah   ALLEN   013   Noah   ALLEN

Noah   B-Apr 18,1763 Greenfield,MA.
Orinda   B-Feb 12,1770 Greenfield,MA.
Lucinda   B-Feb 12,1770 Greenfield,MA.

OTHER INFORMATION:

Phinehas   ALLEN   014   Phinehas   ALLEN
-. ------ Soldier   DAR Patriot Index

RESIDENT DATE: - 1830
TOWN: Sherburne
BIRTH DATE: Apr 6, 1745
BIRTH PLACE: Weston, Massachusetts (Middlesex Co.)
FATHER: Benjamin **Allen**
MOTHER: Eunice **Gale**
DEATH DATE: May 15, 1830
DEATH PLACE: Smyrna, New York
CEMETERY: Christ Church
LOCATION: Sherburne, New York

TOMBSTONE INSCRIPTION: In
                                Memory of
                              Phinehas Allen
                             Who died May 15th
                              1830 aged 85
                                 Years.
                    To earth and friends I bid farewell,
                    Im call'd of God in heaven to dwell,
                     A stranger and a pilgrim here,
                       A glorified spirit there.

SERVICE: Soldier from Massachusetts.

FAMILY INFORMATION: Married Mar 6, 1769 at Lincoln, Massachusetts to Abigail **Foster**, a daughter of Abiel and Hannah (**Russell**) **Foster** .She was born Apr 6, 1745 in Haverhill, Essex County, Massachusetts and died May 18, 1770 in Lincoln, Massachusetts. He married second Sep 14, 1775 at Lexington, Massachusetts to Sarah **Danforth**, a daughter of Benjamin or Thomas and Sarah **Danforth**. She was born Jun 18, 1749 in Dunstable, Middlesex County, Massachusetts. He married third Nov 21, 1784 at Fitchburg, Massachusetts to Dolly **Flagg** a daughter of Ebenezer and Lydia **Flagg**. She was born Oct 13, 1756 in Worcester, Worcester County, Massachusetts.

Phinehas   ALLEN   014   Phinehas   ALLEN

Children:
Second wife
  Benjamin   B-Nov 04,1777 Lincoln,MA. M-Asenath
             Colman (B-Oct 7,1776 Ashby,MA).
             M2-Vashti **Wilder** (B-Aug 26,1788).
  Sally   B-Jan 16,1779 Lincoln,MA. M-Benjamin
             Parker (B-Aug 26,1780 Woburn,MA).
  Dolly   B-Jan 15,1781 Weston,MA. M-Aaron **Kemp**
             (B-1781).
Third wife
  Lydia   B-Aug 28,1785 Fitchburg,MA. M-Samuel
             Parker (B-Dec 23,1784 Woburn,MA).
  Abigail   B-Dec 08,1786 Fitchburg,MA. M-Jonathan
             Thurston (B-1786).
  Phineas   B-Dec 06,1788 Fitchburg,MA. M-Sally
             Campbell (B-1788).
  Eunice   B-Mar 18,1790 Fitchburg,MA. M-Abel
             Thurston (B-1790).
  John   B-Nov 05,1791 Fitchburg,MA.
  Samuel   B-Nov 28,1793 Fitchburg,MA.
  Betsey   B-Apr 27,1795 Fitchburg,MA. M-John
             Campbell (B-1795).
  Abijah   B-Jun 29,1797 Fitchburg,Ma. M-Abigail
             Bacon (B-1796; D-Dec 30,1842).
             D-Mar 3,1843. Both bur Christ Church
             Cem, Sherburne,NY.

OTHER INFORMATION:

Moses   **ALLIS**   015   Moses   **ALLIS**
         S. 8021   Sergeant   DAR Patriot Index

RESIDENT DATE: 1795 - 1830
TOWN: Coventry
BIRTH DATE: Feb 13, 1756
BIRTH PLACE: Montague, Massachusetts
FATHER: Zebediah **Allis**
MOTHER: Mary **Baker**
DEATH DATE: Mar 30, 1842
DEATH PLACE: Laport, Ohio
CEMETERY:
LOCATION:

TOMBSTONE INSCRIPTION: Here lies Bathsheba
                                 Wife of Moses
  (assume to be second wife)   Allis died March
  (In Wylie Cem., Coventry)   19th 1810 Ae t 46 y

Moses ALLIS 015 **Moses ALLIS**

SERVICE: He served throughout the war. He was a private in Captain Israel Chapin's Company, Colonel John Fellows Regiment; muster roll dated Aug 1, 1775; enlisted Apr 27, 1775; service three months twelve days; also Company return dated Oct 8, 1775; also order for bounty coat or its equivalent in money, dated Dorchester, Dec 18, 1775; also return of men enlisted into Continental Army from Captain Moses Harvey's fifth Company, 6th Hampshire Regiment, dated Mar 5, 1778; enlisted for town of Montague; joined Jan 15, 1777, served as first sergeant in Captain Ephraim Cleveland's Company, Colonel Michael Jackson's Eighth Massachusetts Regiment; enlisted three years. Was discharged Dec 13, 1779.

FAMILY INFORMATION: He married Dec 18, 1781 in Deerfield, Franklin County, Massachusetts to Anna **Newton**, a daughter of Solomon and Mary (**Taylor**) **Newton**. She was born in 1760 at Deerfield, Franklin County, Massachusetts and died Oct 21, 1808.

Children:
- Leonard B-Jan 24,1786. M-1814 to Roxey **Converse** (B-Sep 7,1796; D-May 29,1833). M2-Polly **Risley** (B-Feb 15,1798; M1-Zeba **Spencer** [B-1798; D-Feb 5,1832]. D-Jan 14,1887). D-Feb 29,1844. All four bur Coventry Cem, Coventry, NY.
- Fanny B-Nov 24,1790. M-Jan 1,1811 to Clark **Provin** (D-Sep 2,1864 in Clinton, IL).
- William B-Sep 15,1793. First white child born Coventry,NY. M-1817 to Betsy **Wilson**. D-Oct 31, 1864.
- Calvin B-Apr 03, 1797. D-Oct 20, 1800.
- Luther B-Sep 05, 1799. D-Mar 28, 1800.

OTHER INFORMATION: He lived in Montague, Massachusetts for several years after his marriage, then in 1795 moved to New York State settling three miles south of Coventry, Chenango County, New York. He was allowed pension on his application executed May 2, 1818, at which time he was a resident of Coventry, Chenango County, New York. He was a farmer by occupation and is also said to have been a shoemaker. About 1830 he moved again, this time to Laport, Ohio with his son William and spent the remainder of his life there. He relinquished the pension under the Act of March 18, 1818, and was allowed pension under the Act of June 7, 1832, on an application executed Jul 16, 1834. He was living in Carlisle, Lorain County, Ohio.

John **AMBLER** 016 John **AMBLER**
S. 11978 Private

RESIDENT DATE: 1797 -
TOWN: New Berlin
BIRTH DATE: Jun 10, 1759
BIRTH PLACE: Stanford, Connecticut (Fairfield Co.)
FATHER: John **Ambler**
MOTHER: Sarah
DEATH DATE: Oct 13, 1835
DEATH PLACE: Nassau, New York (Rensselaer County)
CEMETERY: *Nassau Schodack
LOCATION: Nassau, New York

*Described in some documentation as "Maplewood" This may be prior cemetery name or stone could have been moved from another site.

TOMBSTONE INSCRIPTION: (Section 3 - row 17)
John Ambler
Died
Oct 13 1835,
In the 76 year
Of his age

SERVICE: While a resident of Salem, Westchester County, New York in January 1776 he enlisted for three months in Captain Cornelius Stienrod's Company, Colonel McDugal's Regiment. He was engaged in fortifying at Horns Hook on the North river. At the end of the three months, without leaving service, he reenlisted for an additional nine months under the same officers. He was stationed at Grand Battery, Governors Island near Bulls Head, Long Island, Frogs Neck, and White Plains, New York. He served three months as a substitute in Captain Wood's Company of Boston, Massachusetts. During the years 1777, 1778, 1779, while living at Salem he was frequently called out in the militia and guarded the lines. In 1777, while serving in Captain Samuel Lawrence's Company, Colonel Drake's Regiment, his brother was killed in a battle they were in, as Bedford was burned. He was also out under other officers as Danbury was burned and in the battle of Richfield, where the British were in retreat and General Worcester was killed.

FAMILY INFORMATION: Married Dec 7, 1780 in Salem, Westchester County, New York to Ruth **Cooley**. She was born Apr 6, 1758 in South Salem, New York and died Sep 18, 1842 in Massena, New York.

John AMBLER   016   John AMBLER

Children:
    Sarah   B-Sep 23,1781 in Westchester County,NY.
                M-Spencertown,NY Robert **Bell** (B-1779;
                D-Oct 15,1822; Bur Wightman Cem,
                New Berlin,NY).
    Ephriam   B-Jan 25,1784. D-Mar 10,1801.
    Elizabeth   B-Nov 25,1787. M-Spencertown,NY to D____
                Parmalee. D-Aug 14,1832.
    John   B-Sep 23,1790. M-Mary **Wheeler** (B-1797;
                D-Apr 18,1827; Bur Rich Sage Cem,
                New Berlin,NY).
    Lydia   B-Jul 07,1793. M-Jan 21,1813 to James W
                Averell (B-Dec 18,1789; D-Jul 8,1861).
                D-Feb 27,1885 in Ogdensburg,NY.
    Stephen   B-Oct 13,1795. M-Pamelia **Ritter**.
                D-Truxton,NY.
    Daniel C   B-Apr 12,1798 in New Berlin,NY.
                M-Laura **Stow**. D-Apr 4,1866 In St Johns,
                FL by drowning.
    Ruth   B-Sep 25,1801 in New Berlin,NY.
                M-Sep 17,1817 Asa Matthew **Caulkins**
                (B-Nov 10,1796; son of Matthew and Lois
                [**Smith**] **Caulkins**; D-Aug 26,1872
                Palmyra,NY). D-Aug 2,1841 New Berlin,NY.

OTHER INFORMATION: He removed from Stanford, Fairfield County, Connecticut when he was about 16 years old to Westchester County, New York. He lived there several years before moving to Dutchess County, New York. From there he went to Columbia County, New York before going to Truxton, Cortland County, New York. In August, 1805 John **Ambler** bought of Robert **Bell** of Hillsdale, Columbia County, New York 150 acres of land in the town of Norwich, Chenango County, New York being lot #91 of the 10th township.

John AMES   017   John AMES
       W. 20601 Marine   DAR Patriot Index

RESIDENT DATE: 1803 - 1844
TOWN: Plymouth
BIRTH DATE: May 17 1762
BIRTH PLACE: Voluntown, Connecticut (New London Co)
FATHER: John **Ames**
MOTHER: Mary **Selden**
DEATH DATE: October 11, 1844
DEATH PLACE: Plymouth, New York
CEMETERY: North
LOCATION: Plymouth, New York

John   AMES   017   John   AMES

TOMBSTONE INSCRIPTION: John Ames
   Sarah   Died
   Wife   Oct 11
   John Ames   1844
   Died   Aged 84 years
   March 14 1862   Soldier of the Revolution
   Ae 95 & 5 m

SERVICE: Enlisted for the term of a cruise on board the United States ship "Confederacy", commanded by Captain Seth Hardin on March of 1779, in the state of Connecticut Continental establishment. He continued to serve on board for sixteen months until discharged from the said ship in Philadelphia, Pennsylvania.

FAMILY INFORMATION: Married on November 24, 1785 in Montville, Connecticut to Sarah **Fargo** daughter of William and Mercy (**Beebe**) **Fargo**. Sarah was born in 1767, died March 14, 1862 and is buried with her husband.

Children: (11)
  Alice   B-October 27,1787 Stonington,CT.M-Nov, 1810
           Phineas **Newton** (B-Jul 29,1786; son of
           Winslow and Ann [**Blemis**] **Newton**;
           D-1867).D-Plymouth,NY 1870. Both bur Mt
           Hope Cem, Norwich,NY.
  Mehitable B-1789. M-Jonathan **Morton** (B-1790; son of
  (Hitty)   James and Jane [**Holmes**] **Morton**; D-1841
           fall of a tree near Edmeston,NY; Bur
           Doolittle farm Cem between New Berlin
           and Edmeston on Rt 80). D-Nov 2,1876.
           Bur South Side Cem, Plymouth, NY.
  John F   M-_____.
  Sally   M-Leander **Haskins**. Resided in Fabius, NY.
  Robert   B-Dec 31,1794. Soldier War of 1812. M-1817
           Celma **Atkins** (B-May 3,1799;
           D-Sep 18,1891). D-Nov. 22, 1826.
  Seldom   D-young from epidemic.
  Samuel   D-young from epidemic.
  William   D-young from epidemic.
  Rufus   D-young from epidemic.
  Joseph   B-1805. M-Melissa **Babcock** (Dau. of Lodowick
           and Mary [**Davis**] **Babcock**). D-1958.
           Bur North Cem, Plymouth,NY.

John AMES   017   John AMES

OTHER INFORMATION: He was allowed a pension April 27, 1818. After two years it was discontinued because he owned property consisting of 10 acres with a log home in Plymouth. His widow reapplied and was given a pension April 5, 1845.

Alexander ANDERSON   018   Alexander ANDERSON
          S. 45215 Private

RESIDENT DATE: 1818
TOWN: Smyrna
BIRTH DATE:
BIRTH PLACE:
FATHER:
MOTHER:
DEATH DATE:
DEATH PLACE:
CEMETERY:
LOCATION:

TOMBSTONE INSCRIPTION:

SERVICE: He enlisted Jan 1, 1777, at Johnstown, New York, serving in Captains. James Robichaux and John Baptist Allen's Companies, Colonel Livingston's New York Regiment, and in Colonel Van Cortland's New York Regiment, was in the battle of Fort Stanwix, the battle of White Plains and in the taking of Cornwallis at Yorktown and was discharged at the close of the war, having served more than six years.

FAMILY INFORMATION: Married to _____.
  Children:
     (son)   B-1802
     (daughter)   B-1805
     (daughter)   B-1810

OTHER INFORMATION: He was allowed pension on his application executed May 8, 1818, while residing in Chenango County, New York.

Samuel ANDERSON   019   Samuel ANDERSON
-. ------ Private

RESIDENT DATE: 1796 -
TOWN: New Berlin
BIRTH DATE: 1758
BIRTH PLACE: Blandford, Massachusetts
FATHER: Samuel Anderson
MOTHER: Mary (aka Mollie)
DEATH DATE: Mar 23, 1834
DEATH PLACE: Unadilla, New York   (Delaware County)
CEMETERY: Pioneer
LOCATION: Sidney, New York (Delaware County)

TOMBSTONE INSCRIPTION: Here lies
                            The remains of
                            Samuel Ander-
                            son died March
                            23 1834 ae 73
                                Years
                       Regreted by a numerous circle
                       of friends and relations he has
                     gone down to the grave but the earth
                       covers not the remains of a more
                       affectionate father or a warmer
                            hearted friend

SERVICE: He served in the Revolutionary War from
Blandford and shown as "three Months Men", August to
October 1780; at the Northward return of men raised by
order of Brigadier General Danielson for service in
the Continental Army, dated Hampshire County, Oct 26,
1780, for the town of Blandford, for the term of three
months. Mustered by Lieutenant Colonel Timothy
Robinson.

FAMILY INFORMATION: Married Dec 25, 1786 in Fonda,
Montgomery County, New York to Jerusha **Lyon**, a
daughter of Samuel and Zerviah (**Grosvenor**) **Lyon**. She
was born Feb 8, 1762 in Pomfret, Windham County,
Connecticut.

  Children:
   Zerviah   B-Jan 25,1788 Blandford,MA. D-Dec 11,1814
              at New Berlin,NY.
   Augustus A B-Jul 04,1789 Blandford,MA. M-Oct 3,1816
              at Chenango Co,NY to Sally **Hathaway**
              (B-Jan 20,1796 in Middleboro,MA; Dau of
              Dr Levi and Caroline [**Leonard**]
              Hathaway; D-Nov 20,1857 in LaPorte,IN).
              D-Sep 23,1836 Unadilla,NY. Bur Pioneer
              Cem, Sidney,NY.

Samuel ANDERSON   019   Samuel ANDERSON

    Armella   B-Apr 13,1791, NY. D-State of NY.
    Pollina   B-Dec 08,1792, NY. M-Aug 29,1816 in
              Chenango Co, NY to Stephen **Greenleaf**
              (B-Sep 12,1790 in Bolton; son of Israel
              and Ursula [**Woods**] **Greenleaf**;
              M2-Aug 29,1858 to Amanda A. **Fountain**
              of Iowa; D-Sep 14,1868).
              D-Aug 12,1855 in Bloomfield,IA.
    Aaron B   B-Nov 17,1794 Chenango Co, NY.
              D-Feb 11, 1816 in Chenango Co, NY.
    Elieh   B-Sep 10, 1796 in Chenango Co, NY.
    Mary   B-May 04, 1798 in Chenango Co, NY.
              M-_____ **Bennett**. D-Mar 5, 1874.

OTHER INFORMATION: It appears that he and his family were in the Town of Canajoharie, Montgomery County, New York, for the census of 1790, however, he could not have remained there but a short while, since he had established himself in the town of Norwich before 1796, when he returned to Blandford for the sale of property that he owned there. On the third day of January 1797 he purchased 250 acres of land in Chenango County on the west side of the Unadilla River. This land was known as lot No. 76. This lot along with lot No. 77 owned by Silas **Burlingame** was settled as the village of New Berlin. Samuel and Silas are referred to as "The fathers of New Berlin" He later resided in the town of Butternuts, Otsego County, New York.

Samuel ANGELL   020   Samuel ANGELL
           -. ------- Captain   DAR Patriot Index

RESIDENT DATE: 1793 - 1795
TOWN: New Berlin
BIRTH DATE: Oct 24, 1742
BIRTH PLACE: Scituate, Rhode Island
FATHER: Joshua **Angell**
MOTHER: Elizabeth **Taylor**
DEATH DATE: Jan 24, 1795
DEATH PLACE: New Berlin, New York
CEMETERY:
LOCATION:

TOMBSTONE INSCRIPTION:

SERVICE: Commanded a company of Rhode Island Artillery under Colonel Elliott.

Samuel ANGELL   020   Samuel ANGELL

FAMILY INFORMATION: Married Lydia **Medbury** on Oct 4, 1767 in Scituate, Rhode Island. Lydia was born April 9, 1749 in Scituate, Rhode Island to parents Isaac and Lydia (**Sprague**) **Medbury**. She died in New Berlin, New York.

Children: all born in Scituate, Rhode Island.
  Mutably B-Jul 29,1768. M-Jabez **Andrew**.
           D-Jul 27,1825. Bur Medbury Cem, New
           Berlin,NY.
  Emory   B-Aug 26,1770. M-Lydia **Rice**.
  Daniel   B-Jul 2,1773. M-Dec 13,1801, Cynthia
           Burlingame (B-Jul,1778, Apr 24,1839,
           New Berlin,NY). D-Oct 2,1840, New Berlin,
           NY. Both bur Medbury Cem, New Berlin,NY.
  Isaac M B-Feb 6,1780. M-1812 to Rebecca **Church**.
           D-Feb 13,1859.
  Samuel   B-Mar 2,1783. M-Betsey **Williams**. M2-
           Triphosa **Williams** (B-1795;
           D-Feb 3,1874). D-Jan 20,1860. All three
           bur Medbury Cem, New Berlin,NY.
  John   B-1793. M-Mary Elizabeth **Sayles**.
           D-New York City.

OTHER INFORMATION: Samuel cultivated hired farms in Scituate; then he and his sons, and son-in-law all moved to New Berlin, not far from where the relatives of his wife settled. He purchased wild land, cleared a small lot and built a house. He returned to Rhode Island for his family. The trip was so exhausting that he was taken sick for a time.

Caleb ARNOLD   021   Caleb ARNOLD
       S. 12003 Fife Major   DAR Patriot Index

RESIDENT DATE: 1805 - 1838
TOWN: Norwich
BIRTH DATE: July 5, 1757
BIRTH PLACE: Smithfield, Rhode Island
FATHER: Caleb **Arnold**
MOTHER: Patience **Brown**
DEATH DATE: October 16, 1838
DEATH PLACE: Norwich, New York
CEMETERY: Evergreen (White's Store)
LOCATION: Norwich, New York

Caleb ARNOLD   021   Caleb ARNOLD

TOMBSTONE INSCRIPTION:

Mary Arnold
Died Feb 19,
1841
Aged 82 years &
10 m

Caleb Arnold
died Oct 16
1838
aged 81 years
But drops of grief can never pay
The debt of love I owe
Here Lord I give myself away
Tis all that I can do.

SERVICE: While residing in Gloucester, Rhode Island, he enlisted in March 1775, and served in the Rhode Island Troops as private and fife major, at various times, under Captains Stephen Kimball, Timothy Willmarth, Samuel Meag and Colonels Daniel Hitchcock and Chad Brown. He was in Spencer's and Sullivan's expeditions and served until 1781, in all thirteen and one-half months; in Company A, Colonel Robert Elliott's Regiment; he was also in Captain Stephen Kimball's Company and was promoted to fife major in 1778.

FAMILY INFORMATION: Married to Mary **Arnold** daughter of Stephen **Arnold** of Gloucester. She was born in 1759, died Feb 10, 1841 and is buried with her husband.

Children:
Stephen   M-Jun, 1805 Lydia **Richmond**.
             (B-Sep 26,1785; dau of David and Nancy
             [**Davis**] **Richmond**; D-Oct 1850 at Tully,
             NY).
Thomas
William   B-1785. M-Eliza **Greene** (B-1788; dau of
             Edward & Prudence [**Davis**] **Greene**;
             D-Nov 9,1876). D-Nov 19,1846. Both bur
             Evergreen Cem, Norwich,NY.
John   M-Cynthia **Westcott** (B-Dec 13,1795; dau
             of Amos and Abigail [**Keith**] **Westcott**)
Peleg   B-1788. M-Armenia **Bennett** (B-1799;
             D-Jun 21,1878). Was a Capt. in the War of
             1812. D-Nov 30,1865.
             Both bur Evergreen Cem, Norwich,NY.

OTHER INFORMATION: He was allowed pension on his application executed Feb 13, 1833, while a resident of Norwich, Chenango County, New York.

Jabez ARNOLD   022   Jabez ARNOLD
      W. 20630 Private   DAR Patriot Index

RESIDENT DATE: 1802 - 1839
TOWN: New Berlin
BIRTH DATE: Jun 10, 1755
BIRTH PLACE: Smithfield, Rhode Island
FATHER: Caleb **Arnold**
MOTHER: Patience **Brown**
DEATH DATE: July 9, 1839
DEATH PLACE: New Berlin, New York
CEMETERY: Arnold
LOCATION: New Berlin, New York

TOMBSTONE INSCRIPTION:
    Jabez Arnold   Rachel
       Died   Wife of
   July 9, 1839.   Jabez Arnold
     Ae 84 yr's   Died May 31, 1854.
                        Ae 89 yrs.

SERVICE: He enlisted for eight months on May 1, 1775 while a resident of Gloucester, Providence County, Rhode Island, in Captain Stephen Gimble's Company, Colonel Hitchcock's Regiment of Rhode Island state troops. He was mustered at Providence and marched to Boston, was attached to General Greene's brigade. He was at Cambridge and on Prospect Hill. Upon discharge at Prospect Hill on January 1st 1776 he reenlisted for one year, marched to New York, was there at a hospital at the time of the battle of Long Island, was in the retreat through New Jersey in the fall, was at the battle of Princeton, went into winter quarters at Morristown. He extended his service another month and was discharged at Morristown, New Jersey, February 1, 1777. Served one month in October 1777 going from Gloucester, Rhode Island in Colonel Cornell's Regiment of drafted militia to Providence. In September 1777 went from Gloucester, Rhode Island in Colonel Cornell's Regiment to Warwick.

FAMILY INFORMATION: Married first to Lucinda **Hunter**. Married second May, 1788 at Gloucester, Rhode Island to Rachel **Phetteplace**. She was born in 1765, died May 31, 1854 and is buried with her husband.

   Children: All born in Gloucester except William.
    Othniel   B-1780. M-Polly ____ (B-1780;
                  D-Jul 27,1866; Bur Village Cem, New
                  Berlin, NY)D-Aug 22,1854. Bur with
                  parents.
    Benjamin

Jabez   ARNOLD   022   Jabez   ARNOLD

Thomas   M-Johannah **Medbury** (B-1785; dau of Joseph
            and Mary [**Potter**] **Medbury**;
            D-Feb 13,1867; Bur Medbury Arnold Cem,
            New Berlin, NY).
Second wife
Lucy
Lucretia   M-Charles **Medbury**.
Samuel
Eddy
Jabez
Welcome   B-May 11,1795. D-May 19, 1891.
William   B-1803 in New Berlin, NY. D-Jul 9,1839
            and is buried with his parents.

OTHER INFORMATION: Jabez and his brother Othniel marched into the Battle of Bunker Hill together. Othniel had a premonition that he would be killed and asked Jabez "if I am killed in this battle, will you marry my sweetheart Rachel **Phetteplace**?" Othniel was wounded, returned home, and after a while died with Rachel mourning his loss. Jabez returned home, but married Lucinda **Hunter** who had 4 or 5 of his children. She died and Jabez then married Othniel's former sweetheart, Rachel. He moved to New Berlin, Chenango County, New York and settled about one and one-fourth miles west of New Berlin. His application for pension was dated Aug 13, 1832 while a resident of New Berlin, Chenango County, New York.

Zebulon   ASHBY   023   Zebulon   ASHBY
          S.   6536 Private

RESIDENT DATE: 1807 - +1833
TOWN: Guilford
BIRTH DATE: Aug 10, 1754
BIRTH PLACE: Groton, Connecticut.(New London County)
FATHER:
MOTHER:
DEATH DATE:
DEATH PLACE:
CEMETERY:
LOCATION:

TOMBSTONE INSCRIPTION:

Zebulon ASHBY   023   Zebulon ASHBY

SERVICE: He volunteered at Paulings, Dutchess County, New York on Aug 1, 1776 for five months in Captain William Pearce's Company, Lieutenants Benjamin Elliott and Nathaniel Brewster, Colonel Jacobus Swartout's Regiment. Served on the lines at White Plains and near New York and was discharged at Kings Bridge. In the spring of 1777 he enlisted at Paulings, New York for one year in Captain Daniel Davis's Company, Colonel Field's Regiment. Served at White Plains, North Castle, North River and in various scouting and foraging, in one of which he was wounded in the left leg by a musket ball. He then engaged again for a nine-month period being discharged at Fredericksburg in the fall of 1778. After returning home he was frequently called out on alarms.

FAMILY INFORMATION: Married ?
   Children: ?

OTHER INFORMATION: He continued to reside in Paulings Town after the war. He removed to Guilford, New York in 1807. A pension was granted on May 05, 1833 while a resident of Guilford, Chenango County, New York.

Cornelius ATHERTON   024   Cornelius ATHERTON
  - ------ Patriotic Service   DAR Patriot Index

RESIDENT DATE: 1804 - 1809
TOWN: Afton
BIRTH DATE: May 8, 1737
BIRTH PLACE: Harvard, Massachusetts (Worcester Co)
FATHER: John **Atherton**
MOTHER: Phebe **Wright**
DEATH DATE: Dec 4, 1809
DEATH PLACE:
CEMETERY: Vallonia Springs
LOCATION: Vallonia Springs, New York (Broome Co.)

TOMBSTONE INSCRIPTION: In memory of   Jane
                           Cornelius   Wife of
         (His stone down)   Atherton   Cornelius
                          Died Decr 4th   Atherton
                          1809 AE 73 y   Died
                                             Aug 13 1848

Cornelius ATHERTON   024   Cornelius ATHERTON

SERVICE: He was a blacksmith by trade, and having discovered the process of converting iron into American steel, in 1772 he entered into a contract with the Messrs. Reed, merchants of Amenia, New York, to superintend the erection of a steel works, to be constructed by them, and to instruct their workmen in the art. The works were erected and were in sucessful operation during the War of the Revolution. From Amenia he returned to Cambridge, where he superintended an armory belonging to John and Samuel Adams and John Hancock, which was burned by the British soldiers during the Revolutionary War. In 1775/6 he removed to Plymouth, Luzerne County, Pennsylvania, where he worked at his trade. He was drafted at the time of the Wyoming massacre, but his place was taken by his eldest son, Jabez, who volunteered to become his substitute. The youthful patriot fell in that engagement and his name heads the list on the Wyoming monument. Cornelius' wife, by whom he had seven children, died soon after the Wyoming massacre.

FAMILY INFORMATION: Married first to Mary **Delano**, a daughter of Nathaniel and Elizabeth **(Durfee) Delano**. She died in 1784. He married second Jane **Johnson**. She was born in 1767, died on Aug 13, 1848 and is buried with her husband.

Children:
  Jabez   B-? D-Jul 1-4, 1778 at Wyoming, PA
              (Revolutionary War Battle)
  John
  ?
  ?
  ?
  ?
  ?

Second marriage
  Humphrey B-1787. M-Experience ____ (B-Aug 14,1796;
           D-Oct 9,1835; Bur Mt Hope Cem, Norwich,
           NY). M2-widow **Wicks**.
           D-Dec 11,1849. Bur Vallonia Springs,NY.
  Angelia   B-1791. M-Ira **Church** (B-1791; son of
           Richard and Polly **[Pollard] Church**;
           Vet War 1812; D-Mar 12,1861 Morris, NY).
           D-Jul 15,1847. Both bur East Cem, Afton,
           NY.
  Charles   B-1793. M-____ **Bramhill** (D-Friendship,
           Allegany Co, NY). D-May 13, 1869 at
           Emporium, Cameron Co, PA.

Cornelius ATHERTON   024   Cornelius ATHERTON

  Hiram   B-Jun 16,1796. M-Lovina **Sisson**
               (B-Jul 17,1801; D-Aug 11,1883).
               D-Mar 19,1870 at Greene,NY.
               Both Bur North Canal Cem,Greene,NY.
  Christianna
  William   B-1802. M-Jane E **Hamlin** (D-Patterson,NJ).
               D-Aug 2,1879 at Patterson,NJ.
  Cornelius

OTHER INFORMATION: Residence had been Cambridge, Massachusetts, Amenia, New York in 1763, Plymouth, Pennsylvania in 1775/1776, to Afton, New York in 1803/1804. He was a blacksmith and gun maker.

Joseph ATKINS   025   Joseph ATKINS
  -. -------Private   DAR Patriot Index

RESIDENT DATE: 1805 - 1820
TOWN: Smyrna
BIRTH DATE: 1743a
BIRTH PLACE: Hartford, Connecticut (Hartford County)
FATHER: Joseph **Atkins**
MOTHER: Abigail **Rich**
DEATH DATE: Apr 5, 1820
DEATH PLACE: Smyrna, New York
CEMETERY: West Hill
LOCATION: Sherburne, New York

TOMBSTONE INSCRIPTION: (not found--- reported by DAR in 1972)

SERVICE: He was a private from the State of Connecticut.

FAMILY INFORMATION: Married Jul 30, 1767 in Waterbury, New Haven, Connecticut to Phebe **Hall**. She died in the summer of 1828.

  Children:
  Rosannah B-Mar 05,1768. M-Jonas **Heacock** of
              Waterbury, CT. D-Jan 11,1790.
  Sylvia   B-Nov 03,1769. D-Jan 11,1790.
  Asahel   B-Feb 26,1772. M-Sarah **Warner**. M2-widow
              Prudence **Metcalf** (B-1785;
              D-Apr 14,1849; Bur Frink Cem, Pharsalia,
              NY). D-Apr 06,1857.
  Samuel   B-Jan 01,1774.
  Xenia   B-Jun 30,1776. D-Jan 08,1777.
  Adah   B-Jan 09,1778. D-Oct 1778.

Joseph   ATKINS   025   Joseph   ATKINS

Phebe   B-May 26,1780. M-Joseph **Twitchell** of
            Wolcott, CT.
Abigail   B-Jun 07,1783. M-Ziba **Norton** of Wolcott,
            CT.
Joseph   B-Feb 10,1786   } twins
Joel   B-Feb 10,1786   }

OTHER INFORMATION: Joseph was a deacon in the church at Wolcott Connecticut for 19 years.

Jonathan   **ATWATER**   026   Jonathan   ATWATER
           R. 00298 Private

RESIDENT DATE: - 1849
TOWN: Coventry
BIRTH DATE: Jun 20, 1765
BIRTH PLACE: Woodbridge, Connecticut
FATHER: Jonathan **Atwater**
MOTHER: Miriam **Canfield**
DEATH DATE: Feb 10, 1849
DEATH PLACE:
CEMETERY: Chapel
LOCATION: Coventry, New York

TOMBSTONE INSCRIPTION: NOT FOUND.
   DAR reading-- Jonathan Atwater D-Feb 10, 1849 Ae 84
                 Eunice Atwater   D-May 07, 1849 Ae 78

SERVICE: While a resident of Woodbridge, Connecticut, in Sepember 1781, he was drafted into Captain Lazarus Toller's Company of militia, and marched to New Haven, Connecticut; served three months and 12 days. In the fall (Sep) of the following year he was drafted into Captain Trumbull's Company of militia under Sergeant Murray and once again marched to New Haven, Connecticut; served for three months.

FAMILY INFORMATION: Married to Eunice _____, a widow of Adda **Downs**. She was born in 1771, died May 7, 1849 and is buried with her husband.

Jonathan   ATWATER   026   Jonathan   ATWATER

Children:
Amanda   B-17--. M-Jan 31,1822 at Coventry,NY
              to Larkin **Packard** (B-Sep 21,1794 at
              Bridgewater,MA; son of Rev. War Vet.
              Oliver and Mercy [**Dunbar**] **Packard**;
              War of 1812 Vet; M2-Oct 5,1864 at
              Colesville,NY to Betsy **Montgomery**
              [B-1802; widow of Asa **Montgomery**];
              D-Apr 16,1880 at Colesville,NY).
              D-Sep 4,1863 at Coventry,NY.
              Both bur Coventry Cem, Coventry,NY.
Garret   B-Jun 02, 1800.
Polly   BP-Sep 09, 1804. M-Aaron **Winslow**.

OTHER INFORMATION: Following the Revolution he removed to Waterbury, Connecticut, then nine years later went to Coventry, Chenango County, New York. He applied for a pension on an application dated Jan 18, 1839, while a resident of Coventry, New York.

Abraham   AVERY   027   Abraham   AVERY
        S. 28626 Sergeant   DAR Patriot Index

RESIDENT DATE: 1800 - 1840
TOWN: Preston
BIRTH DATE: May 20, 1754
BIRTH PLACE: Stonington, Connecticut
FATHER: William **Avery**
MOTHER: Sarah **Walker**
DEATH DATE: Nov 30, 1844
DEATH PLACE: Earlville, New York
CEMETERY: Whitman Clark farm
LOCATION: Lebanon, New York (Madison County)

TOMBSTONE INSCRIPTION:

SERVICE: On July first 17-- he enlisted at Stonington as a corporal in a company commanded by Nathan Hale, a part of the 7th Regiment of Connecticut, under Colonel James Webb.

FAMILY INFORMATION: Married about 1780 at Guilford, Windham County, Vermont to Mercy **Packer**, daughter of Ichabod and Esther (**Burrows**) **Packer**. She was born in 1761 and died Jun 20, 1843.

Abraham   AVERY   027   Abraham   AVERY

Children:
Elias P   B-Aug 16,1781 at Guilford,VT.
             M-Mar 13,1806 Preston,NY to Sally **Covil**
             (B-Oct 20,1783; dau of David and Sarah
             [**Marsh**] **Covil**; D-May 7,1863 Averyville,
             MI). D-Dec 16,1846. Resided in Galina,
             Davis Co., IL in 1844.
Hubbard B   B-Dec 29,1784 Colerain,MA. M-Jul 21,1816
             at Preston,NY to Mary Stanton **Mason**
             (B-May 7,1788 Lebanon; dau of James and
             Abigail [**Beaumont**] **Mason**; D-Jan 29,1868
             Norwich,NY). D-Mar 7,1849 Preston,NY.
             Both bur Wait Cem, Preston, NY.
Amos W   B-May 24,1787 Colerain,MA. M-Jul 5,1808
             Preston,NY to Nancy **McCutcheon**
             (B-May 6,1787 Stowe,VT; dau of Hugh and
             Jane [**Wallace**] **McCutcheon**;
             D-Dec 11,1869 in MI). D-Jun 1,1863 at
             LaSalle,Monroe Co.,MI.
Ichabod D   B-1792. M-Eliza **Steward** (B-1800;
             D-Nov 13,1877). D-Apr 23,1869. Both bur
             South Side Cem, Plymouth,NY.
Abigail   D-single.
Esther   B-1802. M-Macon **Johnson** (B-Jun 8,1799
             Colerain, MA; M2-Sabrina **Sprague**
             [B-Jun 13,1818; D-Jan 5,1917];
             D-Jul 22,1865). D-Jan 24,1839. All three
             bur Brown Cem, Plymouth,NY.

OTHER INFORMATION: He was a blacksmith and an armorer.
About 1800 he settled on the land given to him by the
State of New York, about 2.5 miles from Preston on the
Norwich road. Applied for a pension Oct 16, 1818 which
was granted but dropped in May 1820 as he had over
$300 worth of property. He was reinstated to the rolls
on Jun 1, 1832. He moved to Earlville, Madison County,
New York in 1840.

John   AVERY   028   John   AVERY

RESIDENT DATE: 1840
TOWN: Preston
BIRTH DATE: Dec 14, 1755
BIRTH PLACE: Preston, Connecticut (New London Co.)
FATHER: John **Avery**
MOTHER: Mary **Park**
DEATH DATE: Jan 30, 1836
DEATH PLACE:

John   AVERY   028   John   AVERY

CEMETERY: Widger
LOCATION: Preston, New York

TOMBSTONE INSCRIPTION:

SERVICE:

FAMILY INFORMATION: Married August 23, 1795, Groton, New London County, Connecticut to Sarah **Denison**. She was born in 1760 in New London, Connecticut, died November 9, 1830 and is buried with her husband.

Children: ?

OTHER INFORMATION: Listed in the 1840 census of Revolutionary War pensioners in Preston, Chenango County, New York. (son?)

Uriah   AVERY   029   Uriah   AVERY
         S. 16612 Lieutenant   DAR Patriot Index

RESIDENT DATE: 1798 - 1834
TOWN: Norwich
BIRTH DATE: Aug 23, 1760
BIRTH PLACE: Norwich, Connecticut (New London Co)
FATHER: Jonathan **Avery**
MOTHER: Dorothy (**Denison**) Copp
DEATH DATE: Aug 25, 1843
DEATH PLACE: Norwich, New York
CEMETERY: Mt Hope
LOCATION: Norwich, New York

TOMBSTONE INSCRIPTION: Died   Sibbel
                        Uriah Avery   Wife of
                        Aug 25 1843   Uriah Avery
                        Aged 83 years   Died Aug 14, 1838
                                            Ae 80 yrs

SERVICE: While residing in Norwich, Connecticut he volunteered in April 1776, served as a private in Captain Oliver Coit's Company, Colonel Ely's Connecticut Regiment, was employed in erecting Fort Griswold at Groton, Connecticut, marched to New York and was in the battle of White Plains, length of service, six months and fifteen days. He volunteered in December, 1776, under Captain Jedadiah Hyde, Captain of Marines, entered on board the ship "Warren" that cruised to the West Indies, captured two British ships and took them into Boston harbor. He was discharged in April 1777, having served five months.

Uriah   AVERY   029   Uriah   AVERY

FAMILY INFORMATION: Married Jan 28, 1783 at Lebanon, Connecticut to Sybil **Little**. She was baptised Jun 29, 1758 in Lebanon, New London County, Connecticut, died Aug 14, 1838 and is buried with her husband.

Children:
  Eliza   M-_____ Carey (son of Judge **Carey**)
  William
  Sophia   B-Jul 23, 1792 Old Hadley,MA.
  Hariot   B-1793. D-Mar 18,1816. Bur Mt Hope Cem, Norwich, NY.

OTHER INFORMATION: After the Revolution he resided in Canterbury and Hampton, Connecticut; Sturbridge and Hadley, Massachusetts; Pownal, Vermont; Florida, Montgomery County, New York and Norwich, Chenango County, New York. He was a saddler and harness maker, the first in the settlements. A pension was allowed on Feb 11, 1834 while residing in Norwich, Chenango County, New York.

Arthur   AYLESWORTH   030   Arthur   AYLESWORTH
         W. 16495 Private

RESIDENT DATE: 1832
TOWN: Guilford
BIRTH DATE: Nov 10, 1755
BIRTH PLACE: West Greenwich, Rhode Island
FATHER: Joseph **Aylesworth**
MOTHER:
DEATH DATE: Apr 20, 1834/5
DEATH PLACE: Unadilla, New York
CEMETERY: Spencer
LOCATION: Unadilla, New York (Otsego County)

TOMBSTONE INSCRIPTION: Arthur
                                 Aylesworth
                              A Revolutionary
                                 Soldier

SERVICE: While residing in Pawlingstown, Dutchess County, New York, he enlisted sometime in 1775, and served six months in Captain Whiting Parks' New York Company; he enlisted about April 1, 1776, and served nine months in Captain William Clark's Company, Colonel Vanderburg's New York Regiment; he enlisted about June 1, 1777, and served three months in Captain William Calkin's Company, Colonel Henry Luddington's New York Regiment. While on a visit to West Greenwich, Rhode Island, he enlisted there and served three

Arthur AYLESWORTH   030   Arthur AYLESWORTH

months as a private in Captain Job Angell's Company, Colonel John Brown's Rhode Island Regiment; he again enlisted in the spring of 1781, in Pawlingstown, New York and served nine months in Captain William Pierce's Company, Colonel Morehouse's New York Regiment. He was in a number of skirmishes: he was also at Danbury, Connecticut, when it was burned.

FAMILY INFORMATION: Married January 1777, in Pauling township, Dutchess County, New York to Polly **Fish**. She was born Jul 30, 1759 in Pauling Township, New York.

Children: ?

OTHER INFORMATION: After the Revolution, he resided in Dutchess County, New York; he moved from there about 1818 or 1819 to Otsego, Otsego County, New York. He was allowed pension on his application executed Sep. 17, 1832, at which time he was residing in Guilford, Chenango County, New York, where he had lived for a short time. His widow was allowed pension on her application executed Feb 17, 1837, while residing in Unadilla, Otsego County, New York. In 1832 the soldier's brother, Joseph **Aylesworth**, was residing in Harpersfield, New York. His widow was listed in the 1840 census of pensioners in Guilford, New York.

Peleg AYLESWORTH   031   Peleg AYLESWORTH
-, ------ Private

RESIDENT DATE: 1820 - 1824
TOWN: New Berlin
BIRTH DATE: Aug 27, 1749
BIRTH PLACE: Foster, Rhode Island
FATHER: Chad **Aylesworth**
MOTHER: Mary **Wood**
DEATH DATE: Aug 20, 1824
DEATH PLACE: New Berlin, New York
CEMETERY: Aylesworth
LOCATION: New Berlin, New York

Peleg AYLESWORTH   031   Peleg   AYLESWORTH

TOMBSTONE INSCRIPTION:

In
Memory of
Mr Peleg Aylesworth
Who departed this
life August 20th 1824
Aged 75 years on the
day of his death.

Anna
Wife of
Peleg Aylesworth
Died Jan. 12. 1844
Ae 88 years

SERVICE: He was on a list of men mustered between Jan 20, 1777 and Jun 1, 1778, in Berkshire County, Massachusetts by Truman Wheeler, Muster Master. He served in Captain Satterly's Company, Colonel Hazen's Regiment, an enlistment of three years.

FAMILY INFORMATION: Married Nov 26, 1772 to Anna **Cole**. She was born Mar 23, 1755, a dau of Daniel and Anna (**Young**) **Cole**, died Jan 12, 1844 and is buried with her husband.

Children:
- Daniel   B-Jan 28,1774. M-in RI to Anna **Hopkins**. Resided in Marengo,Wayne Co,NY.
- Abel   B-Mar 12,1776. M-Apr 2,1809 Susanna **Leach** (B-Aug 26,1786 New London,CT; dau of Stephen and Susanna [**Smith**] **Leach**). D-Aug 5,1836. Bur Aylesworth Cem, New Berlin,NY.
- Rhoda   B-Feb 09,1778. D-Dec 23,1797.
- Mary   B-Aug 30,1781. Unmarried - Invalid. D-Aug 11,1830 at New Berlin,NY. Bur Aylesworth Cem,New Berlin,NY.
- Sarah   B-Oct 11,1783. Unmarried. D-May 16,1861 at New Berlin,NY. Bur Aylesworth Cem, New Berlin,NY.
- Anna   B-May 11,1786. M-Apr 1,1804 to Nehemiah **Leach** (B-Oct 27,1779; son of Stephen and Susanna [**Smith**] **Leach**; D-Apr 23,1846; Bur King Settlement Cem, North Norwich,NY).
- Martha   B-Apr 11,1788. M-Mar 1,1807 to George **Davis** (B-Jul 23,1786 in Scituate,RI; son of William **Davis**; D-Feb 1842). D-Aug 6,1836 in Fulton Co,IL.
- Peleg   B-Feb 28,1790. M-Sep 12,1812 to Hannah **Wilcox** (Dau of Ebenezer and Elizabeth [**Hiram**] **Wilcox** of Oxford, Chenango Co, NY; D-Jan 29,1858 Abington,PA). D-Jan 9,1858 at Abington, Luzerne Co,PA.

Peleg AYLESWORTH   031   Peleg AYLESWORTH

David   B-Sep 08,1792. M-Jan 18,1816 Ada **Curtis**
          (B-1797; D-Feb 14,1890). D-Feb 8,1876 at
          New Berlin,NY. Both bur Aylesworth Cem,
          New Berlin,NY.

Amy   B-Jan 03,1795. M-Oct 17,1818 Myron **Toles**
          (B-Jan 16,1799; son of Ebenezer and Lucy
          [**Fitch**] **Toles** of Edmeston, NY;
          D-Mar 7,1871 Butternuts, Otsego Co,NY).
          D-Apr 16,1862 Butternuts,NY.

Philip   B-Apr 20,1797. M-Dec 2,1827 Sagamore Co,IL
          to Chloe **Goodell** (B-May 11,1809;
          D-Jul 19,1839 Fulton Co,IL).
          M2-Elizabeth **Beers**(B-Apr 7,1822;
          D-Jul 9,1859). M3-Cynthia **Aylesworth**
          (dau of Allen and Lefee [**Tibbets**]
          Aylesworth; D-Mar 11,1863).
          D-Dec 22,1883.

Elizabeth B-Aug 11,1799. D-at age 2 or 3.

OTHER INFORMATION: The family left Foster, Rhode Island in the autumn of 1797, and settled in Edmeston, Otsego County, New York, between Wharton Creek and the Unadilla River, west of Edmeston Centre, where they dwelt until the year 1820, when they removed to the western part of the town of New Berlin, Chenango County, New York.

Christopher BABCOCK   032 Christopher BABCOCK
        Lieutenant   DAR Patriot Index

RESIDENT DATE: - 1815
TOWN: Smyrna
BIRTH DATE: Sep 12, 1734
BIRTH PLACE: Westerly, Rhode Island
FATHER: William **Babcock**
MOTHER: Sarah **Denison**
DEATH DATE: Mar 15, 1815
DEATH PLACE: Smyrna, New York
CEMETERY: Stover
LOCATION: Smyrna, New York

TOMBSTONE INSCRIPTION: No stone was erected at his grave, but years later his son Stephen had a gravestone placed beside the grave of his wife Mehitable, in Westerly, Rhode Island.

Christopher BABCOCK 032 Christopher BABCOCK

SERVICE: In 1767 he was a lieutenant in Captain Champlain's Train Band, Westerly Militia.

FAMILY INFORMATION: Married in 1754 to his stepsister Mehitable **Chalker**, a daughter of Stephen and Mehitable (**Chapman**) **Chalker**. She was born Sep 9, 1733 at Saybrook, Connecticut and died Jun 8, 1810 in Westerly, Rhode Island.

Children: (All born at Westerly, Rhode Island)
- William B-Dec 10,1755. M-Sep 8,1781 Westerly,RI. Mary **Babcock** (B-Apr 8,1765 Westerly, RI; Dau of Ichabod and Sarah [**Stanton**] **Babcock**). D-Lebanon Springs,NY.
- Amy B-Jun 12,1757. M-____ **Coffin**.
- Joshua B-Mar 15,1759. D-Oct 1786 at Westerly,RI.
- Christopher B-Jul 26,1761. M-1783 at Westerly,RI. to Polly **Burdick** (B-Nov 9,1761 at Westerly, RI; Dau of Oliver and Susannah **Burdick**; D-Sep 2,1828 Coeymans, NY). D-Albany, NY.
- Sarah B-Mar 10,1763. M-Joseph **Babcock**. M2-Thomas **Grant**.
- Eunice B-Dec 28,1764.
- Jeremiah B-Mar 23,1766. M-Jan 5,1792 to Amy **Angell** (Dau of William **Angell**; D-Feb 17,1835 at Champion,NY). D-Apr 9,1847 at Champion,NY.
- Asa B-Jul 06,1768. D-Apr 1777.
- Wealthy B-Jun 12,1770. D-Jun 1772.
- Stephen B-Feb 27,1772. M-Mar 22,1801 Westerly, RI. to Phebe **Burch** (B-Nov 22,1774 at Stonington,CT.; Dau of Henry and Mary [**Irish**] **Burch**; D-Nov 10,1837 at Stonington,CT.). D-Mar 22,1852 at Stonington,CT.
- Elias B-Oct 26,1773. D-Apr 1794 at sea, while returning from the West Indies.
- Phineas B-Feb 14, 1776. M-Nov 28, 1801 Westerly, RI. to Thankful **Babcock** (B-1775; Dau of Joseph and Hannah [**Ross**] **Babcock**). M2-at North East, Pa. to ____ **Huntington**. D-Jul 12,1844 at North East,Pa.

Christopher BABCOCK 032 Christopher BABCOCK

Asa   B-Oct 1777. M-Jan 16,1800 at Westerly, RI.
            to Molly Babcock (B-Mar 2,1778 at
            Westerly, RI; Dau of Joseph and Hannah
            [Ross] Babcock; D-Dec 31, 1802 at
            Westerly,RI). M2-Dec 19,1805 at
            Hopkinton,RI. to Elizabeth Barber
            (B-Oct 17,1779; Dau of Thomas and Mary
            [Barney] Barber; D-Dec 3,1823 Pitcher,
            NY). D-Dec 26,1851 at Champion,NY.

OTHER INFORMATION: He owned a farm near the seashore in the town of Westerly, Rhode Island. He served as the Justice of the Peace. In 1813 his son Asa sold the farm and moved to Smyrna, New York. Evidently Christopher went with him at that time, as he died at the home of his son in Smyrna.

Daniel BABCOCK   033   Daniel BABCOCK
        R.   345 Private

RESIDENT DATE   1827
TOWN: German
BIRTH DATE:
BIRTH PLACE:
FATHER:
MOTHER:
DEATH DATE: Feb 5, 1827
DEATH PLACE: German, New York
CEMETERY:
LOCATION:

TOMBSTONE INSCRIPTION:

SERVICE: While residing at Mansfield, Connecticut he volunteered and served about 6 weeks in the vicinity of Boston, Massachusetts. Sometime in the year 1776 he volunteered into Captain Amariah Williams' Company and served at Bennington, Vermont for about three months. Again in 1777 he volunteered into Captain Amariah Williams' Company for three months.

FAMILY INFORMATION: Married at Coventry, Connecticut on Nov 16, 1774 to Triphena Scripture, a daughter of Simeon and Ann (Slater) Scripture. She was born Feb 3, 1757 in Coventry Twp., Tolland, Connecticut.

Daniel BABCOCK   033   Daniel BABCOCK

Children:
  Daniel   B-Aug 01,1782 Weathersfield,VT.
  Augustus   B-Mar 09,1784 Weathersfield,VT.
  Eunice D   B-Apr 01,1786 Weathersfield,VT.
  Orin   B-Apr 14,1789 Weathersfield,VT.

OTHER INFORMATION: His wife applied for a pension on Sept 1, 1838 while residing at Greene, Chenango County, New York.

Elisha BABCOCK   034   Elisha BABCOCK
       S. 6029 Private

RESIDENT DATE: 1840
TOWN: New Berlin
BIRTH DATE: 1762
BIRTH PLACE: Stonington, Connecticut (New London Co)
FATHER: Silas Babcock
MOTHER: Phoebe Wood
DEATH DATE:
DEATH PLACE:
CEMETERY:
LOCATION:

TOMBSTONE INSCRIPTION:

SERVICE: Served eleven months. He was a resident of Stephentown, Rensselaer County, New York and a member of the local militia, when he was called out in August 1776 and sent to Scoharie, New York to guard the populace from the Indians and Tories. He was dismissed after ten days of service. On the alarm at the approach of Burgoyne's army from the north, he again was ordered out, under Captain Niles, about Sep 1, 1777. He was in service at Ballstown about one month. Again he was called out on Oct 1, 1777, and marched to Stillwater. After the capitulation of Burgoyne, about three weeks later, he returned to Stephentown. On Apr 1, 1782 he was classed off in the militia, and was detached to the State Troops of New York. He marched to Albany and was there mustered in Captain Peter Tierce's Company of Infantry for nine months. He served in various forts along the Mohawk river, and, after nine months, was discharged at Fort Plain, Dec 31, 1782.

FAMILY INFORMATION: Married ?
  Children: ?
    X   B-

Elisha BABCOCK   034   Elisha BABCOCK

OTHER INFORMATION: After the war he lived in Stephentown, Burlington, Cazenovia, and Edmeston. He was granted a pension on his application dated Oct 16, 1832, while a resident of Edmeston, Otsego County, New York. He was listed in the 1840 census of pensioners at New Berlin, Chenango County, New York.

Jonathan BABCOCK   035   Jonathan BABCOCK
       S. 6589 Private   DAR Patriot Index

RESIDENT DATE: 1840
TOWN: Lincklaen
BIRTH DATE: Jun 5, 1764
BIRTH PLACE: Stonington, Connecticut
FATHER: Silas Babcock
MOTHER: Phobe Wood
DEATH DATE: Feb 10, 1849
DEATH PLACE: Cincinnatus, New York
CEMETERY: Hetty Greene (Burrell Green's farm)
LOCATION: Willett, Cortland County, New York

TOMBSTONE INSCRIPTION: Selinda
    (His stone not found)   Wife of
                             Jonathan Babcock Sen'r
                                    Died
                                July 29, 1845
                                Aged 79 years
   (Note: tree growing against
    stone. Unknown if more
    reading exists)

SERVICE: He enlisted at Stephentown, New York Apr 1, 1782. He marched with the state troops to Albany and mustered there under Captain Peter Tierce in a Company of New York Infantry. They marched to Schenectady and joined Colonel Willet's Regiment at Johnstown. He served nine months as a scout and was on duty at different times on the Mohawk River. He was discharged at Fort Plain, New York Dec 31, 1783.

FAMILY INFORMATION: Married to Selinda Hanks, a daughter of Benjamin and Ruth (Bruster) Hanks. She was born Mar 9, 1766 in Mansfield, Tolland County, Connecticut and died Jul 29, 1845. She is buried with her husband.

Jonathan   BABCOCK   035   Jonathan   BABCOCK

Children:
Jonathan   B-1789. D-Sep 15,1856. Bur Hetty Greene
               Cem,Willett,NY.
Rebecca   M-_____ Parker.

OTHER INFORMATION: He was granted a pension on his application dated Jul 7, 1832 while a resident of Burlington, Otsego County, New York. He is listed in the census of 1840 pensioners at the town of Lincklaen, Chenango County, New York, with the head of household being Harvey Babcock.

Roger   BABCOCK   036   Roger   BABCOCK
         W. 12107 Private   DAR Patriot Index

RESIDENT DATE: 1800 - 1836
TOWN: New Berlin
BIRTH DATE: June 10, 1758
BIRTH PLACE: Coventry, Connecticut
FATHER: William Babcock
MOTHER: Mary Gates
DEATH DATE: May 11, 1836
DEATH PLACE: New Berlin, New York
CEMETERY: Burlington Flats
LOCATION: Burlington Flats, New York (Otsego Co.)

TOMBSTONE INSCRIPTION: Mrs Thankful wife
                          Of Mr Roger Babcock
                          Died March 9th 1822
                             In the 66th year
                               Of her age
                    Jesus to thy dear faithful hand
                         my naked soul I trust
                    and my flesh waits for thy command
              Mr   to drop into my dust
         Roger Babcock
          Died May 11,
         1836 Ae 79 yrs
Behold and see as you pass by
as you are now so once was I
  as I am now so you must be
prepare for death and follow me.

SERVICE: Enlisted in December 1775 and served three months as a private in Captain James Dana's Company, Colonel Moseley's Connecticut Regiment. He reenlisted Feb. 5, 1776 and was a private in Captain Gershorn Barrow's Company, Colonel John Chester's Connecticut Regiment. He was in the battle of Long Island and

Roger BABCOCK   036   Roger   BABCOCK

White Plains and was discharged Dec. 25, 1776. He enlisted in May 1779 or 1780 and served ten months as a private in Captain James Dana's Company, Colonel Levi Well's Connecticut Regiment.

FAMILY INFORMATION: Married to Thankful _____. She was born 1756, died Mar 9, 1822 and is buried with her husband.

Children:
Almiron   B-1781 Burlington, Otsego Co, NY.
Harmonia   B-Dec. 2,1783. M- Sep 2,1803,Daniel Dewey
           Hopkins (B-Mar 21,1776 Burlington,VT).
           D-Oct 30,1809
Chester
Alva

OTHER INFORMATION: He was allowed a pension on his application executed Oct. 9, 1832 while a resident of New Berlin Chenango County New York. Pension began Mar 4, 1831, at the rate of $76.66 per year.

Thomas Gould BACON   037   Thomas Gould BACON

RESIDENT DATE: 1788 - 1821
TOWN: Bainbridge
BIRTH DATE: May 9, 1749
BIRTH PLACE: Middletown, Connecticut (Middlesex Co)
FATHER: John **Bacon**
MOTHER: Rhoda **Gould**
DEATH DATE: Apr 1, 1821
DEATH PLACE: Bainbridge, New York
CEMETERY: Pioneer
LOCATION: Sidney, New York (Delaware County)

TOMBSTONE INSCRIPTION: In
                           Memory of
                           Gold Bacon
                          Died April 1
                          1821 ae 75
             He toiled for heirs he knew not whom
                 and straight was seen no more

SERVICE: The book on The History of Sidney shows that local DAR records indicate he was a Revolutionary soldier.

Thomas Gould   BACON   037   Thomas Gould   BACON

FAMILY INFORMATION: Bachelor
Children: none

OTHER INFORMATION: He came from Connecticut about the year 1788 and settled on lot #76 on the east side of the river, one and one-half miles above Bainbridge. He afterwards removed to the mouth of the Unadilla River. He was an eccentric genius, and a bachelor, living alone in a small log hut, which stood upon a low flat, adjacent to the river. Two interesting anecdotes of his life are contained in "The History of Chenango County" by James Smith.

Nathaniel   BADGER   038   Nathaniel   BADGER
-, ----- Sergeant

RESIDENT DATE: - 1830
TOWN: Coventry
BIRTH DATE: Feb 7, 1752
BIRTH PLACE: Coventry, Connecticut (Tolland County)
FATHER: Enoch **Badger**
MOTHER: Mary **Langdon**
DEATH DATE: Jun 13, 1830
DEATH PLACE:
CEMETERY: Chapel
LOCATION: Coventry, New York

TOMBSTONE INSCRIPTION: Mr
                         Nathaniel Badger
                              Died
                           June 1830
                        Aged 78 years
                           Mehitable
                            Wife of
                         Nathaniel Badger
                              Died
                         Apr 1, 1848
                        Aged 90 years

SERVICE: He served as a private in Captain Samuel Gilbert's Company, Colonel William Prescott's Regiment. He is shown on the muster roll dated Aug 1, 1775, having enlisted on May 20, 1775 for a service of 73 days. He was also listed on a Company return dated Cambridge, Sep 28, 1775. He is listed on an order for bounty coat or its equivalent in money dated Cambridge, Oct. 30, 1775. He enlisted at Morristown on Dec 20, 1776 as a sergeant in Captain Jonathan Wales' Company, Lieutenant Colonel S Williams' Regiment.

Nathaniel BADGER   038   Nathaniel BADGER

He was discharged Mar 23, 1777 for a service of 3 months and 10 days.

FAMILY INFORMATION: Married to Mehitable _____.
She was born in 1758, died Apr 1, 1848 and is buried with her husband.

Children:
Samuel   B-Jan 31,1776/7 in MA. M-Jul 7,1799 to
            Abigail **Miles** (B-Mar 16,1776 in
            Wallingford,CT; Dau of John and Abigail
            [Perkins] **Miles**; D-Apr, 1844 Elmira,
            NY). Major in War of 1812; D-Mar 3,1849
            in Elmira,NY. Both bur Second Street
            Cem, Elmira, NY.
John   B-1778 Elmira,NY.
Bostwick   B-1780 Elmira,NY.
Orrin   B-1781 Elmira,NY.
Oliver   B-1783 Elmira,NY. M-Lucretia _____.
Harvey   B-1785 Elmira,NY.
Joseph   B-1788 Elmira,NY. M-Hannah _____ (B-1805;
            D-Oct 8,1836). M2-Sally _____ (B-1814;
            D-Jun 22,1881). D-Jul 22,1876. All 3 bur
            Chapel Cem, Coventry,NY.

OTHER INFORMATION:

Daniel BAGG   039   Daniel BAGG
-, ----- First Lieutenant   DAR Patriot Index

RESIDENT DATE: 1798 -
TOWN: New Berlin
BIRTH DATE: 1757
BIRTH PLACE: Pittsfield, Massachusetts
FATHER: David **Bagg**
MOTHER: Elizabeth **Morley**
DEATH DATE: May 29, 1829
DEATH PLACE: New Berlin
CEMETERY: Riverside #1
LOCATION: New Berlin, New York

Daniel BAGG   039   Daniel BAGG

TOMBSTONE INSCRIPTION: Mr
                      Dan Bagg
                      Died May 29
                  1829 ae 72 years
    My flesh shall slumber in the ground
    till the last trumpets joyfull sound
    then burst the chains with great surprise
        and in my saviours image rise.
         Peace to thy gentle shade.

SERVICE: Was a private in Captain Peter Porter's Company of Colonel Benjamin Simonds Regiment, enlisted Apr 26, 1777, discharged May 20, 1777. He belonged to the Berkshire County Regiment and marched to Saratoga by order of Major General Gates. Served as a first lieutenant in Captain David Mosley's Company, John Mosley's Regiment, Massachusetts troops.

FAMILY INFORMATION: Married to Thirza **Ingham** (born Nov 23, 1763 in Hebron County to Alexander and Katherine (**Noble**) **Ingham**).

Children:
Oliver
Althea   B-1784. M-William **Jones** (D-May 19,1826).
            D-Mar 29,1867. Both bur Riverside Cem,
            New Berlin, NY.
Lucy   M-_____ **Lewis**
William
Jeremiah
Olive   M-Samuel **Kinney**.
Anna   M-_____ **West**
Henry   M-Harriet **Davis**.
Gamaliel   B-1807. M-Elizabeth **Barrett** (B-1810;
            D-Aug 31,1892). D-Oct 31,1892. Both bur
            Riverside Cem, New Berlin, NY.
Horace
Rhoda
Aaron

OTHER INFORMATION: Daniel's father, David also served in the Revolutionary War when he was past the age of 60.

Jeremiah BAILEY   040   Jeremiah BAILEY
    W. 19191 Private   DAR Patriot Index

RESIDENT DATE: wife
TOWN: New Berlin
BIRTH DATE: Mar 2, 1761
BIRTH PLACE: East Greenwich, Rhode Island (Kent Co.)
FATHER: William Bailey
MOTHER: Phebe
DEATH DATE: Nov --, 1798
DEATH PLACE: on a voyage to St Thomas
CEMETERY: (maybe DAR burial)
LOCATION:

TOMBSTONE INSCRIPTION:

SERVICE: He enlisted and served in the years of 1778 and 1779 as a private in Captain James Parker's Company, Colonel Crary's Rhode Island Regiment. He also served in Colonel John Topham's Rhode Island Regiment.

FAMILY INFORMATION: He married Sep 22, 1785 at Warwick, Rhode Island to Roby **Miller**, a daughter of Nathan **Miller**. She was born Jun 26, 1764 in Warwick, Kent Co, Rhode Island. She married second in Jan, 1811 to Archibald **Dorance** who died Oct, 1817.

  Children:
   Betsy Ann   B-Oct 14,1788 East Greenwich,RI.

OTHER INFORMATION: He sailed on a schooner from East Greenwich bound for St. Thomas, and never was heard from again. His widow applied for pension on an application dated Jan 24, 1846 while a resident of New Berlin, Chenango County, New York.

Timothy   BAILEY   041   Timothy   BAILEY
    W. 15752 Private

RESIDENT DATE: - 1834
TOWN: Lincklaen
BIRTH DATE: 1754
BIRTH PLACE: Harford, Connecticut (Harford County)
FATHER:
MOTHER:
DEATH DATE: Oct 18, 1834
DEATH PLACE: Lincklean, New York
CEMETERY:
LOCATION:

TOMBSTONE INSCRIPTION:

Timothy **BAILEY**   041   Timothy **BAILEY**

SERVICE: He enlisted in May 1775 while a resident of Kinderhook, New York for a term of five months in the Company of Captain John Chadwick, Colonel Brewer's Regiment. After a short time of service at Bunker Hill, he was taken with distemper and spent the remainder of his enlistment in the hospital at Roxbury. His father had to come to take him home. He enlisted for five months at Green River in May 1776 and went to New York with Captain Davey's Company, Colonel Hopkin's Regiment, where he was involved in various actions, involving General Putnam and General Washington. He enlisted, again for five months, in May, 1777 with Captain Joseph Cook's Company, Colonel Joshua Taylor's Regiment at Newtown. They joined General Schuyler forces at Fort Edward. He was part of the forces who captured Burgoyne and was near General Arnot when he jumped his horse over the enemy's breastworks. He enlisted in May 1780 under the same officers for nine months. He had smallpox while at Johnstown. He enlisted in May 1781 for six months under the same officers going to Ballston, guarding against the Tories and Indians.

FAMILY INFORMATION: Married in the spring of 1776 at New Cannan, New York to Jane **Houghtaling** daughter of Jacobus **Houghtaling**, born in 1759 at Phillips Patent, New York, and died Mar 18, 1840.

Children:
John   B-1777 NY.
Nathan G   B-Sep 15,1778 in NY; M-Jan 7,1802 to
                Catharine **Patterson** (B-Mar 29,1786);
                D-Aug 10,1835.
Timothy   B-Feb 14, 1782 Clifton Park, NY.
James   B-1786 NY.
Mary   M-_____ **Moe**.
Lorahanna   M-_____ **Scitton**.

OTHER INFORMATION: After the war he lived in Newtown for several years, then removed to Duanesburgh for a few more years, then removed to Cherry Valley, after which he moved to Lincklaen, Chenango County, New York in 1818. He applied for pension on Aug 24, 1832 while a resident of Lincklaen, New York. His widow was granted a pension thru an application made on Mar 24, 1837, while a resident of Lincklaen, New York.

Abraham BAKER   042   Abraham   BAKER
     R.   404 Private

RESIDENT DATE: 1801 - 1834
TOWN: New Berlin
BIRTH DATE: Jan   1752
BIRTH PLACE: Warwick, Rhode Island (Kent County)
FATHER:
MOTHER:
DEATH DATE: Aug 14, 1834
DEATH PLACE:
CEMETERY: St Andrews
LOCATION: New Berlin, New York

TOMBSTONE INSCRIPTION: Mrs
                              Sarah wife
                             of Abm Baker
                            Died Jan 6, 1825
                             in the 71 year
                              of her age
                    Farewell dear friends I must be gone
         Mr   I have no home to stay with you
       Abraham   I'll take my staff and travel on
      Baker died   till I a better world do view
      Aug 14 1834   Farewell, farewell, farewell
      Ae 82 yrs &   my loving friends farewell.
        7 mths.
He has gone the way of all
                the earth

SERVICE: While a resident of Warwick, Rhode Island, was drafted as a militia man under Captain Thomas Rice in Colonel John Waterman's Regiment. He was employed in guarding the coast and worked on the forts around Warwick. After discharge he continued to serve at short periods from ten to forty days up to the close of the war. He served in Massachusetts under General Spencer and General Sullivan. Was at Howland, Bristots and Fogland Ferries. He was serving at Newport when the French fleet came, as he was at work on a fort under a French engineer, toward the close of the war. He served a total of two years and four months over a seven-year period.

FAMILY INFORMATION: Married May 2, 1773 in Warwick, Kent County, Rhode Island to Sarah **Wescott**. She was born about 1754 in Norwich, New London County, Connecticut and died Jan 6, 1825. She is buried with her husband.

    Children:
     Josiah   B-

Abraham BAKER   042   Abraham BAKER

OTHER INFORMATION: Had a sister Temperance **Sarle** who was born in 1758, a wife of Thomas **Sarle** and a brother named Josiah, who died during the war. He applied for a pension on an application dated Jun 11, 1833. His initial application, which was submitted Jan 18, 1833 was returned for additional information. His application listed Noah **Ely**, Rev War Vet Isaac **Green**, Charles **Knapp**, Charles **Medbury** and Augustus **Welch** as Neighbors.

Joseph BAKER   043   Joseph BAKER

```
RESIDENT DATE:   1827 - 1850
TOWN:            Guilford
BIRTH DATE:      Oct 21, 1755
BIRTH PLACE:     Marlborough, England
FATHER:          Bennett Baker
MOTHER:          Mary Gilbert
DEATH DATE:      Jan 2, 1850
DEATH PLACE:     Guilford, New York
CEMETERY:        North
LOCATION:        Guilford, New York
```

TOMBSTONE INSCRIPTION:

    Joseph Baker   Levinia
      Died   Wife of
    Jan. 2 1850.   Joseph Baker
    Ae 94 yrs 2 m.   Died
      & 12 d   April 9. 1859.
             Aged 94 years

SERVICE: A British soldier. He enlisted in the British army in 1774 after running away from home at London, England. He embarked for America in 1776 and while with General Burgoyne was taken prisoner at Saratoga, New York on Oct 17, 1777. There was an exchange of prisoners soon after and 500 started for New York to sail for England. The first night 300 deserted and the second night 100 more leaving only 100 to proceed to New York City. Joseph was one who deserted the first night. He never heard from his friends in England, not daring to write fearing he might be taken and shot as a deserter. Being told later in life that he might write in safety, as the government would not molest him at that late period, he replied, "I don't know, England has done worse things than that".

Joseph   BAKER   043   Joseph   BAKER

FAMILY INFORMATION: Married Apr 15, 1788 at Princeton, Worcester County, Massachusetts to Lavina **Keyes**, a daughter of Cyprian and Martha (**Bush**) **Keyes**. She was born Mar 22, 1765 in Princeton, Massachusetts and died Apr 9, 1859 at Guilford, New York. She is buried with her husband.

Children:
- John — B-Dec 22,1783 at Princeton,MA.
  M-Feb 16,1809 at Hancock,NH to Martha **Dennis** (B-Mar 29,1786 at Hancock,NH; D-Sep 17,1857 at Marlboro,MA).
  D-Aug 31,1848 at Marlboro,MA.
- Joseph — B-Apr 14,1789 Princeton,MA. M-Rutland,VT. Pamelia **Bartlett** (B-Feb 4,1793 Rutland,MA.; D-Oct 4,1859 East Pharsalia,NY). D-May 14,1885 East Pharsalia,NY. Both bur East Pharsalia Cem, Pharsalia,NY.
- Levinia — B-Oct 10,1801 Princeton,MA. M-Sep 17,1826 John **Gibbs** (B-Jun 5,1798 Princeton,MA; Son of William and Martha [**Cobb**] **Gibbs**; D-Feb 11,1884 in Guilford,NY). D-Nov 7,1900. Both bur North Cem, Guilford,NY.
- Bennett — B-Apr 29,1803 at Princeton,MA. M-Mar 13,1833 at Guilford,NY to Abigail **Miller** (B-Feb 5,1804 at Toringford,CT; D-Jul 5,1877 at Guilford,NY). D-Apr 10,1877 in Guilford,NY. Both bur North Cem, Guilford,NY.
- (daughter) D-young - no date

OTHER INFORMATION: He settled in Princeton, Massachusetts, where he bought 40 acres of very stony land and improved it. When his second son Joseph became of age and married, they bought 20 more acres of land and owned and worked the farm together. In the spring of 1827 they sold it for $1800 and all emigrated to Chenango County, New York. Joseph Sr., in April and Joseph Jr with his family of six children in September.

Henry BALCOM   044   Henry BALCOM
-. ----- Private   DAR Patriot Index

RESIDENT DATE: 1793 - 1812
TOWN: Oxford
BIRTH DATE: Aug 16, 1740
BIRTH PLACE: Sudbury, Massachusetts
FATHER: Joseph **Balcom**
MOTHER: Deborah **Boise**
DEATH DATE: Oct 28, 1812
DEATH PLACE: Oxford, New York
CEMETERY: Balcom
LOCATION: Oxford, New York

TOMBSTONE INSCRIPTION: (Cemetery farmed over)
                       STONE NOT FOUND

SERVICE: While a resident of Newfane, Windham County, Vermont, he fought in the battle of Bennington on an alarm call and served as a private under Captain Joseph Tyler and Jason Duncan. He was present at the surrender of Burgoyne. He is shown by Vermont records, as serving short terms, at three different times, the longest being 123 days in a Company of Rangers. He began service for his native State as a member of the training band, Apr 29, 1757, being but sixteen years of age. Owing to the early death of his father, he as well as his brothers, were apprenticed at an early age, and by entering the service of the State he was able to free himself of such bonds.

FAMILY INFORMATION: Married on Apr. 29, 1761 in Southboro, Middlesex County, Massachusetts to Keziah **Stow**, a daughter of Benjamin and Zebiah **Stow**. She was born Aug 15, 1737 in Sudbury, Middlesex County, Massachusetts and died Sep 26, 1826.

Children:
Rhoda   B-Apr 06,1762. M-Joshua **Davis**.
Frances   B-May 18,1764. M-Darius **Wheeler**.
Joseph   B-Jun 19,1766. D-1766.
Francis   B-Jul 17,1767. M-Priscilla **Kinney**
            (B-Jan 1,1776 in Dutchess Co,NY; Dau of
            Didymus **Kinney**; D-Sep 25,1866 Oxford,
            NY). D-Aug 08, 1850 in Preston, NY.
Leafa   B-Mar 30,1770. D-Sep 04,1853 in Oxford,NY.
            Unmarried.
Samuel   B-Dec 31,1772 in Sudbury,MA. M-1800 at
            Oxford,NY to Polly **Knapp** (B-1777;
            adopted dau. of Elijah **Blackman**; first
            white female in Oxford; D-Oct 7,1852).
            D-Aug 27,1847 at Oxford,NY.

Henry   BALCOM   044   Henry   BALCOM

Olive   B-May 09,1775. M-J **Holland**.
Sally   B-May 21,1780. M-Samuel **Farnham**.
          (B-Dec 16,1775; D-Apr 20,1822).
          D-Feb 16,1859.

OTHER INFORMATION: In about 1774 he removed from Sudbury, Massachusetts to Newfane, Vermont and thence, in 1793 to Oxford, Chenango County, New York. Henry's two sons Francis and Samuel came to Unadilla, New York and thence to Oxford in 1791 or 1792. They assisted in cutting the first road through to Oxford from Unadilla. Henry followed his sons to Oxford in 1793. By occupation, he was a carpenter and joiner and farmer.

Samuel   BALDWIN   045   Samuel   BALDWIN
         S. 10335 Private

RESIDENT DATE: 1804 - 1834
TOWN: Pitcher
BIRTH DATE: Dec 31, 1758
BIRTH PLACE: Cornwall, Connecticut (Litchfield Co.)
FATHER: David **Baldwin**
MOTHER: Joanna
DEATH DATE: Aug 09, 1834
DEATH PLACE: Pitcher, New York
CEMETERY:
LOCATION:

TOMBSTONE INSCRIPTION:

SERVICE: While residing in Cornwall, Connecticut he enlisted in July 1776, served as a private six months in Captain Bazeleel Beebe's Company, Colonel Bradley's Connecticut Regiment; enlisted in June or July 1780, served as private, six months in Captain Sension's (probably meant for St John's) Company, Colonel Bradley's Connecticut Regiment.

FAMILY INFORMATION:
  Children:

OTHER INFORMATION: Following the Revolution Samuel remained in Massachusetts for 23 years before moving to Pitcher, New York.

Dr Samuel   BALDWIN   046   Dr Samuel   BALDWIN
    S. 29599 Minute Man

```
RESIDENT DATE:   1819 - 1842
TOWN:            Oxford
BIRTH DATE:      Nov    1756
BIRTH PLACE:     Egremont, Massachusetts
FATHER:          Ebenezer Baldwin
MOTHER:          Mary
DEATH DATE:      Sep 02, 1842
DEATH PLACE:     Oxford, New York
CEMETERY:        Riverview
LOCATION:        Oxford, New York
```

TOMBSTONE INSCRIPTION: Samuel Baldwin
(on monument with Miller family)   1765 - 1842

SERVICE: At the age of 17 he was drafted into the militia of his native state and served in the continental army at different periods over thirteen months. In the year 1775 he was a minute man, and was called in active service soon after the battle of Lexington on April 19th of that year. He joined the continental troops at Boston, where he remained three months. In the following winter in January 1776, he was one of the volunteers who marched into Canada, in prosecution of one of the most difficult and perilous enterprises undertaken during th conflict. Besides suffering from an attack of smallpox at Montreal, on his way to that place he marched in one day, 60 miles, on Lake Champlain, on the ice, in the spring of "77", the army under General Gates, having been obliged to retreat before the British force of the north. Mr Baldwin returned to Egremont much reduced and feebled by hardships which he had endured. He was drafted again in the following September and once more joined the army under General Gates. He was present at the battle of Saratoga, and witnessed the surrender of Burgoyne on Oct 18, 1777.

FAMILY INFORMATION: Married Dec 20, 1791 in Otis, Berkshire County, Massachusetts to Mehitable **Kingsley**. She was born Jan 6, 1757 in Boston, Suffolk County, Massachusetts.

```
Children:
Elizabeth B-Mar 26,1787 in West Stockbridge,MA.
          M-Jul 14,1810 at Wilkesbarre,PA to
          Epaphras Miller (B-Jun 2,1778 in
          Glastonbury,CT; D-Jul 5,1860 at Oxford,
          NY). D-Jul 14,1853 in Oxford, NY.
Samuel    Bp-Feb 11,1798 Otis,MA. M-Lois _____.
```

Dr Samuel   BALDWIN   046   Dr Samuel   BALDWIN

Sarah   Bp-Feb 11,1798 Otis,MA.
Sophronia   Bp-Feb 11,1798 Otis,MA.
Harriet   Bp-Jul 30,1809 Otis,MA.
Mehitable   Bp-May 31,1801 Otis,MA.

OTHER INFORMATION: After the war he devoted himself to study and acquired a substantial education in the ordinary English branches, with a sufficient knowledge of the languages to enable him to commence the study of medicine, the practice of which he commenced in West Stockbridge, at the age of twenty-eight years. In the year 1800 after the death of his wife, and having been twice a Representative in the Massachusetts Legislature, he removed to Wyoming, Pennsylvania, where he resided with the exception of two years in Ohio, until he removed to Oxford in 1819, where he lived with his daughter. He practiced here a few years, but not, except among his intimate friends, for several years previous to his death. He was a large, powerful man, standing six feet in height, and was a vigorous pedestrian. He had an extensive practice in the Wyoming Valley, and in urgent cases, so well were his great physical powers known, he was often urged by those who solicited his professional services, to go without waiting for his horse. He possessed a rare faculty of threading his way through the almost interminable forests. His mind was singularly inquisitive and discriminating and well furnished with diversified stores of knowledge, which his ready and retentive memory always rendered available.

Stephen   BALDWIN   047   Stephen   BALDWIN
         S. 23111 Private

RESIDENT DATE: 1804 - 1835
TOWN: Pitcher
BIRTH DATE: Jul 4, 1761
BIRTH PLACE: Cornwall, Connecticut (Litchfield Co)
FATHER: David **Baldwin**
MOTHER: Joanna
DEATH DATE: Jun 05, 1835
DEATH PLACE:
CEMETERY:
LOCATION:

TOMBSTONE INSCRIPTION:

Stephen BALDWIN   047   Stephen BALDWIN

SERVICE: While a resident of Cornwall, Connecticut he enlisted in May 1777, and served as private in Captain Gillet's Company, Colonel Enos' Connecticut Regiment and was discharged about Dec 1, 1777. He enlisted in May 1778, and served three months as private in Captain Waugh's Company, Colonel Adams' Connecticut Regiment. He enlisted about Jun 1, 1779, and served three months in Captain David Catlin's Connecticut Company. He enlisted in June 1780, served three months and was stationed around the goal at Litchfield, Connecticut, as one of a sergeant's guard, under Sergeant William Baldwin, no relation shown.

FAMILY INFORMATION:
  Children:

OTHER INFORMATION: He lived for twenty-three years in Massachusetts before moving to Pitcher, New York He was allowed pension on his application executed Sep 21, 1832 as a resident of Pitcher, New York.

Moses   BALLARD   048   Moses   BALLARD
        W. 6074 Private   DAR Patriot Index

RESIDENT DATE: 1812 - 1833
TOWN: Smyrna
BIRTH DATE: Apr 11, 1756
BIRTH PLACE: Montague, Massachusetts (Franklin Co)
FATHER: David Ballard
MOTHER: Mary Russell
DEATH DATE: Apr 4, 1833
DEATH PLACE: Smyrna, New York
CEMETERY: West end
LOCATION: Smyrna, New York

TOMBSTONE INSCRIPTION: In
                           Memory of
                          Moses Ballard
                    A patriot of the Revolution
                         Died April 4
                        1833 ae 76 yrs.

SERVICE: While residing at his fathers home, he volunteered about Jun 1, 1775, and served two months at Boston under Colonels Doolittle and Holden in the Massachusetts troops; he volunteered about May 1, 1776, served in Captain Timothy Child's Massachusetts Company, marched to Ticonderoga and remained there until discharged in November; volunteered again about

Moses BALLARD   048   Moses BALLARD

May 1, 1777, served in Captain Harvey's Massachusetts Company, marched to Bennington, thence to Saratoga, where he was present when Burgoyne surrendered. Granted a furlough in 1777, he did not volunteer again.

FAMILY INFORMATION: Married Feb 2, 1795, in Gill, Franklin County, Massachusetts, to Ruth **Morley**, a daughter of Dimmock and Ruth (**Weston**) **Morley**. His widow remarried Feb 21, 1837 to Bethuel **Slate** of Gill Massachusetts, who died at said Gill, Jan 22, 1848, aged 71 years. She was born on Dec 29, 1776 in Glastonbury, Hartford County, Connecticut and died Feb 18, 1859.

Children:
  Moses Russell   B-Oct 27, 1801 in Franklin,MA.
  Luthur Western   B-Oct 03, 1804 in Gill,MA.

OTHER INFORMATION: After the Revolution, he remained in Montague about two years, lived in Gill and then nearly thirty years in Greenfield, Massachusetts. He then removed to Smyrna, Chenango County New York. Pension was allowed on his application executed Oct 9, 1832, while he was a resident of Smyrna, New York. Ruth **Slate** was allowed pension on account of the services of her former husband, Moses **Ballard**, on her application executed May 19, 1851, at which time she resided in Will County, Illinois. In 1855, she is living in Maine, Cook County, Illinois. In 1832, Patty **Carrier**, sister of the soldier, Moses Ballard, lived in Columbus, Chenango County, New York.

Jeremiah BALLOU   049   Jeremiah BALLOU
       S. 23102 Private

RESIDENT DATE: 1833 - 1838
TOWN: Columbus
BIRTH DATE: Dec 16, 1749
BIRTH PLACE: Gloucester, Rhode Island
FATHER: Jeremiah **Ballou**
MOTHER: Isabella **Ross**
DEATH DATE: 1838
DEATH PLACE: Columbus, New York (at home of Son-in-
CEMETERY: ?   law Charles **Keech**)
LOCATION: Columbus, New York

TOMBSTONE INSCRIPTION:

Jeremiah BALLOU   049   Jeremiah BALLOU

SERVICE: While residing at Smithfield, Providence County, Rhode Island, he enlisted Apr 1, 1775 and served nine months as a private in Captain John Angell's Company, Colonel Hitchcock's Rhode Island Regiment. He enlisted at Killingly, Connecticut and served as a private in the Connecticut troops as follows: In the spring of 1776, ten days in Captain Ephriam Warren's Company, Colonel Dennison's Regiment, and in the fall of the same year, served twenty days in the same Company and Regiment. From January, 1777 six weeks in the same Company and Regiment. In the spring of 1778, fifteen days in the same Company and Regiment and in August of the same year, twenty days in the same Company and Regiment and was in Sullivan's Expedition to Rhode Island. In the fall of 1779, two months in Captain David Cady's Company, Colonel Dennison's Regiment. From October, 1780, one month in Captain Clark's Company.

FAMILY INFORMATION: He married in 1770 at Providence, Rhode Island Abigail **Record**. She was born in 1742 at Providence, Rhode Island.

Children:
  Joseph R   M-Betsey **Ballou** (Dau of Asa and Roba
             [**Williams**] **Ballou**).
  Elisha   Unmarried. D-RI.
  Jeremiah   Unmarried.
  Betsey   B-1778 in Killingly, CT. M-Charles **Keech**.
             D-ab 1850 in Columbus, NY.
  Sally   M-Jacob **Phillips**.

OTHER INFORMATION: He lived at Smithfield, Rhode Island during the war and since the war except for 7 years in New York State and 3 years in New Hampshire. Applied for a pension on Sep 17, 1832, while a resident of Providence County, Rhode Island. Moved to Columbus, Chenango County, New York shortly after making his application for pension. His trade was a blacksmith and went by the nickname of "Bumble Doram".

Samuel BANKS   050   Samuel BANKS
W. 17234 Sergeant &Ensign   DAR Patriot Index

RESIDENT DATE: - 1826
TOWN: Bainbridge
BIRTH DATE: Apr 18, 1755
BIRTH PLACE: Bedford, New York
FATHER: John **Banks**

| Samuel | BANKS | 050 | Samuel | BANKS |

MOTHER: Deborah **Newman**
DEATH DATE: Jun 24, 1826
DEATH PLACE: Bainbridge New York
CEMETERY: St Peters Church
LOCATION: Bainbridge, New York

TOMBSTONE INSCRIPTION:

In
Memory of
Samuel Banks
Who died
June 24, 1826
Aged
71 years

Charity
Wife of
Samuel Banks
Died Dec 2 1848
Ae 88 yrs & 1 mo.

SERVICE: Served as a sergeant and ensign in Captain Benonia Platt's Company, Colonel Gilbert Budd's Regiment. In the fall of 1781, while in an engagement with a party of British Light Horse at a place called Harrison's Purchase, he was made a prisoner by the British and confined in the Old Sugar House prison in New York City. He was in a prisoner exchange the following spring and went home. He went back into the service and acted as a lieutenant, serving until Feb. 15, 1782.

FAMILY INFORMATION: Married Apr 9, 1778 to Charity **Lyon**, dau of Israel and Abigail (**Husted**) **Lyon**, B-Sep 28, 1760 at Bedford, New York, D-Dec 2, 1848 at Bainbridge, New York.

Children:
Mary   B-Jan 23,1779. M-May 1799 Ezra **Clarke**.
        D-May 5,1806.
Samuel B-Aug 04,1780.
Parmelia B-Oct 05,1781. M-Isaac **Seeley**
        (B-Jul 30,1787; son of Eli and Zipporah
        [**Worden**] **Seeley**; M2-Priscilla _____
        (B-1801; D-Dec 9,1866; D-Nov 18,1848).
        D-Apr 6,1828. All 3 bur Baptist Cem,
        Afton, NY.
William B-Sep 27,1783 at North Castle, NY.
        M-May 23,1819 Sarah **Mead** (B-Jul 5,1798,
        Dau of Gideon and Mary (Miller) **Mead**;
        D-Dec 14,1866). D-Mar 24,1855.
Sarah   B-Aug 09,1786. D-Oct 16,1790.
Abigail B-Mar 12,1789. M-Sutton **Pearsall** (Son of
        Thomas **Pearsall**).

Samuel BANKS   050   Samuel BANKS

OTHER INFORMATION: He settled on the west side of the
river, about three fourths of a mile below Bainbridge.
His widow applied for a pension on Feb 6, 1838, while
a resident of Bainbridge, Chenango County, New York.

Abraham BARDEN   051   Abraham BARDEN
         R. 1448 Private

RESIDENT DATE: 1804 - 1808
TOWN: Greene
BIRTH DATE: Apr 29, 1765
BIRTH PLACE: Norfolk, Connecticut (Litchfield Co.)
FATHER: Jacob Barden
MOTHER: Mary
DEATH DATE:
DEATH PLACE:
CEMETERY:
LOCATION:

TOMBSTONE INSCRIPTION:

SERVICE: He resided in Norfolk, Litchfield County,
Connecticut with his father Jacob who was drafted to
serve in April or May, 1780. Abraham took his father's
place and served six months as a private. He went to
Danbury, Connecticut and under Colonel Durgy, marched
to Peekskill, New York, joining the main army under
Captain Converse, Colonel Swift's Regiment under
General Washington. After two or three weeks they
crossed the river and went to Haverstraw, thence to
the State of New Jersey. He went from place to place
within that State during the remainder of his service.
About Nov 1, 1780 he was given a discharge by
Lieutenant Holdridge, but lost it soon after he got
home because he thought it would be of no further use
to him. He was present at the execution of Major
Andre.

FAMILY INFORMATION: He married ?.

   Children: ?

OTHER INFORMATION: Removed to New Britain, New York
for five years, then to Butternuts, Otsego County, New
York two years, then returned to New Britain two
years, then to Kingston, North Carolina three years,
then to Little Hoosick Rensselaer County, New York two
years, then to Manlius, Onondaga County, New York four
years, then to Greene, Chenango County, New York for

Abraham BARDEN   051   Abraham BARDEN

four years, and in 1814 returned Manlius, New York. He filed for a pension on Mar 5, 1833, while a resident of Manlius, New York where he had been a resident for 25 to 26 years.

John BARKER   052   John BARKER

RESIDENT DATE: 1836
TOWN: Greene
BIRTH DATE: Jan 1, 1744
BIRTH PLACE: Bradford, Connecticut (New Haven Co)
FATHER: Edward **Barker**
MOTHER: Hannah **Baldwin**
DEATH DATE: Nov 29, 1836
DEATH PLACE:
CEMETERY: Willard
LOCATION: Greene, New York

TOMBSTONE INSCRIPTION:
Here lies
Mary wife
of John
Barker
Died August
25t 1800
Aet. 56 y.

In
Memory of
John Barker
Died Nov 29th 1836
Aged 94 years
The gospel was his joy and song,
even to his latest breath;
the truth he had proclaim'd so long
was his support in death.

In
Memory
Of
Margaret
Wife of John
Barker died
July 18 1824
Ae 73 y

SERVICE: Served in the Connecticut troops. Was taken prisoner and sent to England for one year.

FAMILY INFORMATION: Married Mar 17, 1765 in Branford, New Haven, Connecticut to Mary **Rodgers**, a daughter of Mary **Allen Barker Rodgers**, wife of Sim **Rodgers**. She was born in 1744, and died Aug 25, 1800. He married second Margaret _____. She was born in 1751 and died Jul 18, 1824. Both are buried with their husband.

John BARKER   052   John BARKER

Children:
Triphenia B-May 30,1765 Branford,CT.
John   B-Mar 15,1767 Branford,CT.
Peter   B-Jun 09,1772 Branford,CT. M-Pamelia
           Livermore (B-Apr 8,1781; Dau of Isaac
           and Hannah **Livermore**). D-Dec 11,1828.
           Bur Willard Cem, Greene,NY.
Mary   B-Mar 24,1774 Branford,CT. M-1792 to
           Simeon **Rogers**. D-Feb 5,1859.
Silas   B-Dec 02,1778 Branford,CT. D-Dec 6,1807.
Asa   B-May 06,1780 Branford,CT. D-Sep 12,1854.
Second wife
Elizabeth Bp-Feb 05,1790 Catskill,Greene Co,NY.
Lena   Bp-May 09,1792 Loonenburg,Greene Co,NY.
?
?
?
?
?   B-Mar 18,1815. D-Nov 21,1882.

OTHER INFORMATION: Settled in Barker, Broome County in 1792. (town was named for him). He purchased of Thomas **Gallop**, his land and improvements and took up his residence with his family in the "Treaty House". This house was erected for the accommodation of the participants in the treaty between the Indians and the commissioners of the Boston Company. It was a large double log house and stood a little Northeast of where the bridge toll house was subsequently erected.

Samuel BARKER   053   Samuel BARKER
        S. 12977 Private

RESIDENT DATE: 1802 - 1838
TOWN: Greene
BIRTH DATE: Jan 8, 1758
BIRTH PLACE: Branford, Connecticut (New Haven Co)
FATHER: Samuel **Barker**
MOTHER: Hannah
DEATH DATE: Jun 20, 1838
DEATH PLACE: Greene, New York
CEMETERY:
LOCATION:

TOMBSTONE INSCRIPTION:

SERVICE: While a resident of Ashford, Windham County, Connecticut, he enlisted in 1776, served as private in Captain John Sumner's Connecticut Company, then he

Samuel BARKER   053   Samuel BARKER

went to Rhode Island where he remained through the summer, was in an engagement with the Hessian troops and was discharged after having served six months; he enlisted in the summer of 1777 under Major Ledyard in the Connecticut troops, went to Groton, Connecticut where he assisted in building a fort and he was discharged in the late fall of that year after having served six months; he volunteered in April 1779, served as private in Captain James Barker's Company, Colonel Eli Fowler's Connecticut Regiment; he was engaged in guarding the seacoast and during this tour of six months was in an engagement with the British when they came to East Haven; he enlisted in the spring of 1780, served four months in Captain John Russell's Connecticut Company, again engaged in guarding the coast until the fall of that year; he enlisted in the spring of 1781, served in Captain Mason Hubbard's Connecticut Company and was discharged in the fall of 1781 after having served about four months; he enlisted in Oct 1781, served about one week, when the war ended, was discharged and returned home.

FAMILY INFORMATION: Married to

Children:
Almira   M-_____ Davis.
Hannah   M-Joseph Smith.
Cynthia   M-_____ Ledyard.

OTHER INFORMATION:

Jonathan BARNES   054   Jonathan BARNES
        S. 44603 Private

RESIDENT DATE: 1810 - 1829
TOWN: Guilford
BIRTH DATE: 1760/62
BIRTH PLACE: Watertown, Connecticut (Litchfield Co)
FATHER:
MOTHER:
DEATH DATE: July 1, 1829
DEATH PLACE:
CEMETERY:
LOCATION:

TOMBSTONE INSCRIPTION:

Jonathan BARNES   054   Jonathan BARNES

SERVICE: Enlisted March 10, 1778, served as private in Captain Henry Champion's Company, Colonel Samuel Wylly's Connecticut Regiment and continued in service until June 7, 1783, when he was discharged at West Point, New York. He received the badge of honor for faithful service.

FAMILY INFORMATION: Married to Mary _____. She was born in 1762.

Children:
(son)   B-?

OTHER INFORMATION: He was allowed a pension on his application executed April 14, 1818, at which time he resided in Guilford. He had a home in Harwinton, Connecticut which burned.

Simon BARNET   055   Simon BARNET
    R.   539 Seaman   DAR Patriot Index

RESIDENT DATE: 1792 - 1838
TOWN: Greene
BIRTH DATE: 1743
BIRTH PLACE: Isle of Martinique, West Indies
FATHER:
MOTHER:
DEATH DATE: Mar 1, 1837
DEATH PLACE: Greene, New York
CEMETERY: Chapel
LOCATION: Greene, New York

TOMBSTONE INSCRIPTION: (All gravestones have been removed from the grave site. The veterans stone was salvaged and is currently located in a descendants garage in Johnson City, New York (Oct 14, 1994)

    (STONE BROKEN)
    Simon Barnet
      Died
    March 1, 1837
    Aged 93 years.
    Marget Barnet
      Died
    March 17, 1836
    Aged 83 years.

SERVICE: While a resident of Philadelphia, Pennsylvania, he was engaged as a ships carpenter: employed for one month by John Whorton and Joshua

Simon BARNET   055   Simon   BARNET

Humphrey to build a Row Galley, which mounted an 18 pounder, stationed in the river to guard the city of Philadelphia; one month building a second galley, by one Simon Shutick, same description, to guard the city; for six weeks, engaged in the yard of Mr Shutick; further engaged for at least six months in the building activity; another six months under Captain Robbins, and Colonel Mash, building boats at "Swatara Creek" which were used in Sullivan's expedition; then enlisted for three months on board the Brig "Fair American" under Captain Stephen Decatur, capturing ships, was wounded in the thigh; second three months with the same Brig and Captain; another three months on board Captain Carson's ship of 20 guns, called the "Rising Sun"; nine months on the ship "Washington", with 20 guns, under Captain Joshia, was on a cruise to France as the war ended.

FAMILY INFORMATION: Married in May of 1769, at Philadelphia, Pennsylvania to Margaret **Sidell** who emigrated with her parents from Germany. She was born in 1753, died March 17, 1836 and is buried with her husband.
  Children:
    Charles F (Rev) B-Nov 23,1792. M-Feb 19,1809 to
              Clarissa Abigail **Whitmore** (B-1790, Dau
              of Nathan **Whitmore**; D-1862).
              D-Oct 8,1885. Both bur Sylvan Lawn Cem,
              Greene,NY.

OTHER INFORMATION: He learned the trade of a ship carpenter and worked at it until he had acquired some property, including a house and lot in Philadelphia, which he exchanged for land in Butternuts where he moved a few years after the close of the war. In 1792 he accompanied some French refugees to their settlement in the village of Greene. He was granted a pension based on his application dated Dec 25, 1832, while a resident of Greene, Chenango County, New York.

Henry   BARTLE   056   Henry   BARTLE
        -, ------ Private   DAR Patriot Index

RESIDENT DATE: - 1833
TOWN: Oxford
BIRTH DATE: Dec 20, 1763
BIRTH PLACE:
FATHER: John W **Bartle**
MOTHER: Margaret **Beard**

Henry BARTLE   056   Henry BARTLE

DEATH DATE: Oct 26, 1833
DEATH PLACE: Oxford, New York
CEMETERY: Ten Broeck
LOCATION: Oxford, New York

TOMBSTONE INSCRIPTION:

> In
> Memory of
> Henry Bartle
> Who departed
> This life
> Oct. 26, 1833.
> In the 70 yr.
> Of his age.

SERVICE: A private from New York State.

FAMILY INFORMATION: Married to Tabitha **White**, a daughter of Josiah and Tabitha **White**. She was born November 6, 1764 in Lominster, Worcester County, Massachusetts.

Children:
  Peter
  Charles A
  Warren
  John H   D-Was deceased at father's probate.
  Catharine   M-Tyler **Smith**.
  Margaret   M-Ellis **Loomis**.
  Sarah   M-Alanson W **Stewart**.
  Cornelia   M-Walter B **Smith**.

OTHER INFORMATION:

John W BARTLE   057   John W BARTLE
-, ----- Private   DAR Patriot Index

RESIDENT DATE: 1791 - 1808
TOWN: Oxford
BIRTH DATE: 1729
BIRTH PLACE: Germany
FATHER:
MOTHER:
DEATH DATE: May 17, 1808
DEATH PLACE: Oxford
CEMETERY: TenBroeck
LOCATION: Oxford, New York

John W BARTLE   057   John W   BARTLE

TOMBSTONE INSCRIPTION:
>   John Bartle died
>   May 17, 1808.
>   In the 79 d.
>   Year of his
>   Age
> Death like an overflowing stream
> sweeps us away our lifes a dream.
>   Mrs
>   Margaret
>   Wife of John Bartle
>   Died March 28th
>   1804 in the 63d
>   Year of her
>   Age
>   All is the Lord's. He rules the wild
>   creation:
>   gives sinners vengeance and the
>   saints salvation.

SERVICE: Served in Colonel Robert Van Rensselaer's Regiment of Albany County Militia, New York State.

FAMILY INFORMATION: Married to Margaret **Beard**. She was born in 1741, died March 28, 1804 and is buried with her husband.

Children:
- John   M-_ Duffey. M2-Lydia **Tuttle**. D-Apr 2,1822.
- Hendrick   B-Dec 20,1763. M-Tabitha **White**. D-Oct 26,1833 in Oxford,NY. Bur TenBroeck Cem, Oxford,NY.
- Andrew   B-Sep 24,1767 Manorton,NY. M-_____. D-Junius,NY.
- Peter   B-Sep 24,1769 Churchtown,NY. M-Caroline ___ (B-1768; D-May 17,1792; Bur TenBroeck Cem, Oxford,NY). M2-May 1795 (first in town) to Tabitha **Loomis** (B-Jun 13,1779; Dau of Benajah and Rachel [**Patterson**] **Loomis**; D-Mar 2,1860 in Delmar,PA). D-Mar 22,1831 in Ohio.
- Philip   B-1772. M2-Betsey **Loomis** (B-Jul 15,1772; Dau of Benajah and Rachel [**Patterson**] **Loomis**; D-Jul 28,1864 at Oxford,NY). D-Oct 1,1861 at Oxford,NY. Both bur TenBroeck Cem, Oxford,NY.
- Elizabeth   Bp-May 10,1774 Pine Plains,NY. M-Henry **Gordon** (B-1771; D-Jun 19, 1820 Oxford, NY). D-Aug 2,1854 at Oxford,NY. Both bur Riverview Cem, Oxford,NY.

John W   BARTLE   057   John W   BARTLE

David   B-Aug 19,1778 Manorton,NY. M-Rhoda **West**
            (1781;D-May 8,1831). D-Nov 22,1830 at
            Oxford,NY. Both bur TenBroeck Cem,
            Oxford,NY.

OTHER INFORMATION: He and his brother Richard, from whom most of the Bartles in this country are supposed to be descended, came from Germany previous to the Revolution, and settled on the Livingston Manor, in Columbia County. Richard afterwards removed to the west, where many of his descendants now live. John removed to Oxford, Chenango County, New York, and failing by some wrong-doing of others to secure the land promised to him, settled on the west side of the river, at the mouth of Bowmans Creek, some four miles below Oxford Village. There he kept the first inn in the town.

Jonathan   BARTON   058   Jonathan   BARTON
           S. 44612 Corporal

RESIDENT DATE: - 1831
TOWN: Bainbridge/New Berlin
BIRTH DATE: Jan 12, 1759
BIRTH PLACE: Sutton, Massachusetts
FATHER: Samuel **Barton**
MOTHER:
DEATH DATE: Mar 31, 1831
DEATH PLACE: New Berlin
CEMETERY:
LOCATION:

TOMBSTONE INSCRIPTION:

SERVICE: While residing at Royalston, Worcester County, Massachusetts on Jan 1, 1776 he enlisted as a volunteer, for one year, in Captain Gleason's Company, Colonel John Nixon's Massachusetts Regiment. After discharge, he immediately reenlisted in the same Company for three years. Again immediately enlisted in Captain Sewell's Company, Colonel Ebenezer Sprout's Massachusetts Regiment. Served at Boston and New York at the taking of Burgoyne, at West Point and in the State of New Jersey until the army was disbanded in 1783. Discharged at New Windsor, New York. He regularly performed his duty; he never had a furlough except one for 60 days, and in consequence of faithfulness was honored with the Badge of Merit, given by his Excellency, General Washington, which

Jonathan   BARTON   058   Jonathan   BARTON

badge was also mentioned in his discharge.

FAMILY INFORMATION: Married Nov 1, 1781 in Cannan, Litchfield County, Connecticut to Mary **Willard**, a daughter of Hezekiah and Lydia **Willard**. She was born June 1, 1756 in Harvard, Worcester County, Massachusetts and died Feb 20, 1835.

Children:
Jerusha	B-Aug 10,1783.
Aly	B-Oct 20,1785.
Ezra	B-Jul 27,1787.
Emma	B-Apr 19,1790.
Hannah	B-May 23,1792.
Anna	B-Jun 02,1794.
Peggy	B-Jul 06,1797.

OTHER INFORMATION: He was allowed pension on his application executed Apr 14, 1818, at which time he was a resident of Bainbridge, Chenango County, New York. He lived in Bainbridge in 1806 then moved to New Berlin in 1828.

Silas   BARTOO   059   Silas   BARTOO
        *S. 44594 Private

RESIDENT DATE: 1829
TOWN: Greene
BIRTH DATE: May 31, 1742
BIRTH PLACE: Hempstead, New York (Nassau County)
FATHER: Francis **Bartoo**
MOTHER: Mary **Ketchum**
DEATH DATE: Nov 7, 1831
DEATH PLACE: Eden, New York   (Erie County)
CEMETERY: Eden Valley
LOCATION: Eden, New York

TOMBSTONE INSCRIPTION: (NEWER)   S
   Silas Bartoo   Jonathan L Bartoo   A   R
       Born   Born   1775
  May 31, 1742,   July 1, 1769,
       Died   Died
  Nov. 7, 1831.   Jan. 16, 1852.   1742   1831
                                             Silas Bartoo
  Ruth his wife,   Silence, his wife   Erected by
       Born   Born   Buffalo Chapter
  Jan. 20, 1745,   Jan. 24, 1771   N. S. D. A. R.
       Died   Died
  Jan. 29, 1839.   Dec. 3, 1832.

Silas   BARTOO   059   Silas   BARTOO

SERVICE: In 1829, while a resident of Greene, Chenango County, New York, he submitted a statement supporting Reuben **Bartoo**'s application for a pension. Silas indicated that he served with Reuben. (See pension file #S 44594 for Reuben **Bartoo**). Reuben enlisted Mar 1, 1776, in Suffolk County, New York, for a term of nine months. He served as a private in Captain Daniel Roe's Company, Colonel James Clinton's New York Regiment, and was discharged Mar 12, 1777 at Fort Montgomery.

*Pension number for brother Reuben.

FAMILY INFORMATION: He married Jun 1, 1768 Martha's Vineyard, Duke County, Massachusetts to Ruth **Luce**, a daughter of Jonathan and Urania **Luce**. She was born Jan 20, 1745 in Tilsbury, Martha's Vineyard, Dukes County, Massachusetts, died Jan 29, 1839 and is buried with her husband.

Children:
Jonathan L   B-Jul 01,1769. M-Sep 8,1790 to Silence
              Linsley (B-Jan 29,1771; D-Dec 3,1832).
              Pioneer mill builder in Erie and
              Chautauqua Counties. D-Jan 16,1852.
              Both bur Eden Valley Cem, Eden,NY.
Polly   B-Sep 13,1770. D-Jun 12,1790.
Urania   B-Mar 02,1772. M-Henry **Vorse** at Greene,
              NY. D-Feb 15,1815.
Anna   B-Jan 15,1774. D-Jun 15,1790.
Jesse   B-Dec 24,1775. M-Eunice **Loomis**
              (B-Oct 17,1778). D-Dec 24,1823.
Morris   B-Apr 12,1778. D-Jun 09,1779.
Ruth   B-Jul 16,1782.
Ellis   B-Dec 14,1783. M-1799 to William **Davis** at
              Catskill,NY. D-Oct 28,1884 Rushford,NY.
Nancy   B-Apr 14,1785. M-___ **Hall**. Moved west.
Silas   B-Jan 13,1788.

OTHER INFORMATION: As a young man he was engaged in the whale fishery. At one time, his family had to seek protection in the fort. Sinking their pewter in a pond near by, and putting clothes and bedding in a dry well, they covered it with boards. Their house was burned, and their bedding and clothes also. In 1783 Silas lived in Connecticut and in 1791 moved to Catskill, New York. He lived in Chenango County with his son Jesse for some time, and in 1830 lived with his son Jonathan in Erie County.

James   BASFORD   060   James   BASFORD
        W. 39952 Private

RESIDENT DATE: 1840 - 1842
TOWN: Bainbridge
BIRTH DATE: Sep 27, 1762
BIRTH PLACE: Chester, New Hampshire (Rockingham Co)
FATHER: Joseph Basford
MOTHER: Elizabeth Goodhue
DEATH DATE: Sep 1845
DEATH PLACE:
CEMETERY:
LOCATION:

TOMBSTONE INSCRIPTION:

SERVICE: Served as a private in the Pennsylvania line. He enlisted in Newburgh, New York in 1777 or 1778 in the Company of Captain John Craig, of the fourth Pennsylvania Regiment of Dragoons. He served through the war, and was discharged at Lancaster, Pennsylvania June 30, 1783. He was at the taking of Cornwallis, the Battle of Charleston, South Carolina and several skirmishes with Indians, Tories and British in the State of Georgia.

FAMILY INFORMATION: Married in 1812 to Tammer _____. She was born in 1768.

Children:
    James   B-1813

OTHER INFORMATION: He was granted a pension Apr 21, 1818. He Made his statement of resources in 1820, at Kingston, New York being a resident of Warsink in Ulster County. On Apr 26, 1826 he filed a petition to have his residence transferred to Franklin County, Vermont. On Mar 11, 1829 he made application to have his pension records transferred to Poughkeepsie, Dutchess County, New York. On Mar 16, 1840 he petitioned to have his pension record transferred to Chenango County, New York. On Jun 30, 1842 he petitioned to have his pension sent to him in Susquehanna County, Pennsylvania where he was residing with his son. He was listed in the 1840 census in Bainbridge, Chenango County, New York.

Jonathan **BATES**   061   Jonathan **BATES**
—. ————— Private

RESIDENT DATE: 1792 - 1793
TOWN: Bainbridge
BIRTH DATE: Apr 15, 1755
BIRTH PLACE: Canterbury, Connecticut (Windham Co.)
FATHER: John **Bates**
MOTHER: Sarah
DEATH DATE: Apr 20, 1827
DEATH PLACE: Lebanon, New York
CEMETERY: Bates family
LOCATION: Eaton, New York   (Madison County)

TOMBSTONE INSCRIPTION: Jonathan Bates
                         1755 - 1827
                      Revolutionary soldier
                      Pioneer of this region
                         Elizabeth Bates
         Memorial———   1750 - 1827
                  First white woman in what is
                     now the town of Lebanon
            Erected by the State Education Department
                  James Madison chapter D.A.R.
              Thomas L. Hall Madison County Historian
                              1886

         In memory of   In memory of
         Jonathan Baits   Elizabeth Baits
       Who died 20th April   Wife of
               1827   Jonathan Baits
         Aged 72 years   Who died 25th April
                                         1827
                                   Aged 77 years
              (Double stone + double foot stone)

SERVICE: Served in the Militia at various times. In
the alarm of Oct 1780. Was private in Captain Bigelow
Lawrence's Company, Colonel Herrick's Regiment. He was
enrolled in Ethan Allen's Green Mountain Volunteers
while in Vermont. His green uniform with red facings
has been in the possession of his descendants.

FAMILY INFORMATION: Married to Elizabeth _____. She
was born in 1750 and died Apr 25, 1827, just five days
after her husband. She is buried with her husband.

   Children:
   Reuben   B-before 1790. M-Neomi **Carmel**. Went to
              Columbia Co.,WI.
   Hovy B   B-1792. M-Electa _____. D-Aug 14,1831.
              Bur Bates family Cem, Eaton,NY

Jonathan **BATES** 061 Jonathan **BATES**

    Lydia   M-Abel Wedge, son of Daniel **Wedge**.(Abel's 2nd marriage)
    Eunice   M-Stephen **Wakeman** (son of Hill and Dorcus [**Saunders**] **Wakeman**). Went to Columbia Co.,WI.
    Stephen   B-May 22,1798 Smyrna,NY. M-Aug 4,1822, Pamelia **Wakeman** (B-Jul 22,1805; Dau of Hill and Dorcus [**Saunders**] **Wakeman**).

OTHER INFORMATION: He along with some others came to Lebanon, Madison County in the autumn of 1792. They erected a bark shanty and chopped the timber on twenty acres of land before the winter came. As the cold storms of the season approached, their discomfort warned them of the lack of protection by their shelter. The party removed to Bainbridge, Chenango County, New York to spend the winter among friends, who were settlers there from Vermont. After removing to New York State Jonathan became a small farmer. He increased his living by making and mending shoes, a trade which he seemed to have learned in his youth.

Benjamin **BEADLE** 062 Benjamin **BEADLE**
    W. 20705 Private

RESIDENT DATE: 1801 - 1810
TOWN: Sherburne
BIRTH DATE: Dec 18, 1741
BIRTH PLACE: Wethersfield, Connecticut
FATHER: David **Beadle**
MOTHER: Abigail **Beadle** (cousin)
DEATH DATE: Jun 24, 1810
DEATH PLACE: Sherburne, New York
CEMETERY:
LOCATION:

TOMBSTONE INSCRIPTION:

SERVICE: He had six months service as a private in a company of the Connecticut Coast Guard commanded by Captain Couch. He served in two campaigns. In one, his unit marched against General Burgoyne but did not arrive until after Burgoyne had surrendered at Saratoga in October, 1777.
    Benjamin's war story most vividly recalled by his son, Flavel in 1839, was his assignment to take care of soldiers who were ill with smallpox, a disease which Benjamin had had before entering service. While he was nursing these patients, "orders were given by

Benjamin   BEADLE   062   Benjamin   BEADLE

the physician that no rum was to be given to those sick with the smallpox... Benjamin, believing spirits was good for those thus sick, said he dare not give it to them, but would leave a bottle of rum where the sick could reach it, and then go away, so as to afford an opportunity for them to get it and drink, which they did, and every one who drank got well.

FAMILY INFORMATION: He was married Feb 6, 1766 in Colchester, Connecticut to Mary **Munn**. She was born Jan 27, 1741 in Colchester, the daughter of James Jr and Martha (**Smith**) **Munn** and died Jan 31, 1781 at Colchester. He married second Oct 21, 1781, in Hebron, Conn., to Sibyl **Gillet**. She was born Oct 4, 1753, in Colchester, a daughter of Israel and Mary (**Coleman**) **Gillet** and died Jan 11, 1789 in Colchester. He married third Mar 4, 1789 in Lebanon, Connecticut to Rhoda **Hinckley**. She was born Jun 19, 1754 and died Dec 21, 1841 in Columbus, Pennsylvania at the home of her daughter Sophia **York**.

```
Children:   all born in Colchester except last two in
                                  Otsego, New York.
  Benjamin  B-Jun 01,1766. M-_____ (D-1818).
  David     B-Jun 08,1767. M-Elizabeth Coleman.
            D-Mar 14,1802 in Otsego,NY.
  Mary      B-Dec 24,1768. D-Niagara Co,NY.
  Jonathan  B-Dec 22,1770. M-Oct 24,1802 to Lydia
            Green. D-Feb 28,1805.
  Abigail   B-Oct 20,1772. M-Jun 4,1794 in Colchester
            to Orlando Mack. M2-_____
            D-Oct 19,1862 in Marshall,MI.
  (male)    B-Sep 12,1774. D-after one hour.
  James     B-Feb 05,1776. Unmarried. D-Mar 2,1816 in
            Otsego.
  (male)    B-Jan 26,1778. Still born.
  (male)    B-Jan 18,1779. D-in one hour.
  (female)  B-Feb 25,1780. D-in a few minutes.
  (female)  B-Jan 31,1781. Still born.
Second wife
  Harvey    B-Aug 15,1782. M-_____. D-1826 in Ohio.
  Henry     B-Aug 15,1782. M-Susan _____ (B-1787;
            D-Jul 14,1849 in Cooperstown,NY).
            D-Sep 12,1837 at Cooperstown,NY.
  Sibyl     B-Aug 25,1784. D-May 30,1814 Otsego,NY.
  Horace    B-Nov 21,1785. M-Polly Bourne
            (B-Jul 9,1791 in Fly Creek,NY;
            D-Mar 1,1875 at Schuyler Lake,NY).
            D-Jun 9,1853 at Schuyler Lake,NY.
```

Benjamin   BEADLE   062   Benjamin   BEADLE

Homer   B-Nov 21,1785. M-Nancy W **Newell** (B-1785;
            D-Aug 25,1839 at Otsego,NY).
            M2-Dec 24,1840 in Cooperstown,NY to Amy
            Williams (B-1801; D-Nov 12,1859 at
            Cooperstown,NY). D-Apr 10,1843 at
            Otsego,NY.
Flavel   B-Mar 13,1788. M-Dec 7,1809 in Otsego,NY
            to Polly **Tuller** (B-Oct 11,1787 at
            Stockbridge,MA. D-Apr 12,1864 Franklin,
            NY). D-Aug 1,1854 at Otsego,NY.
Third wife
Rhoda   B-Nov 15,1789. M-Henry **Sawdy** (B-1791 RI).
Chauncey   B-Jun 25,1791. M-Jan 15,1823 to Orinda
            Converse (B-Jan 25,1794; Dau of Col.
            Israel **Converse**; D-Jan 19,1885 in St
            Catharines,Canada). D-Mar 24,1863 in
            St Catharines, Canada.
Hoel   B-Jan 23,1793. M-Aug 27,1818 to Abigail
            Hardy (B-Apr 17,1801; D-Dec 20,1865 in
            Westfield,NY). D-Jan 15,1878 in
            Barcelona,NY.
Sally   B-Nov 08,1794. Unmarried.
Sophia   B-Mar 01,1798. M-David L **York** (D-1849).
            D-Jun 22,1866.
Joel H   B-Dec 03,1800. D-Aug 27,1829.

OTHER INFORMATION: After service in the Revolutionary
War, emigrated from his Connecticut home in 1796 by
way of Long Island Sound to New York City and then by
boat up the Hudson River to Lansingburg, thence by
team of oxen and covered wagon rumbled over the hills
to Otsego County. He settled with his family near the
head of Otsego Lake. He later went to Chenango County.
His widow applied for a pension on Apr 20, 1840, while
a resident of Westfield, Chautauqua County, New York.

Azariah   BEAL   063   Azariah   BEAL
           W.   5811 Private

RESIDENT DATE: Wife
TOWN: Preston
BIRTH DATE: Dec 15, 1753
BIRTH PLACE: Bridgewater, Massachusetts
FATHER: Jonathan **Beal**   (Plymouth County)
MOTHER: Abigail **Harlow**
DEATH DATE: Feb 25, 1811
DEATH PLACE: Plainfield,Massachusetts (Hampshire Co)
CEMETERY:
LOCATION:

Azariah BEAL   063   Azariah BEAL

TOMBSTONE INSCRIPTION:

SERVICE: He resided at Bridgewater, Plymouth County, Massachusetts at enlistment and served as a private in the Massachusetts Line as follows: in 1775, six months in Captain Orr's Company; in 1776, one and one-half months in Captain Orr's Company; in 1776 and 1777, four months in Captain Truant's Company; in 1777, three months in Captain Washburn's Company, Colonel Sprout's Regiment; in 1778, one and one-half months on Rhode Island under Colonel Carpenter.

FAMILY INFORMATION: He married May 10, 1776 at Bridgewater, Massachusetts to Bathsheba **Bisbee**, a daughter of Ebenezer and Bathsheba **Bisbee**. She was born Apr 21, 1753 in Bridgewater, Massachusetts and died Mar 22, 1844 at Pine Valley, Pennsylvania.

Children:
David	B-May 31,1778.
Ezra B	B-Feb 20,1781. In 1855 resided Pine Valley,PA.
Roxana	B-May 12,1784. M-____ Andrews. Resided in Preston,NY in 1837.
Clarisa	B-May 07,1787. D-Sep 18,178-.
Levi B	B-May 18,1789.
Patty M	B-Jul 04,1792.

OTHER INFORMATION: His widow was allowed a pension on an application executed Jan 12, 1837, while residing in Preston, Chenango County, New York. In 1841 she was living with her son in Columbus, Warren County, Pennsylvania. His brother Jonathan in 1836 lived in Charlemont, Massachusetts and stated he served two tours with Azariah.

William BEATMAN   064   William BEATMAN
       S. 44645 First Lieutenant

RESIDENT DATE: - 1810
TOWN: Bainbridge - Afton
BIRTH DATE: May 14, 1741
BIRTH PLACE:
FATHER:
MOTHER:
DEATH DATE: 1810
DEATH PLACE:
CEMETERY: North
LOCATION: Afton, New York

William BEATMAN   064   William BEATMAN

TOMBSTONE INSCRIPTION: (Also DAR plaque placed by
                                        Cunahunta Chapter)
                                    Captain
    Thankful A.   William Beatman
     Wife of   1745 - 1810
  William Beatman   Revolutionary Soldier
      Died   With Washington
   June 17 1835   At Valley Forge - 1778
  Still remembered   Erected by his descendants
                                      1958

SERVICE: While residing in Sandisfield, Berkshire County, Massachusetts, he volunteered within a week after the battle of Lexington, marched to Roxbury, Massachusetts, where he immediately received a warrant as orderly sergeant in Captain Soule's Company, Colonel John Fellow's Massachusetts Regiment, length of this tour nine months. At the expiration of this tour he was commissioned lieutenant in Captain Charles Dowd's Company, served six months in a campaign at Quebec in a detachment commanded by Major Jeremiah Cady. While at Quebec, he was commissioned first lieutenant and served in that rank in Captain William Bacon's Company, Colonel Elisha Porter's Massachusetts Regiment, length of this tour one year. At the close of this service he was commissioned adjutant in Colonel Samuel Brewer's Massachusetts Regiment, which commission he held to the close of the war; during his service he was in the battle of Hubbardton, the two battles at Stillwater, the battle of Monmouth, and was discharged the latter part of June, 1783.

FAMILY INFORMATION: Married Mar 16, 1774 in Great Barrington, Massachusetts to Rachel **Teal**, a daughter of Oliver and Ruth **Teal**. She was born Jan 15, 1751 in Middletown, Connecticut.

    Children: (eight)
    David   B-1777. M-Margaret **Campbell** (B-1787, Dau
                of John and Lydia [**Whiting**] **Campbell**;
                D-Sep 5,1862 at Bainbridge,NY).
                D-Jun 7,1866.
    Nathan   B-1786. M-Dorothy **Nichols** (B-Aug 23,1788;
                Dau of Samuel and Dorothy [**Blodgett**]
                Nichols). D-Afton,NY.
    Philander BP-Jun 29,1791.

William BEATMAN   064   William BEATMAN

OTHER INFORMATION: An Irishman. He was allowed pension on his application executed Apr 10, 1818, while a resident of Bainbridge. In 1820 he was still a resident of Bainbridge.

Dr Daniel BECKLEY   065   Dr Daniel BECKLEY
        S. 12199 Private   DAR Patriot Index

RESIDENT DATE: 1832
TOWN: Greene
BIRTH DATE: Jun 11, 1758
BIRTH PLACE: Berlin Connecticut
FATHER: Daniel **Beckley**
MOTHER: Ruth **Hart**
DEATH DATE: Nov 9, 1843
DEATH PLACE: Utica, New York
CEMETERY: *Forest Hill
LOCATION: Utica, New York (Oneida County)
                *Buried Potter Street Cemetery then
                                        removed in 1916

TOMBSTONE INSCRIPTION: (Location not found in the office records for the Forest Hill Cemetery).

SERVICE: Enlisted 1776 under Captain Samuel Hart. Thought General Washington and General Putnam were in command. After two months at Boston was dismissed and returned home. A few weeks thereafter enlisted under Captain Gad Stanley and Colonel Gay of Farmington. They went to New York and were stationed in the city a month or six weeks; thence to Long Island; returned to New York in the night; thence to Turtle Bay about two weeks; thence retreated to White Plains and Harlem where they were dismissed- six months from his enlistment. In the summer of 1779 he joined a Company under Captain John Allen and went to New Haven; thence to East Haven; thence to West Haven where he enlisted in the Matross Company under Captain Azel Kimberley and remained there during the winter; dismissed about Apr 1, 1780 after serving eight months and returned home. He then took the place of his brother Jonathan who was drafted for two months. He was out two weeks at the burning of Danbury.

FAMILY INFORMATION: Married Mar 22, 1787 in Waterbury, Connecticut on Mar 22, 1787 to Levia **Lewis** a daughter of Captain John and Sarah (**Gordon**) **Lewis**. She was born Jul 25, 1770 in Connecticut and died at Waterbury, Connecticut Feb 16, 1797.

Dr Daniel   BECKLEY   065   Dr Daniel   BECKLEY

Children:
Gordon Lewis B-Oct 17,1788 at Waterbury,CT.
             M-Oct 25,1815 Southington,CT. to Phebe
             Barnes, (B-Jul 15,1794; Dau of Thomas
             and Phebe [**Langdon**] Barnes;
             D-Feb 9,1851 Nunda,IL). D-Jan 5,1883
             in Nunda,IL.
Flora   B-Apr 27,1791 Waterbury,CT. M-Nov 1,1812
             to Clark **Scott** (B-Mar 16,1790; son of
             Samuel and Susanna [**Clark**] Scott;
             D-Apr 29,1867 near Cheshire,OH).
             D-Apr 29,1865 at Berkshire twp.,OH.
Levia   B-Feb 28,1795 at Naugatuck,CT.
             M-Jan 1,1816 at Waterbury,CT. to Ely
             Platt (B-Jul 3,1793; Son of Nathan
             and Ruby [**Smith**] Platt; D-Feb 13,1865
             Norwich,CT). D-Jun 15,1880 at Albany,NY.

OTHER INFORMATION: Upon his return home from the war he studied medicine and obtained his M.D. and continued in practice until his death, which took place at the home of his daughter Levia **Platt**, in the city of Utica, New York. He was buried with full military honors. He applied for pension on Jul 30, 1832 with a residence at Greene, New York.

Joseph   BECKWITH   066   Joseph   BECKWITH
          S. 9278 Teamster

RESIDENT DATE: ---- - 1833
TOWN: Preston/Smyrna
BIRTH DATE: Jun 15, 1761
BIRTH PLACE: Lyme, Connecticut   (New London County)
FATHER: Joshua **Beckwith**
MOTHER:
DEATH DATE: Jun 2, 1853
DEATH PLACE: Morris, New York   (Otsego County)
CEMETERY: Old Harmony
LOCATION: Morris, New York

TOMBSTONE INSCRIPTION:
        (laying flat & 3/4 buried)
              Joseph Beckwith
                   Died
                June 2 1853
               Aged 92 yrs.
To soft remembrance drop a silent tear
and holy friendship sets a mourner here

Joseph BECKWITH   066   Joseph BECKWITH

                Desiah   Anna
               Wife of   Wife of
           Joseph Beckwith   Joseph Beckwith
                 Died   Died April 19th
          March 23, 1850 Ae.   1819
               78 years   In the 57th year
                                                 of her age
                                    Lo soft remembrance drops
                                    a pious tear
                                    and holy friendship sets a
                                    mourner here

SERVICE: He enlisted in March 1780 at Lyme, New London County, Connecticut for two years under Captain Roswell Ransom. He served as a cook and a teamster, with his father, Joshua, furnishing six oxen for his use. After marching to Peekskill to join General Washington's army, he transported military stores and provisions during the summer and fall of 1780. He returned to Lyme, Connecticut and drew boards and logs for construction of barracks. During the winter he gathered fodder and attended the teams. In April he returned to Peekskill. He was sent to Yorktown, Virginia where he carried a brass field piece into the entrenchments at the battle in which Cornwallis surrendered. While at Yorktown his oxen became sick and died. He was discharged in April 1782.

FAMILY INFORMATION: He married Nov 29, 1787 at Palmer, Massachusetts to Anna **Farrell**, a daughter of Robert and Mary **Farrell**. She was born in 1762, died Apr 19, 1819 and is buried in the Prentice Burying Ground at Butternuts, Otsego County, New York along with her mother. He married second Desiah (**Sylvester**) **Halbert**, a daughter of Eleakim **Sylvester** and the widow of John **Halbert**. She had married John on January 25, 1790 at Chesterfield, Massachusetts and had ten children by him. Mr & Mrs **Halbert** moved from Chesterfield to Salem, New York in 1792/3, then about 1800 to Butternuts, Otsego County, New York. He died November 1807 in Lisle, New York. She was born in 1772, died in Laurens, New York Mar 23, 1850 and is buried with Joseph.

Children:
  Zenus   In the War Of 1812. Bur Butternuts,NY.
  (female)   M-Metins **Hulbert**.
  Phila   M-Jacob **Slater**.
  Daniel   M-Lucy **Perkins**.

Joseph   BECKWITH   066   Joseph   BECKWITH

OTHER INFORMATION: He moved to Palmer, Massachusetts for 15 years; then moved to Otsego County, New York; then in 1827 to Hamby, Steuben County, New York; then to Preston and Smyrna, Chenango County, New York; then in 1833 to Butternuts, Otsego County. He applied for pension on an application dated Feb 4, 1834, while a resident of Butternuts. He was one of the organizers of the Butternuts Baptist Church in 1805.

Amon   BEEBE   067   Amon   BEEBE
         S. 49302 Private   DAR Patriot Index

RESIDENT DATE: 1800 - 1813
TOWN: Guilford
BIRTH DATE: May 7, 1750
BIRTH PLACE: New London, Connecticut
FATHER: Gideon Beebe
MOTHER: Ruth Clark
DEATH DATE: Jan 21, 1830
DEATH PLACE: French Creek, N.Y. (Chautauqua County)
CEMETERY: Tefft   (located on Amon's farm)
LOCATION: French Creek, New York

TOMBSTONE INSCRIPTION: -Brass markers dedicated
                                            July 18, 1981-

         Amon Beebe   Eunice Pease Beebe
Pvt Co B 1 Regt. Conn Line   Wife of Amon
      Revolutionary War   July 1749   Circa 1827
May 7 1750   Jan 21 1830

SERVICE: He enlisted at New Fairfield, Connecticut, on May 9, 1775, for eight months, in Captain Nehemiah Bradley's Company, Colonel Waterbury's Regiment. This tour of duty was spent in the northern theater of operations in Brigadier General Richard Montgomery's command. From Ticonderoga he continued north to fort St John and participated in the siege there, continuing on duty in the Lake Champlain area until his discharge Dec 5, 1775. He enlisted at Norwich, Connecticut on May 10, 1777, for three years in Captain Shumway's Company, Colonel Jedediah Huntington's Regiment. During this term of service he shared the winter-spring encampment at Valley Forge 1777 - 1778, fought in the battle of Monmouth June 28, 1778, and was discharged at Morristown, New Jersey on May 10, 1780. While a resident of Ludlow, Massachusetts, he enlisted again at Boston, Massachusetts, on Jun 20, 1781, for three years in

Amon BEEBE   067   Amon BEEBE

Captain David Holbrook's Company, Colonel William Shepard's fourth Regiment, and was discharged at West Point in Dec, 1783. He had served all three enlistments as an infantry foot soldier, and also performed duty as a blacksmith.

FAMILY INFORMATION: Married 1773 at Norwich, Connecticut to Eunice **Pease**, daughter of Job and Eunice (_____) **Pease**. She was born in July, 1749 at Martha's Vineyard, died about 1827 and is buried with her husband. He married second May 31, 1829 to Mrs. Elizabeth **Warson**. She was born in 1773.

Children:
- Amos   B-1774. M-Oxford,NY to Lois **Pier** (B-1779; Dau of Levi and Anna [**Dewey**] **Pier**). Settled in Quincy, IL. about 1822.
- David   B-1776. M-_____. Accompanied Amos to IL.
- Eunice B-1778. M-Elijah **Pier** (B-1777; son of Levi and Anna [**Dewey**] **Pier**; D-1802 in Chenango Co.). M2-Elijah **Gilbert**.
- Amon   B-1784. M-Joann **Northrup** (Dau Thomas **Northrup**). D-in 1845 at Macon Co.,MO.

OTHER INFORMATION: He was a farmer who lived in Ludlow, Massachusetts, selling his land there Jan 5, 1784. Next, in the 1790 census, he is in Danby, Rutland County, Vermont with a wife and four children- three boys and one girl. The 1800 census carries him in Guilford, Chenango County, New York. He applied for a pension on his application dated May 23, 1818, while a resident of Chautauqua County, New York. A follow up statement was made on Feb 21, 1822, while he was a resident of Clymer, Chautauqua County, New York. His family had moved to Clymer, later split off as French Creek, New York in 1813, being among the first three settlers of this part of the Holland land Purchase, then a trackless wooded wilderness.

David   BEEBE   068   David   BEEBE
        W. 16838 Private

RESIDENT DATE: - 1832
TOWN: Coventry
BIRTH DATE: 1759
BIRTH PLACE: Lyme, Connecticut (New London County)
FATHER: David **Beebe**
MOTHER: Sarah **Lord**
DEATH DATE: Aug 24, 1832

David   BEEBE   068   David   BEEBE

DEATH PLACE: Coventry, New York
CEMETERY: Coventryville
LOCATION: Coventry, New York

TOMBSTONE INSCRIPTION: In   In memory of
                         Memory of   Sarah
                        David Beebe   Wife of
                         Who died   David Beebe
                       Aug. 24 1832   Died
                        Ae. 73 yrs.   Dec. 29 1847
                                           In the 90th year
                                             of her age.

SERVICE: He served seven months, in 1775, in Captain Joseph Smith's Company, Colonel Waterbury's Regiment at New York, St Johns and Ticonderoga. In Oct, 1780 he volunteered with a Company of militia commanded by Captain Ephraim Barnum, and joined said Company in Bethel, a part of Danbury, Connecticut, marched to Horseneck; served one month.

FAMILY INFORMATION: Married Jun 8, 1780 at New Milford, Litchfield County, Connecticut to Sarah **Beach**, a daughter of David and Ruth (**Hawley**) **Beach**. She was born Apr 12, 1758 in North Stratford, Fairfield County, Connecticut, died Dec 29, 1847 and is buried with her husband.

Children: (All born Danbury, Fairfield County,
                   Connecticut except David)
Sally   B-Sep 11,1781.
Ruth Ann   B-Sep 11,1781. M-Eliakin **Benedict**
            (B-Mar 9,1778; son of Benjamin and Mary
            [**Bouton**] **Benedict**; D-Feb 7,1839
            Coventry,NY; Bur Coventryville Cem,
            Coventry,NY). D-Sep 1,1868.
Rebecca   B-Dec 23,1784.
Rachel   B-Dec 23,1784.
Eunice   B-May 23,1787. M-_____ **Dean**. Resided
            Broome Co.,NY.
Sarah   B-Jun 25,1789.
Jonathan   B-Apr 21,1791.
David   Resided Steuben Co.,IN.

OTHER INFORMATION: His widow applied for a pension on her application dated Sep 8, 1838, while a resident of Coventry, Chenango County, New York. Supporting statements were made by David's brother John, dated Nov 30, 1838, while a resident of Marshall, Oneida County, New York; a daughter Eunice **Dean**, dated Jun

David BEEBE   068   David BEEBE

29, 1855, while a resident of Broome County, New York; and a son David Beebe, dated Feb 24, 1854, while a resident of Steuben County, Indiana.

Joseph BEEBE   069   Joseph BEEBE
S. 12997 Sergeant   DAR Patriot Index

RESIDENT DATE: 1817 - 1833
TOWN: Columbus
BIRTH DATE: Jan 16, 1746
BIRTH PLACE: Saybrook, Connecticut (Middlesex Co.)
FATHER:
MOTHER:
DEATH DATE: Mar 17, 1833
DEATH PLACE:
CEMETERY: Columbus Center
LOCATION: Columbus, New York

TOMBSTONE INSCRIPTION: Mr
                  Joseph Beebe died
                    March 17, 1833
                  In the 86 yr of his
                         Age
      Beneath this stone an honored parent lies
   death will not stay for pleading childrens cries
       no fond companion can afford one breath
           when fastened in thy arms O death

SERVICE: Entered service early in 1775, as a minuteman in Captain John Lewis Company, Colonel Jonathan Baldwin's Connecticut Regiment and served two months; He enlisted May 1, 1775 and served seven months as corporal in Captain Samuel Peck's Company, Colonel Wooster's Connecticut Regiment, during which he went north and was at the siege of St. Johns. He enlisted in 1776, about the time of the battle of White Plains, and served two months as sergeant in Captain Josiah Terrill's Company, Colonel Jonathan Baldwin's Connecticut Regiment. In 1777, he served three tours as sergeant in Captain Terrill's Company, one tour under Colonel Mosely and another under Colonel Baldwin, amounting in all to eleven weeks; in 1778 or 1779, he served two weeks as sergeant under Ensign Hezekiah Hine, and at the time Norwalk and Fairfield were burned, two weeks as sergeant in Captain Terrill's Connecticut Company; in the fall of 1781, he served one month as sergeant in Captain Moses Foot's Connecticut Company.

Joseph   BEEBE   069   Joseph   BEEBE

FAMILY INFORMATION: Married April 15, 1773 at Waterbury, New Haven County, Connecticut to Thameson **Terrill**, a daughter of Moses and Susannah (**Barnes**) **Terrill**. She was born Apr 9, 1752 at Waterbury, New Haven, Connecticut.

Children: ?

OTHER INFORMATION: He continued to reside in Waterbury, New Haven County, Connecticut until 1806, moved then to Colebrook, Litchfield County, Connecticut until 1817, when he moved to Columbus, Chenango County, New York. He was allowed pension on his application executed Aug. 6, 1832.

Amos   BEECHER   070   Amos   BEECHER
-. ----- Sergeant

RESIDENT DATE: 1828 - 1832
TOWN: Greene
BIRTH DATE: May 16, 1749
BIRTH PLACE: New Haven, Connecticut
FATHER: Samuel **Beecher**
MOTHER: Mary **Thomas**
DEATH DATE: Aug 29, 1832
DEATH PLACE:
CEMETERY: Willard
LOCATION: Greene, New York

TOMBSTONE INSCRIPTION: Amos Beecher
                         Died Aug. 29, 1832
                           Aged 83 yrs.

SERVICE: A volunteer in Colonel Willis' State Troops in 1775; also in Captain Shipman's Company in Colonel Webb's Regiment of State Troops; also a private under Captain Clark on an armed schooner crossing the river at New York; helped build the fort at Dorchester Heights; was in the battle of White Plains.

FAMILY INFORMATION: Married ?

Children: ?

OTHER INFORMATION: Lived in Chenango, Broome County in 1828.

Abijah BENEDICT   071   Abijah BENEDICT

RESIDENT DATE:	1800 - 1843
TOWN:	Coventry
BIRTH DATE:	Apr 30, 1765
BIRTH PLACE:	Danbury, Connecticut
FATHER:	Benjamin **Benedict**
MOTHER:	Mary **Bouton**
DEATH DATE:	Apr 18, 1843
DEATH PLACE:	Coventry, New York
CEMETERY:	Coventryville
LOCATION:	Coventry, New York

TOMBSTONE INSCRIPTION:

His stone not found.

In
Memory of
Abigail wife of
Abijah Benedict
Who died Feb
24th 1818
Ae s 50 y

SERVICE: Listed as a Revolutionary War veteran in the book "Revolutionary War Veterans in Broome County" - SAR 1960.

FAMILY INFORMATION: Married Jun 11, 1789 to Abigail **Corbin**, a daughter of Peter **Corbin**. She was born Feb 20, 1766 and died Feb 24, 1818, having been buried in the Coventryville cemetery. He married second Polly **Olmstead**, the widow of Joseph **Rundell**. She was born in 1769 and died Dec 25, 1840.

Children:
Daniel   B-Feb 26,1790. M-Polly **Stoddard** (B-Sep 22,1792; Dau of Deacon John **Stoddard**; widow of Sylvester **Stephens**; D-1876 in Coventry,NY). D-Apr 12,1854 at Coventry,NY. Both bur Coventryville Cem, Coventry,NY.
Sylvester   B-Dec 4,1794. M-Emily ___ (M2-___ **Harvey**).
Amos S   D-Dec 10,1823 at Montezuma by falling 104 ft. into a salt well.
Alvin   Went to California.
Uriah   B-Feb 07,1801. M-Jonathan **Peck**. D-May 30, 1866.
Levi   B-Mar 10,1807. M-Oct 1,1829 Betsey **Corbin** (B-1800; Dau of Jno. P **Corbin** of Woodstock,CT; D-Jun 16,1880). D-Oct 21,1863 at Greene,NY. Both Bur Brisben Church Cem, Greene,NY.

Abijah BENEDICT   071   Abijah BENEDICT
OTHER INFORMATION: Moved to Coventry, Chenango County,
New York in the spring of 1800. Resided in Broome
County, New York.

Benjamin BENEDICT   072   Benjamin BENEDICT
-. ----- Lieutenant   DAR Patriot Index

RESIDENT DATE: 1807 - 1823
TOWN: Coventry
BIRTH DATE: Sep 27, 1740
BIRTH PLACE: Danbury, Connecticut
FATHER: Benjamin **Benedict**
MOTHER: Abigail **Potter**
DEATH DATE: Sep 27, 1823
DEATH PLACE: Coventryville, New York
CEMETERY: Coventryville
LOCATION: Coventry, New York

TOMBSTONE INSCRIPTION: In
                          Memory of Benj
                          Benedict who died
                          Sep 27th 1823 ae 83
                          & Mary his wife
                          Died July 16th
                          1818 ae 77 y

SERVICE: Served as a private in Captain David Beebe's
Company, Colonel Roger Enos' Regiment, Connecticut
State troops. He served as a lieutenant of the
Militia.

FAMILY INFORMATION: Married May 27, 1762 in Danbury,
Fairfield County, Connecticut to Mary **Boughton**, a
daughter of Samuel and Abigail **Boughton**. She was born
Jun 11, 1742 in Danbury, Connecticut, died Jul 16,
1818 and is buried with her husband.

Children:
  Noah   B-May 25,1763 in Danbury,CT. M-May 22,1788
               to Chloe **Andrus** (B-1768; Dau of Capt.
               Abraham and Sarah [**Taylor**] **Andrus**;
               D-May 7,1849 at Unadilla,NY).
               D-Jul 3,1851 at Unadilla,NY. Both bur
               St Matthews Churchyard Cem, Unadilla,NY.

Benjamin   BENEDICT   072   Benjamin   BENEDICT

Abijah   B-Apr 30,1765 Danbury,CT. M-Jun 11,1789 to
          Abigail **Corbin** (B-Feb 20,1766; dau of
          Peter **Corbin**; D-Feb 24,1818) M2-Polly
          Olmstead (B-1769; widow of Joseph
          Rundell; D-Dec 25,1840). D-Apr 18,1843
          at Coventry,NY. He, with first wife bur
          Coventryville Cem, Coventry,NY.
Benjamin B-Jul 18,1767. M-Jul 3,1788 Sybil **Loomis**
          (B-Jun 25,1770; D-Nov 26,1836). M2-Patty
          (___) **Ives** (B-1774;Widow of Amasa **Ives**;
          D-Mar 16,1858). D-Jul 22,1850 at
          Coventry,NY. All 4 Bur Coventryville
          Cem, Coventry,NY.
Eden   B-May 08,1770. M-Miranda **Culver** (B-1775;
          D-Feb 10,1828). D-Sep 15,1842 Coventry,
          NY. Both bur Coventryville Cem,
          Coventry,NY.
Mary   B-Nov 10,1772. M-Oct 25,1792 to Levi
          Bronson (son of Col. Ozias **Bronson**).
          D-Mar 9,1824.
Phebe   B-May 01,1775. M-Aug 1,1796 to Levi **Daw**.
          D-1848.
Eliakim   B-Mar 09,1778. M-May 28,1798 to Ruth Anna
          Beebe (B-Sep 11,1781; Dau of David
          Beebe; D-Sep 1,1868). D-Feb 7,1839 at
          Coventry,NY. Bur Coventryville Cem,
          Coventry,NY.
Huldah   B-Apr 06,1782. M-Oct 6,1799 to Lorrin
          Sweet (B-Sep 17,1778; son of Peter
          Sweet; D-Jun 28,1867). D-Aug 29,1851.
          Both bur Coventryville Cem, Coventry,
          NY.

OTHER INFORMATION: He settled in Winchester in 1770;
was chosen highway surveyor at the first annual town
meeting, 1771. His first deed in the town is dated Apr
4, 1771. First represented the town in the general
assembly, in 1787, and several times afterwards. He
removed to Coventry, Chenango County, New York in
1807.

Noah   BENEDICT   073   Noah   BENEDICT
        S. 12987 Private

RESIDENT DATE: 1804 - 1832
TOWN: Coventry
BIRTH DATE: May 25, 1763
BIRTH PLACE: Danbury, Connecticut
FATHER: Benjamin **Benedict**

Noah **BENEDICT**   073   Noah **BENEDICT**

MOTHER: Mary **Bouton**
DEATH DATE: Jul 4, 1849
DEATH PLACE: Unadilla, New York
CEMETERY: St Matthews Churchyard
LOCATION: Unadilla, New York

TOMBSTONE INSCRIPTION:
                              (NOT FOUND)

SERVICE: While living at Winchester, Connecticut, he volunteered on Jan 1, 1781, for nine months service with Capt. Matthew L_____ Company, attached to General David Waterbury's Brigade of Connecticut troops. Occasionally went out on scouting parties. Remained with the troops at Horseneck until Oct, 1781, when he went with the Company to Stamford, Connecticut to guard General Waterbury's home. In Jan 1782 he went with the Company to White Plains, New York, where they went into winter quarters at a fort which he helped build. In Mar of 1782 he was discharged and returned home.

FAMILY INFORMATION: Married May 22, 1788 at Winchester, Litchfield County, Connecticut to Chloe **Andrus**, a daughter of Capt. Abraham and Sarah (**Taylor**) **Andrus** of Westchester, Connecticut. She was born in 1768 and died May 7, 1849 at Unadilla, New York.

Children:
Noah   B-Mar 18,1789. M-_____. D-1814 in CT.
Hiel   B-Feb 05,1791. M-Sep 25,1814 Lydia **Warren**
            (B-May 20,1794; Dau of Elisha and Louisa
            Warren of Coventry; D-Oct 28,1863).
            D-Mar 18,1824 at Unadilla,NY. Both bur
            St Matthews Cem, Unadilla,NY.
Cyrus K   M-Ann **Ives**. Resided in Detroit,MI.
Hiram   B-Aug 29,1802. M-Nov 11,1825 to Nancy Ann
            Chapman (B-Sep 25,1806 Colchester,CT;
            Dau of Gurdon and Sarah **Chapman**;
            D-Feb 5,1890). D-Apr 21,1864 Unadilla,
            NY. Both bur St Matthews Churchyard,
            Unadilla,NY.
Theron L   B-1805. M-Catharine H **Chapman** (M2-_____
            Arnold). D-Jan 1,1836. Bur
            Coventryville Cem, Coventry,NY.
Chloe   M-William **Roberts**.
Orpha   M-William **Stuart**.

Noah **BENEDICT**   073   Noah **BENEDICT**

OTHER INFORMATION: He lived at Winchester, Connecticut until 1804 when he removed to Coventry, Chenango County, New York. Application for a pension was made on Aug 13, 1832 while a resident of Coventry, New York and was granted on Oct 26, 1832.

Darius **BENJAMIN**   074   Darius **BENJAMIN**
S. 23122 Private   DAR Patriot Index

RESIDENT DATE: - 1850
TOWN: Lincklaen
BIRTH DATE: Jan 17, 1758
BIRTH PLACE: Preston, Connecticut
FATHER: Elijah **Benjamin**
MOTHER: Hannah **Taft**
DEATH DATE: Feb 12, 1850
DEATH PLACE: Lincklaen, New York
CEMETERY: Cuyler Hill
LOCATION: Cuyler, New York (Cortland County)

TOMBSTONE INSCRIPTION:

Darius Benjamin
Died
Feb 12, 1850
Aged 92 years

Charity
Wife of
Derius Benjamin
Died
Nov. 17, 1835:
Aged 72 years
3 months &
19 days

Write, blessed are the dead, which die in the Lord, from hence forth, yea, saith the spirit, that they may rest from their labours, and their works do follow them.

SERVICE: While residing in Town of Rochester, Ulster County, New York he enlisted July 1, 1776 for six months, as a private in Captain Benjamin Kortright's Company, Colonel Levi Pawling's New York Regiment. On May 1, 1777 he enlisted for three months in Captain Hans Hordenbergh's Company, Colonel Levi Paulding's Regiment. In August 1777 he enlisted for a half month in Captain Schoonmaker's Company, under Major Wyncoop. He was at the battle of White Plains. He assisted in the building of Fort Clinton.

FAMILY INFORMATION: Married about 1782 in Dutchess County, New York to Charity **Rice** who was born Aug 29, 1763, died on Nov 17, 1835 and is buried alongside her husband.

Darius BENJAMIN   074   Darius BENJAMIN

Children:
  Ann   B-1783 in Dutchess Co,NY.
  Samuel   B-1784/5 Dutchess Co,NY. M-Charlotte ____
              (B-1782; D-1812). M2-Hulda ____ (B-1787;
              D-1829). M3-Betsey ____ (B-1789; D-1833).
              D-Nov,1863 at DeRuyter,NY.
  James   B-Jul,1786 at Putnam Co,NY. M-Jun 20,1811
              Sally **Spears** (B-Apr 9,1796 Shutesbury,
              MA; Dau of Eli and Jane H [**Tower**]
              Spears; D-Feb 12,1876 at DeRuyter,NY).
              D-Oct 4,1867 at DeRuyter,NY.
  Annie   B-1788 in Dutchess Co,NY. M-Edward **Wilcox**
              (B-1779; D-1869).
  Deborah   B-1790 in Dutchess Co,NY.
  Harry   B-1796 at DeRuyter,NY.
  Sarah   B-1800 at DeRuyter,NY.
  Content   B-1800 at DeRuyter,NY. M-____ **Graves**.
  Charity   B-1803 at DeRuyter,NY. M-Nov 10,1827 at
              DeRuyter,NY Ezra **Burdick** (B-Apr 23,1798
              at Hopkinton,RI; Son of Capt. James
              Reed and Martha [**Coon**] **Burdick**).
  Darius   B-1805 at DeRuyter,NY. M-1828 to Ursula
              Bristol (B-1810; D-Jun 24,1880).
              D-Apr 25,1885 at Lincklaen,NY. Both bur
              in Woodlawn Cem, Lincklaen,NY.
  Melissa   B-Apr 26,1807 DeRuyter,NY. M-1825 Maxon
              Burdick (B-1803; D-1857). D-Apr,1885 at
              Carbondale,KS. Bur at Nortonville,KS.

OTHER INFORMATION: About the year 1774/5 he moved from Fredericksburg, Dutchess County, New York to Ulster County in the same state. He was a pioneer in Madison County, New York and had an original deed to lot #37, dated Jun 30, 1794. He cleared the land and set out a small orchard near the Cemetery. He was allowed pension on his application executed Sep 25, 1832 while a resident of Truxton, Cortland County, New York.

Amos **BENNETT**   075   Amos **BENNETT**
         W. 3377 Private   DAR Patriot Index

RESIDENT DATE: 1807 - 1810
TOWN: Norwich
BIRTH DATE: 1758
BIRTH PLACE: Norwich, Connecticut (New London Co.)
FATHER:
MOTHER:
DEATH DATE: Aug 18, 1840
DEATH PLACE: Auburn, Pennsylvania (Susquehanna Co.)

Amos BENNETT   075   Amos BENNETT

CEMETERY:
LOCATION:

TOMBSTONE INSCRIPTION:

SERVICE: While a resident of Plainfield, Windham County, Connecticut, he volunteered May 9, 1775, and served until Dec 15, 1775, as a private in Captain Waterman Clift's Company, Colonel Samuel H Parsons' Connecticut Regiment. He enlisted at Roxbury, Massachusetts, in February, 1776, served as a private in Captain Edmond's Company, Colonel John Tyler's Connecticut Regiment, was transferred to Captain Christopher Darrow's Company of Rangers and was engaged in watching the British along Long Island Sound; length of this service twelve months. He volunteered May 26, 1781, at New London, Connecticut, and served between three and four months as a private in Captain Avery's Company, Colonel Ledyard's Connecticut Regiment. During this service he was in the cannonading of Dorchester, in the battle on "York Island", and in several skirmishes on the day of the battle of White Plains.

FAMILY INFORMATION: He married Apr 29, 1792, at Preston, New London County, Connecticut to Wealthy **Stafford**, a daughter of John and Mary **(Johnson) Stafford**. She was born in May, 1772 at Preston, Connecticut.

   Children:
Daniel F   Resided in Auburn,PA. in 1841.

OTHER INFORMATION: After the war he remained at New London for one year; then moved to Charleston County, New Hampshire for ten years; then back to New London for seven years; then to Norwich, Chenango County, New York for three years; then to Wilkes-Barre, Luzerne County, Pennsylvania for five years; then to Auburn Township, Pennsylvania. He applied for a pension on an application dated Sep 10, 1832 while a resident of Auburn, Susquehanna County, Pennsylvania. His widow applied on Feb 8, 1841, while a resident of Susquehanna County, Pennsylvania. She also applied for a land warrant on May 7, 1855.

Caleb **BENNETT** 076 Caleb **BENNETT**
W. 24645 Private

RESIDENT DATE: 1786 - 1830
TOWN: Bainbridge
BIRTH DATE: Apr 23, 1758
BIRTH PLACE: Coventry, Rhode Island (Kent County)
FATHER: Phineas **Bennett**
MOTHER: Abigail
DEATH DATE: Mar 22, 1830
DEATH PLACE: Bainbridge, New York
CEMETERY: Bennettsville
LOCATION: Bainbridge, New York

TOMBSTONE INSCRIPTION:
                Elizabeth
                Wife of
            Caleb Bennett
                Died
            June 25, 1849;
            Aged 89 y'rs.

      Mr   Behold and see as you pass by
 Caleb Bennet as you are now so once was I
Died March 22, as I am now soon you must be
    1830   prepare to die and follow me.
  Ae 72 yrs.
By death relieved of earthly cares
   I slumber in the dust
and leave my family and friends
   in God alone to trust

SERVICE: He entered the service under Captain Nathaniel Seely in company with his father and served in the Vermont Militia for a period of seven months and fifteen days.

FAMILY INFORMATION: Married Nov 8, 1782 to Elizabeth **Potter**, a daughter of Robert **Potter**. She was born Jul 18, 1760, in Charleston, Washington County, Rhode Island, died Jun 25, 1849 at Bainbridge, New York and is buried with her husband.

Children:
Anna   B-Feb 03,1783. M-Thomas **Cornell** (B-1771; Son of Rev War Vet Samuel and Thankful [___] **Cornell**; D-Feb 12,1841 Afton,NY). D-Feb 27,1860 at Afton,NY. Both bur East Cem, Afton,NY.
Phineas B-Dec 25,1784. M-Sophia **Chandler** (B-1785; Dau of Henry **Chandler**; D-Aug 24,1863). D-Dec 28,1856. Both bur Bennettsville Cem, Bainbridge,NY.

Caleb   BENNETT   076   Caleb   BENNETT

Abel   B-Dec 25,1784. M-Flavilla **Hoag** (B-1796;
            D-Sep 8,1875). D-Oct 23,1860 at
            Bennettsville,NY. Both bur Bennettsville
            Cem, Bainbridge,NY.
Prudence   B-1789. M-Enos **Goodman** (B-1783;
            D-Dec 2,1861). D-Oct 9,1864. Both bur
            Bennettsville Cem, Bainbridge,NY.
Hannah   B-1790. M-Charles S. **Merritt** (B-1789;
            D-Apr 12,1862 at Bennettsville,NY).
            D-Nov 17,1884. Both bur Bennettsville
            Cem, Bainbridge,NY.
Hiram   B-1803. M-Gratie **Chandler** (B-1802;
            D-Sep 21,1873 at Bennettsville,NY).
            D-Sep 4,1826 at Bennettsville,NY. Both
            bur Bennettsville Cem, Bainbridge,NY.
Arnold   M-Nancy **Forbes** (B-1810; D-May 15,1833;
            Bur Bixby Cem, Bainbridge,NY.
Eunice   D-in childhood.
Nabby   M-Jeremiah **Thurber**. D-Apr 19,1812.

OTHER INFORMATION: The first settlement within the limits of the town of Bainbridge, was made, in the summer of 1786 by Caleb **Bennett**, who came in company with his bothers Phineas, Silas, and Reuben, from Pownal, Vermont. He settled on the southeast corner of the Cemetery in the village of Bennettsville, which derives its name from him. He and his brother, Reuben, built the first mills at Bennettsville in 1798, on the stream which bears his name. This was the first grist mill in the town. His sister Prudence **Arnold** was a resident of Sidney, Delaware County, New York at 79 years of age in 1847.

James   **BENNETT**   077   James   **BENNETT**
         W. 16191 Lieutenant

RESIDENT DATE: 1810
TOWN: Oxford
BIRTH DATE:
BIRTH PLACE:
FATHER:
MOTHER: Abigail **Fowler**
DEATH DATE: Nov 14, 1819
DEATH PLACE: Homer, New York (Cortland County)
CEMETERY: Cortland
LOCATION: Cortlandville, New York (Cortland Co.)

James   BENNETT   077   James   BENNETT

TOMBSTONE INSCRIPTION:
(Stone not located - from file)
Death is a debt to nature due
which I have paid and so must you
weep not my friends, dry up your tears
I shall lie here till Christ appears.

Catherine
Wife of
James Bennet
Died
July, 28 1812,
Aged 77 years

SERVICE: He enlisted in the forepart of 1775, and served until Dec 31, 1775, as sergeant in Captain Daniel Wills' Company in Colonel James Holmes' New York Regiment. He enlisted in the forepart of Jan 1776, and served until Dec 31, 1776, as sergeant major in Colonel Goose Van Schaick's New York Regiment. In 1777, he was commissioned ensign in Colonel Heman Swift's Connecticut Regiment and served as such until Sep 1, 1778, when he was commissioned lieutenant in Colonel Heman Swift's Connecticut Regiment. He was in the battle of Monmouth, where he received a wound in the lower jaw and was discharged in June, 1783.

FAMILY INFORMATION: Married Nov 21, 1784 at Catskill, New York to Catherine **Bogardus** a daughter of Egbert and Annaetje (**Person**) **Bogardus**. She was baptized Dec 25, 1764 at the Dutch Reformed Church in Catskill, Greene County, New York and died Jul 28, 1842. She is buried in the Riverview Cemetery in Oxford, New York. A brother John **Bogardus** was living in Catskill, New York in 1838, age 71 years.

Children:
Adolphus B M-Harriet **Carey** (B-Jul 29,1789; Dau of
            Anson and Hannah [**Carew**] **Carey**;
            D-Aug 9,1863 Oxford,NY; Bur Riverview
            Cem, Oxford,NY). D-Brantford,Canada.
Nancy   B-1789. M-Samuel **Wheeler** (B-1791; Son of
            Samuel and Elizabeth [**Daniels**]
            Wheeler; M1-Tamer **Barnes**;
            D-Mar 26,1847). D-Dec 27,1860. Samuel
            and she bur Riverview Cem, Oxford,NY.
James A   M-Apr 9,1814 to Christena **Tompkins**.
Egbert   M-Gertrude **Reichtmier**. D-Jun,1882
            Des Moines,IA.
Angeline   M-Reuben **Bancroft** (B-1815;
            D-Jan 21,1847; Bur Riverview Cem,
            Oxford,NY).
Eugene   M-Jan 22,1828 to Betsey **Anable**.
Catherine   B-1793. M-Oct 18,1833 to Cyrus **Tuttle**
            (B-1793; D-Jul 20,1870). D-Nov 23,1867.
            Both bur Riverview Cem, Oxford,NY.

James BENNETT   077   James BENNETT

OTHER INFORMATION: He was allowed pension on his application executed Apr 13, 1818, at which time he was living in Homer, Cortland County, New York. His widow was allowed pension on her application executed Aug 29, 1838, while a resident of Oxford, Chenango County, New York. He was listed on the 1810 census in Oxford, New York.

Jared   BENNETT   078   Jared   BENNETT
        -. ----- Private

RESIDENT DATE: - 1845
TOWN: Smyrna
BIRTH DATE: 1764
BIRTH PLACE:
FATHER:
MOTHER:
DEATH DATE: Apr 28 1845
DEATH PLACE: Smyrna, New York
CEMETERY: East
LOCATION: Smyrna, New York

TOMBSTONE INSCRIPTION: Jared Bennett   Parthena
                        Died Apr 28   Wife of
                           1845   Jared Bennett
                        Aged 81 yrs   Died
                                             Nov 10th. 1859
                                             Aged 89 yrs 5
                                             Mo & 25 days.

SERVICE: Toward the end of the Revolution he enlisted as a private in the Commissary department.

FAMILY INFORMATION: Married to Parthena **West**. She was born May 15, 1770 in Lebanon, New London County, Connecticut, died Nov 10, 1859 and is buried with her husband.

    Children:
    Nancy   B-Dec 21,1800. M-1823 to Cyrus **Simons**
                (B-Aug 17,1795 in NY; son of Joseph and
                Elizabeth [**Wells**] **Simons**;
                D-Oct 6,1844). D-Dec 23,1891. Both bur
                East Side Cem, Smyrna,NY.

OTHER INFORMATION: They came from Saybrook, Connecticut to German Flats, Otsego County, New York and a few years later came to Smyrna Hill. He was a carpenter by trade and built a number of houses.

John BENNETT   079   John BENNETT
        S. 45252 Private

RESIDENT DATE: 1831
TOWN: Greene
BIRTH DATE: May 10, 1759
BIRTH PLACE: Ridgefield, Connecticut (Fairfield Co.)
FATHER: Samuel Bennett
MOTHER: Abigail
DEATH DATE: Dec 7, 1842
DEATH PLACE:
CEMETERY: Hudson City   (section 1A)
LOCATION: Hudson, New York (Columbia County)

TOMBSTONE INSCRIPTION: In
            In   Memory
        Memmory of   Mary,
       John Bennett   Wife of
     Who died Dec 7, 1842   John Bennett
       In his 81st year   Who died
                                Dec 9th 1835 in the 77 year
                                        Of her age

SERVICE: He enlisted at Litchfield, Connecticut in 1781 for a term of three years in the Company of Captain Staunton, Colonel Elisha Sheldon's Cavalry. He was discharged after two years because of the termination of the war. He was in the battle of White Plains, at the defeat of General St Clair and in various battles with the Indians.

FAMILY INFORMATION: He married in 1782 in Fairfield County, Connecticut to Mary Selvester. She was born in 1758 In Warwick, England and died Dec 9, 1835. She is buried with her husband.

Children: yes

OTHER INFORMATION: He filed an application for pension on May 7, 1818, while a resident of Mount Washington, Massachusetts. On Aug 28, 1820 he filed a statement while a resident of Columbia County, New York saying he had no permanent residence but had alternately been in Kinderhook and Schodack for the past thirteen years. He was in Fairfield County, Connecticut on Aug 8, 1826 and stated he had children there and had recently married. On Apr 6, 1831 he was in Chenango County, New York and stated he had a brother there and he wished to be near him.

Nathan BENNETT   080   **Nathan BENNETT**
    S. 15325 Corporal

```
RESIDENT DATE:    - 1845
TOWN:             Greene
BIRTH DATE:       Nov 10, 1750
BIRTH PLACE:      Leominster,Massachusetts (Worcester Co)
FATHER:           Nathan Bennett
MOTHER:           Abigail
DEATH DATE:       Aug 17, 1845
DEATH PLACE:      Greene, New York
CEMETERY:         Elliott
LOCATION:         Greene, New York
```

TOMBSTONE INSCRIPTION:
    Nathan Bennett
      died
    Aug 17, 1845
    aged 93 years

In early life my country called
    And I its voice obeyed
By foes my body was enthralled
    And now in Earth is laid.

                          In
                     Memory of
                Violetta wife of
                Nathan Bennett
             Died Aug 15, 1822
              Ae 56 yrs 4 ms
                  & 11 days
With her last breath triumphantly
  she could this anthem sing
  O grave where is thy victory
  O death where is thy sting.

SERVICE: While residing in Old Stockbridge, Berkshire County, Massachusetts, he enlisted in May, 1777 and served as Corporal in Captain Orringh Stoddard's Company, Colonel Vose's Massachusetts Regiment, was at the taking of General Burgoyne and in the battle of Monmouth and was discharged after having served three years.

FAMILY INFORMATION: Married to Violetta _____. She was born Apr 4, 1766, died Aug. 15, 1822 and is buried with her husband.

    Children:
      William   B-1781. M-Lydia _ (B-1781; D-Feb 20,1853).
                D-Dec 9,1857. Both bur Elliott Cem,
                Greene,NY.

Nathan BENNETT   080   Nathan BENNETT

Polly   M-Isaac **Page**
Sally   M-Richard **Rummer**
Nathan
Lovicy   M-James **Ferris**
Clarissa   M-John **Voorhis**
David   M-Irene _____ (B-1805; D-Mar 8,1853).
           D-Jun 13, ---- ae 66. Both bur Elliott
           Cem, Greene,NY.
Eliza   M-Nathan **Marsh**

OTHER INFORMATION: He was allowed a pension on his application executed Jul 30, 1832, at which time he was aged seventy-seven and a resident of Greene, New York.

Wolcott BENNETT   081   Wolcott BENNETT
    W. 17264 sergeant   DAR Patriot Index

RESIDENT DATE: - 1831
TOWN: Lincklaen
BIRTH DATE: 1757
BIRTH PLACE: Fairfield Connecticut (Fairfield Co.)
FATHER:
MOTHER:
DEATH DATE: Dec 6, 1831
DEATH PLACE: Lincklaen, New York
CEMETERY: Woodlawn
LOCATION: Lincklaen, New York

TOMBSTONE INSCRIPTION:
    Soldier of Revolution   Joanna
            In   Wife of
        Memory of   Wolcott Bennett
      Wolcott Bennett   Died
        Who died   June 17, 1843
      Dec. 6, 1831,   Ae 88 years
        Ae. 75 y.
Death is a debt to nature due,
    which I have paid,
    and so must you

SERVICE: Resided at Fairfield, Connecticut in 1776 when drafted for six weeks. He served under Captain Aaron Hawley and Captain Aaron Benjamin. In the same year he enlisted for six months and went to New York. Was in the retreat from Long Island. Again enlisted for one year in Captain Josiah Lacy's Company. Was wounded at White Plains. Also served in Captain Isaac Jarvis's Company and was in the Coast Guard duty.

Wolcott   BENNETT   081   Wolcott   BENNETT

FAMILY INFORMATION: Married on Feb 17, 1777 at Stratfield, Connecticut while on a furlough from White Plains, to Joanna **Patchin**, a daughter of David and Elizabeth (**Hull**) **Patchin**. She was born in 1756 in Fairfield, Connecticut, died Jun 17, 1843 and is buried with her husband.

Children:
  Joseph   B-Oct 17,1777.
  David
  Ellen
  Esther
  Rufus   B-1799. M-Clarissa _____ (B-1806; D-1866).
             D-1863. Both bur Woodlawn Cem, Lincklaen,NY.
  Wolcott

OTHER INFORMATION: He settled in Lincklaen, Chenango County, New York and settled about two miles north of Collin's Settlement. His widow was granted a pension based on her declaration dated Jul 13, 1837, while a resident of Lincklaen, Chenango County, New York.

Peleg   BERRY   082   Peleg   BERRY
        W. 10406 Lieutenant   DAR Patriot Index

RESIDENT DATE: wife
TOWN: Preston
BIRTH DATE: May 30, 1746
BIRTH PLACE: Westerly, Rhode Island (Washington Co.)
FATHER: Richard **Berry**
MOTHER: Susannah
DEATH DATE: Jun 30, 1796
DEATH PLACE: Westerly, Rhode Island
CEMETERY:
LOCATION:

TOMBSTONE INSCRIPTION:

SERVICE: While residing in Westerly, Rhode Island, was commissioned October, 1775 an ensign in Captain Wells' Company, Colonel Richmond's Rhode Island Regiment. He was commissioned August, 1776 lieutenant in the same Regiment and December, 1777 was commissioned first lieutenant in Captain Thompson's Company, Colonel Stanton's Regiment and resigned December, 1777.

Peleg   BERRY   082   Peleg   BERRY
FAMILY INFORMATION: He married Apr 17, 1774 at Westerly, Rhode Island to Mary **Kinyon**, a daughter of David and Mary **Kinyon**. She was born Jul 26, 1755 in Richmond Twp., Washington County, Rhode Island.

Children:
  Peleg   B-Jun 10,1775 Westerly,RI. M-Hannah _____
              (B-1773; D-1854). D-1830. Both bur
              East Hill Cem, Sherburne,NY.
  George   B-Jun 11,1778 Westerly,RI.
  Anna   B-Apr 29,1780 Westerly,RI.
  Richard Wain B-Jun 01,1782 Westerly,RI. Resided in
              Preston,NY.
  Elizabeth B-Oct 17,1784,Westerly,RI.
  Elijah   B-Mar 14,1787,Westerly,RI.
  John Simeon B-Aug 28,1789 Westerly,RI.
  Elisha   B-Dec 20,1792 Westerly,RI.

OTHER INFORMATION: His widow applied for pension on an application dated Oct 31, 1836 while a resident of Preston, Chenango County, New York.

Peter   BESANCON   083   Peter   BESANCON
     R.   803 Lieutenant

RESIDENT DATE: 1792 - 1799
TOWN: Norwich
BIRTH DATE: Feb 4, 1762
BIRTH PLACE: Besancon, France
FATHER:
MOTHER:
DEATH DATE: May 15, 1855
DEATH PLACE: Pike, New York (Wyoming County)
CEMETERY: Elmwood
LOCATION: Pike, New York

TOMBSTONE INSCRIPTION: from town of Pike historian
                           reference cards--
                  Besancon, Peter   1764 - 1856
                           Elizabeth 1779 - 1856

           Peter Besancon
                Died
             May 15, 1855.
             Aged 94 yrs.

              Elizabeth

      (cemented in so unreadable)

Peter BESANCON   083   Peter BESANCON

SERVICE: Signed up with LaFayette while living in Paris, at age of 16, in 1778; was present at the execution of Major Andre, in 1780; was commissioned a lieutenant at Valley Forge; served under Captain Benjamin Walker, Baron Steuben, General Chas. Lee, General LaFayette, General Sullivan in the battle of Rhode Island; stayed with the army until the end of the war, in 1783; was initiated into the Masonic fraternity by General Washington, date unknown.

FAMILY INFORMATION: Married Nov 1, 1798 to Elizabeth **Hayes**, a daughter of James and Elizabeth **Hayes**. She was born Nov 1, 1778, died May 5, 1856 in Pike, New York and is buried with her husband.

Children:
- Paschal   B-Aug 23,1799 Lewisville, town of Butternuts,NY. M-Nov 18,1828 New York City to Elizabeth **Garthwaite**. D-Oct 3,1840 Portage Wood Co.,OH.
- Julia   B-Dec 17,1801. M-George **Cornwall** of Canada at Cooperstown,NY. D-May 29,1844 Hillsboro,IL.
- Peter   B-1804. D-1805.
- Peter   B-1806. M-1852 to Mantoria **McCaleb** of New Orleans and Natchez.
- Edward   B-1808. Unmarried. D-1847 New Orleans,LA.
- James   B-May 13,1810 at Lewisville, Butternuts, NY. M-May 23,1839 at Palmyra,NY to Mary W **Tyler** (B-Aug 21,1819 at Owego,NY; D-1902). D-Jan 13,1882 at Wiscoy,NY. Both bur Elmwood Cem, Pike,NY.
- Lorenzo   B-Jul 1,1812 in Cooperstown,NY. M-May 10, 1838 New Orleans,LA. to Mary Octavia **Woodruff**. D-Jan 21,1853.

OTHER INFORMATION: After the war he returned to France for an unknown period between 1783 and 1798. He purchased 535 acres of land in Otsego County, New York, town of Butternuts, village known as Lewisville, later Morris, on Jul 22, 1799, and he is identified in the deed as Peter **Besancon** of Norwich, Chenango County. He moved to Cooperstown in 1811. Was identified in Butternuts as a "farmer' and in Cooperstown as a "doctor". Moved to Palmyra with son James in 1840, later to Pike, Perry, Middlebury, and again Pike, where he died at the home of his son James. Was a member of the Baptist Church for 51 years; member of Masonic fraternity; honorary member of Odd Fellows and of Good Templars.

Zopher **BETTS**　　　　　084　　　　Zopher **BETTS**
　　　S. 9812 Private　　　DAR Patriot Index

RESIDENT DATE:　　　- 1842
TOWN:　　　　　　　　Oxford
BIRTH DATE:　　　　　Jan 1, 1761
BIRTH PLACE:　　　　Sharon, Connecticut (Litchfield County)
FATHER:　　　　　　　Zopher **Betts**
MOTHER:　　　　　　　Elizabeth **Marvin**
DEATH DATE:　　　　　Mar 10, 1842
DEATH PLACE:　　　　Oxford, New York
CEMETERY:　　　　　　TenBroeck
LOCATION:　　　　　　Oxford, New York

TOMBSTONE INSCRIPTION:
　　　　　　In　　　　　　　　　　In
　　　　Memory of　　　　　　Memory of
　　　　Zopher Betts　　　　　Jane,
　　　　Died Mar. 10.　　　　Wife of
　　　　　　1842　　　　　　　Zopher Betts
　　　　Ae 81 yrs.　　　　　　　Died
　　　　　　　　　　　　　　　Feb 14, 1844
　　　　　　　　　　　　　　　Ae 76 yrs.

SERVICE: While residing at Sharon, he enlisted – served as a private with the Connecticut Troop S as follows: In 1777 six weeks in Captain Sturtevant's Company, Colonel Porter's Regiment; from October 1777 – three weeks in Captain Griswold's Company; from September 1778 – one month in Captain Roger Moore's Company, Colonel Eben Gay's Regiment; from June 1779 – nine months in Captain Joshua Stanton's Company, Colonel Mead's Regiment; from May 1780 – nine months in Captain Baldwin's Company, Colonel Swift's Regiment and in Captain Sturtevant's Company; from May 1781 – one month date and officers not given. He was in several skirmishes.

FAMILY INFORMATION: Married to Jane **Warren**, a daughter of Nehemiah and Anna (**Fuller**) **Warren**. She was born in 1765 at Sharon, Litchfield County, Connecticut, died on Feb 14, 1841 and was buried with her husband.

Children:
　Rachel　　　B-1782. M-Blodget **Smith** (B-1783; D-Jul 6,1856). D-Nov 2,1852. Both bur TenBroeck cem, Oxford,NY.
　Prudence　　B-1788. M-William D **Wheeler** (B-1788; Son of Samuel and Elizabeth [**Daniels**] **Wheeler**; In War of 1812; D-Aug 6,1866). D-Jan 19,1854. Both bur Brisben Church Cem, Greene,NY.

| Zopher | BETTS | 084 | Zopher BETTS |

Annie	B-1794. M-Jeremiah **TenBroeck** (B-1791; Bp-Jan 1,1796; Son of John and Livina [**Miller**] **TenBroeck**; D-Jun 5,1833). D-Aug 5,1880. Both bur TenBroeck Cem, Oxford,NY.
Silas	B-1797. M-Jeanette **Wheeler** (B-1801; Dau of Samuel and Elizabeth [**Daniels**] **Wheeler**; D-Apr 16,1845). M2-Betsey H _____ (B-1800; D-May 20,1889). D-Feb 9,1878. All 3 bur Brisben Church Cem, Greene,NY.
Warren	B-1799. M-Alice _____ (B-1805; D-Mar 5,1844). D-Oct 2,1843. Both bur TenBroeck Cem, Oxford,NY.
Annis	B-1802. M-Wheaton **Race** (B-1800; D-Jul 8,1874). D-Jun 29,1869 at Oxford. Both bur TenBroeck Cem, Oxford,NY.
Polly	B-1806. M-Loren **Miller** (B-1806; D-Sep 2,1879). D-Oct 3,1870. Both bur TenBroeck Cem, Oxford,NY.
Erastus	B-1819. D-Feb 15,1836. Bur TenBroeck Cem, Oxford,NY.

OTHER INFORMATION: A man of large stature. After the Revolution, he lived at Egremont, Berkshire County, Mass., then at Oxford, Chenango County, New York. He was allowed pension on his application executed Jul 30, 1832, while residing in Oxford, Chenango County at age 80, living with his son Warren.

| Benjamin BIRDSALL | 085 | Benjamin BIRDSALL |
| -. ------ Lieutenant Colonel | | DAR Patriot Index |

RESIDENT DATE: 1816 - 1829
TOWN: Greene
BIRTH DATE: Aug 4, 1743
BIRTH PLACE: Dutchess County, New York
FATHER: Nathan **Birdsall**
MOTHER: Jane **Langdon**
DEATH DATE: Oct 08, 1828
DEATH PLACE: Greene, New York
CEMETERY: Canal St
LOCATION: Greene, New York

Benjamin BIRDSALL   085   **Benjamin BIRDSALL**

TOMBSTONE INSCRIPTION:
In memory of
Elizabeth
Wife of
Col Benjamin Birdsall
Died
Sept 9 1836
Aged 83 years.

In memory of
Col. Benjamin Birdsall
Died
October 8, 1828
Aged 84 years

> Revolutionary
> Soldier
> 1775   1783
> placed by the
> GO-Won-Go
> Chapter

SERVICE: Served in Fifth Dutchess County Militia. He was lieutenant colonel in the Regiment of Colonel Morris Graham.

FAMILY INFORMATION: Married to Elizabeth **VanAken**, a daughter of Johannes and Marya (**VanGarden**) **VanAken**. She was baptized Nov 3, 1754 at the Dutch Reformed Church, Machackemeck, Orange County, New York, died Sep 9, 1836 and is buried with her husband.

Children:
- Lewis   B-Jan 22,1770. M-1790 to Patience **Lee** (B-Feb 2,1771). D-1843.
- Mary P   B-Jul 10,1772. M-Jul 14,1794, at Cherry Valley,NY. to Samuel **Stark**.
- Albert   B-1776. M-_____.
- Henry H   B-1780. M-Rachel **Erwin**.
- Benjamin   B-1781. M-Lydia **Bushnell** at Greene,NY.
- James   B-1783. M-at Norwich,NY. to Rispah **Steere** (B-Jan 24,1792; Dau of Stephen and Rispah [**Smith**] **Steere**; D-Fenton,MI). D-Jul 10,1856 at Fentonville, MI.
- Maurice   B-1784. M-Ann **Pixley** (B-1778; D-Jun 12,1829). M2-Anna **Purple** (B-Mar 30,1793, D-Nov 24,1880). D-Jan 7,1852 at Greene,NY. All 3 bur Canal St. Cem, Greene,NY.
- Judith   B-1785. M-Joseph **Hagaman** (B-1782; D-Jan 19,1830). D-Aug 25,1877. Both bur Canal St Cem, Greene,NY.
- George A   B-1785. M-Sarah **Hagaman**.
- Elizabeth   M-_____ **Pixley**
- Sarah   M-George **Amigh**

Benjamin BIRDSALL   085   Benjamin BIRDSALL

OTHER INFORMATION: A personal friend of George Washington. He was educated as a Quaker, yet when the crisis came which stirred the patriotism and the hearts of our people he abandoned the principles of non-resistance and in opposition to a majority of his convictions and early friends, declared for his country. His known ability and undoubted integrity at once procured his commission of a Colonel in the militia under which he was frequently called to the defense of his country, in the most perilous times, and suffered in common with the heroes of liberty, the privation and hardships peculiar to that eventful period. Perhaps few individuals of that day suffered more from the malicious ravages of the Tories. They not only pillaged his stables, drove and butchered his cattle to feed the enemy, but pursued his life with an avidity that required his utmost vigilance to elude.

A few years after the termination of the struggle, he removed to Columbia County, where he was repeatedly honored by the suffrages of his fellow citizens with a seat in the State Legislature and other offices of trust which he filled with credit to himself and satisfaction to his constituents. He then removed to Greene N.Y. where he lived out his life.

John BIRGE   086   John BIRGE
         W. 17309 Private   DAR Patriot Index

RESIDENT DATE: – 1838
TOWN: Coventry
BIRTH DATE: Jun 9, 1755
BIRTH PLACE: Hebron, Connecticut
FATHER: Daniel Birge
MOTHER: Elizabeth
DEATH DATE: May 17, 1838
DEATH PLACE:
CEMETERY: Coventry
LOCATION: Coventry, New York

TOMBSTONE INSCRIPTION:
                 John N. Birge,   Ruhamah R.
                    Died   Birge
                 May 17, 1838:   Died Aug 12, 1856
                 Aged 84 years   Ae 97 yrs.

SERVICE: While residing at Hebron, Tolland County, Connecticut, he was drafted on Sep 1, 1776, as private under Captain Daniel Tarbox, Lieutenant Solomon Tarbox, Colonel Obadiah Hosford and marched to New

John   BIRGE   086   John   BIRGE

Rochelle, New York and served three months. Again, on September 1, 1777 he was drafted for three months, as a private under Captain Samuel Gilbert, Colonel Joel Jones and marched to New London to guard against attacks from the enemy. In September 1778 he was drafted for three months under Captain Gad Talcott, Colonel Joel Jones, and marched to New London, once again to guard against enemy attacks. In August or September 1780 he volunteered for a one month period as private under Captain Went and arrived at New London within two or three days after the burning of that place by the British. He was employed at repairing the fort which had been destroyed.

FAMILY INFORMATION: Married Sep 15, 1777 Hebron, Connecticut to Ruhama **Foote**. She was born in 1761, died Aug 2, 1856 and is buried with her husband.

Children:
Daniel   B-Jan 30,1779 Hebron,CT. M-Mehitable
            Little (B-1774; D-Oct 12,1831).
Betsy   B-Sep 06,1781 Hebron,CT.
Pamela   B-Jan 17,1785 Hebron,CT.
John   B-Jun 18,1789 Hebron CT. In War of 1812.
Alfred   B-Jan 04,1791 Hebron,CT.
Polly   B-Jun 17,1794 Hebron,CT.
Demis   B-Feb 18,1802 Hebron,CT.
Charlotte   B-Jun 06,1803 Hebron,CT.

OTHER INFORMATION: Resided at Hebron, Connecticut before removing to Franklin, Delaware County, New York around the year 1800. He applied for a pension on an application dated Oct 9, 1832, while a resident of Franklin, New York. His widow applied for a pension on an application dated Aug 22, 1838, while a resident of Coventry, Chenango County, New York.

John   BISHOP   087   John   BISHOP
         W. 2588 Private

RESIDENT DATE: 1836
TOWN: Otselic
BIRTH DATE: Jan 26, 1759
BIRTH PLACE: Stanford, Connecticut (Fairfield Co.)
FATHER: Job **Bishop**
MOTHER: Mercy **Slason**
DEATH DATE: Apr 3, 1842
DEATH PLACE:
CEMETERY:

John BISHOP   087   John BISHOP

LOCATION:

TOMBSTONE INSCRIPTION:

SERVICE: He enlisted at Hancock, Massachusetts in September 1776 and served for two months in the Massachusetts line marching through Greenfield to New Rochell and thence to White Plains.
 Enlisted December 1776 for three months under Captain William Douglas. They marched through Lebanon, Bethleham, Greenbush to Stillwater. From there to Fort Edward and Fort Miller then Whitehall. From there to Ticonderoga.
 In June or July 1777 he was drafted for the army at Stillwater, proceeded to Fort Ann under the command of General Gates. He was in a skirmish with the Indians and retreated before Burgoyne down the Hudson to Ford Edward. He accompanied a scouting party to Fort George and Fort Edward returning home in August 1777 having served about five or six weeks.
 In August 1777 he was drafted and on his way to Bennington came down with the measles, returning home for recovery. Afterwards marched under the command of Captain Lusk to Stillwater where he joined General Gates' Army. He was at the Highlands until the day before Burgoyne's surrender. He returned home Oct 22, 1777.

FAMILY INFORMATION: He married Aug 10, 1797 to Sarah **Kimball**. She was born in 1772.

Children:
  Selah   B-Mar 31,1794 Canterbury,CT.
  Lucy W   B-May 24,1798 Lyme,NH.
  John   B-Mar 15,1800. M-Lydia L_____ (B-1804; D-Oct 18,1867). D-Sep 23,1885. Both bur Maple Grove Cem, Otselic,NY.

OTHER INFORMATION: He applied for a pension on Aug 27, 1832, while a resident of Lyme, New Hampshire. He had lived in New Bedford, New York for eight years, Cantisbury, New Hampshire six years and Lyme, New Hampshire for thirty-three years. On Mar 5, 1836 he had moved to Chenango County, New York. He was in the 1840 pension census at Lyme, Grafton County, New Hampshire with Samuel **Hervey** as head of the household. His widow applied on Nov 14, 1848, while a resident of Grafton County, New Hampshire.

Samuel BIXBY 088 Samuel BIXBY
S. 18317 Sergeant   DAR Patriot Index

RESIDENT DATE: 1788 - 1825
TOWN: Bainbridge
BIRTH DATE: 1740
BIRTH PLACE: Shrewsbury, Massachusetts
FATHER: Samuel **Bixby**
MOTHER: Mary **Buck**
DEATH DATE: 1825
DEATH PLACE: Bainbridge, New York
CEMETERY: Bixby
LOCATION: Bainbridge, New York

TOMBSTONE INSCRIPTION: Original stones were thought to have been removed to The Farmers Museum at Cooperstown, New York. A check did not locate them. The following newer stones were found in Greenlawn Cemetery Bainbridge, New York.

   Samuel
   Bixby 2nd   Hanna Powers
   1740 - 1820   Bixby
   Revolutionary   1739 - 1819
   Soldier
   Vermont

SERVICE: Enlisted Aug 29, 1777 and served until Sep 23, 1777 as sergeant in the company commanded by Captain Josiah Boyden in Colonel William Williams' Regiment which marched to Bennington, Vermont. Also he spent six days in the Company of Captain Charles Nelson, raised by an order to defend the frontier, from March 20 to 26, 1781. His name also appears on the muster rolls of New York State troops as a sergeant in Williams' Regiment, the year not given.

FAMILY INFORMATION: Married Mar 4, 1762 at Lancaster, Massachusetts to Hannah **Powers** born there Jan 10, 1739 to parents Jonathan and Hannah (**Sawyer**) **Powers**. She died in 1819 at Bainbridge, New York.

Children:
 Hannah B-Dec 13,1762 Princeton,MA. M-in Vt. Asa **Stowell** (son of Hezekiah and Hepzibah [Rice] **Stowell**, D-Nov 3,1826 in Bainbridge,NY). D-Sep 18,1850 in Bainbridge,NY. Both bur Broad Cem, Afton,NY.

Samuel   BIXBY   088   Samuel   BIXBY

Sibyl   B-Oct 01,1765 at Princeton,MA. M-Edward
           Davidson on Feb 23,1786 Guilford VT;
           M-second Henry **Evans**(B-Jun 8,1770 son
           of Major Henry **Evans**; D-Jul 29,1833 at
           Bainbridge,NY). D-Jul 21,1846 at
           Bainbridge,NY.
Priscilla B-Dec 29,1767 at Princeton,MA. M-in VT. to
           Henry **Ward**.
Asahel   B-Oct 23,1770 Guilford,VT. M-Nov 10,1793
           Bainbridge,NY, Clarina **Smith**
           (B-Jul 27, 1775; Dau of Deacon Israel
           and Abigail [**Chandler**] **Smith**;
           D-May 22,1847). D-Oct 05,1862.
Samuel   B-Jan 25,1774 Guilford,VT. M-Jan 23,1800
           Cheshire,CT. to Lois **Moss** (B-Oct 2,1776
           Cheshire,CT. to Joel and Mary [**Atwater**]
           Moss; D-Apr 2,1852 at Bainbridge,NY).
           Was in the War of 1812; D-Jul 23,1857 at
           Bainbridge,NY. Both were bur Bixby Cem,
           Bainbridge,NY.
Elizabeth B-Apr 08,1778 at Guilford,VT. M-Russell
           Redfield(B-May 6,1775; Son of Levi and
           Sybil [**Wilcox**] **Redfield**;
           D-Mar 13,1853). D-1858 at Bartoo,WI.

OTHER INFORMATION: He also took part in the old
French War in 1758. He served in many elected
capacities in both Guilford, Vermont and in Guilford,
New York. One of the original members and a trustee of
the Presbyterian church, called the church of Silesia.

Elijah   BLACKMAN   089   Elijah   BLACKMAN
 -. ------ Private   DAR Patriot Index

RESIDENT DATE: 1790 - 1825
TOWN: Oxford
BIRTH DATE: Feb 27, 1740
BIRTH PLACE: Coventry, Connecticut
FATHER: Benjamin **Blackman**
MOTHER: Sarah **Phelps**
DEATH DATE: 1825
DEATH PLACE: Oxford, New York
CEMETERY:
LOCATION:

TOMBSTONE INSCRIPTION:

Elijah BLACKMAN   089   **Elijah BLACKMAN**

SERVICE: While a resident of Southwick, Massachusetts he enlisted for eight months as a private in Captain Lebben Ball's Company, Colonel William Shepard's Regiment. He was reported sick at Stanford. Reported as discharged October 12, 1778. On April 2, 1779 he enlisted for eight months as a private in Captain Silas Fowler's Company of the Hampshire County Regiment.

FAMILY INFORMATION: Married to Mary **Atherton**, a daughter of Simon and Mary **Atherton**. She was born Oct 15, 1744 in Coventry, Tolland County, Connecticut.

Children:
   Elijah   B-Jan 23,1767 in Coventry, Ct. M-1787 prob. Southwick, MA to Lucinda **Austin**. Removed from the town in 1813. D-Aug 16,1852. Bur Evergreen Cem, Alden, Erie Co, NY.
   Jabez   B-Mar 26,1772 in Coventry, CT. M-Hannah **Trisket** (B-1785; D-Oct 30,1839). D-Jan 17,1849. Both bur Blackman Cem, Oxford, NY.
   *Polly Knapp (adopted daughter) B-1777. Became first white woman to live in Oxford, NY. M-1800 to Col. Samuel **Balcom** (B-Dec 31,1772 in Sudbury, MA; Son of Henry and Keziah [**Stowe**] **Balcom**; D-Aug 27,1847 in Oxford, NY). D-Oct 7,1852.

OTHER INFORMATION: In the fall of 1790 he came to Oxford, Chenango County, New York from Connecticut and squatted on the little island in the Chenango River, within the limits of Oxford Village, commonly known as "Cork Island". This land was purchased by General **Hovey**. When he came to take possession of his land, he gave to **Blackman**, in consideration of the improvements he had made on his island, a piece of land about a mile and a half up the river, on lot #3 of the Gore. This was supposed to contain one hundred acres, but which, when surveyed, proved to contain one hundred and twenty-eight acres.

   * She was the first white female in the town of Oxford. She was only 10 years of age, and was brought in upon the shoulders of her foster brothers, who had returned to their native state for supplies, and wearied of a life in the lonely backwoods, devoid of female companionship.

Enoch **BLACKMAN**   090   Enoch **BLACKMAN**
   W. 2059 private   DAR Patriot Index

RESIDENT DATE: - 1846
TOWN: Lincklaen
BIRTH DATE: Sep 15, 1760
BIRTH PLACE: Hartford, Connecticut (Hartford County)
FATHER:
MOTHER:
DEATH DATE: Aug 30, 1844
DEATH PLACE: Cincinnatus, New York (Cortland County)
CEMETERY:
LOCATION: Lincklaen, New York

TOMBSTONE INSCRIPTION: In
  (6" thick tree in front)   Memory of
                                         Betsey
                                         Wife of
                              Enoch Blackman & formerly
                                        Consort of
                                       Joseph Morse.
                              Died April 2, 1830 Aged
                                        54 years.

SERVICE: While a resident of Stratford, Connecticut he enlisted on Dec 1, 1776, for three months, as a private with Captain Samuel Comstock, Colonel Samuel Whitney's Connecticut Regiment; May 1777, for one month with Captain Joseph Birdsey, Colonel Samuel Whitney's Connecticut Regiment; May 1, 1780 to January 1781 as a private for Colonel Bradley's 5th Regiment; March, 1781 for one year as a private under Captain Jabez Fitch to guard the seacoast.

FAMILY INFORMATION: Married July 25, 1782 at Stratford, Fairfield County, Connecticut to Abigail **Clark**. She was born Sep 22, 1760 in Connecticut. He was married second to Betsey, former consort of Joseph **Morse**. Betsey was born in 1776, died Apr 2, 1830 and is buried beside Joseph in the Woodlawn Cemetery in Lincklaen, New York. He married third to Lydia **David** at Taylor, New York on September 5, 1837. She was born in 1758.

Children:
  Nathan Clark   B-Dec 27,1782 Stratford,CT.
  Abby Betty   B-Nov 06,1784 Stratford,CT.
  Jaine Sharlotte   B-Mar 21,1787 Stratford,CT.
  Elizabeth Sarah   B-Dec 16,1789 Stratford,CT.
  Roswell   B-Oct 22,1791.In the War of 1812.
                      M-Apr 29,1819 Lorinda **Hayward**
                      (B-Aug 21,1799).

Enoch BLACKMAN   090   Enoch BLACKMAN

OTHER INFORMATION: Lived since the war in Stratford until 1806; removed to DeRuyter, New York; in 1832 went to Cortlandville New York. His application for pension in 1818 was turned down because he had not served long enough. He applied for a pension on September 2, 1832, while residing at Cortlandville, Cortland. He was in Taylor September 5, 1837. His widow was granted a pension based on application dated March 8, 1853, while a resident of Taylor, New York. He is listed in the 1840 census at Cincinnatus, Cortland County, New York.

Samuel BLACKMAN   091   Samuel BLACKMAN
         W. 23625 Private   DAR Patriot Index

RESIDENT DATE: 1837
TOWN: Columbus/Sherburne
BIRTH DATE: Nov 4, 1762
BIRTH PLACE: Lebanon, Connecticut (New London Co.)
FATHER: Samuel **Blackman**
MOTHER: Mehitable **Long**
DEATH DATE: Jan 28, 1857 (95 years old)
DEATH PLACE:
CEMETERY: Liverpool
LOCATION: Salina, New York (Onondaga County)

TOMBSTONE INSCRIPTION:
  Samuel Blackman   Jerusha Blackmon
    a soldier   died
  of the Revolution   Feb 17, 1860,
       died   Aged 89 Y'rs
   Jan. 28, 1857   & 11 Mo's.
   Ae. 96 Y'rs.   When her weak hand grew palsied,
                  and her eye dim with the mist of years
                    then it was her time to die.

SERVICE: On the 9th of July, 1777, at Northhampton, Massachusetts, while living with the late Governor Strong, he enlisted in the Massachusetts line for nine months under Captain Williams, and Colonel Brewer. He served mostly at West Point. He went into winter quarters at Fishkill where he was discharged.

FAMILY INFORMATION: Married on Mar 06, 1791 in Coventry, Tolland County, Connecticut to Jerusha **Babcock**, daughter of William and Mary (**Gates**) **Babcock**. She was born on Mar 12, 1771 in Coventry, Connecticut, died Feb 17, 1860 and is buried with her husband.

Samuel BLACKMAN   091   Samuel BLACKMAN

Children:
- Mary G   B-Jan 23,1793. M-Oct 11,1809 to Ransom **Stevens**. D-May 11,1822.
- Silvester   B-Jun 23,1795. M-May 10,1815 to Claricy **Leak**.
- Hiram   B-Dec 09,1796. M-Jun 22,1823 to Harriet _____. D-Feb 07,1838.
- Eliza   B-Aug 29,1798. M-Oct 17,1821 to Ebenezer **Wheeler**. D-Jun 22,1839.
- Betsey   B-Aug 28,1800. M-Jun 21,1818 to Horace **Morse**.
- Minerva   B-Dec 07,1802.
- Almanzo   B-Dec 07,1802.
- Milo   B-Nov 18,1804.
- William   B-Dec 29,1806. D-Mar 17,1828.
- Delia Ann   B-Jul 03,1814. D-Mar 09,1818.

OTHER INFORMATION: Apr 30, 1818 was of Lowville, New York; May 20, 1823 was of Oneida County; Oct 20, 1836, living in Defiance, Ohio; Aug 31, 1837, he was in Chenango County; Oct 23, 1844, he was of Henry County, Ohio; Oct 02, 1847 was residing in the town of Clay, New York.

David BLAIR   092   David BLAIR
         -. ----- Sergeant   DAR Patriot Index

RESIDENT DATE: - 1829
TOWN: Plymouth
BIRTH DATE: Mar 30, 1749
BIRTH PLACE: Worcester, Massachusetts
FATHER: Robert **Blair**
MOTHER: Hannah **Thompson**
DEATH DATE: Jul 22, 1829
DEATH PLACE: Plymouth, New York
CEMETERY: North
LOCATION: Plymouth, New York

TOMBSTONE INSCRIPTION:

<table>
<tr><td>In
Memory of
David Blair
Died July 22
1829
Aged 80 years</td><td>In
Memory of
Miriam wife of
David Blair
Died August 25
1827 aged
78 years</td></tr>
</table>

SERVICE: Served two months and four days, as private, in Captain John Ferguson's Company, Colonel Timothy

David BLAIR   092   David BLAIR

Danielson's Regiment, which marched Apr 20, 1775 in response to the alarm of Apr 19, 1775, from Blandford and Murrayfield. On the muster roll of Captain William Knox's Company of Militia in John Mosely's Regiment, who marched to Ticonderoga Oct 21, 1776. He served at Murrayfield, for twenty days, as sergeant in Captain Ferguson's Company of Militiamen. Also sergeant under Captain Shepard & Colonel Mosely, seven days on Bennington alarm and in same Company and Regiment one month and three days on Saratoga alarm. On Aug 26, 1778 he was commissioned second lieutenant in Captain James Black's Company (13th Hampshire County).

FAMILY INFORMATION: Married to Mariam **Boise**, a daughter of John and Anna **(Crooks) Boise**. The marriage intentions were published Dec 20, 1771, in Blandford, Massachusetts. She was born Mar 17, 1749 at Hampden, Massachusetts and died Aug 25, 1827. She is buried beside her husband.

Children:
- Thompson   B-Jan 04,1773 in Becket,MA. M-Jun 6,1794 Groton,CT to Esther **Perkins** (Dau of Obadiah **Perkins**). D-Jan 4,1848.
- Dolly   M-Robert **Henry** (B-1769; D-May 6,1846 at Smyrna,NY; Bur Stover Cem, Smyrna,NY).
- Luther   B-May 06,1777 Becket,MA. M-Sep 2,1799 in Groton,CT to Emblem **Perkins** (B-Jul 17,1778; Dau of Obadiah **Perkins**; D-Nov 1,1852). D-Dec 20,1851.
- Calvin   B-Jun 11,1779 in Becket,MA. M-Jun 6,1802 to Fanny **Tyrell**. Went West.
- David   Resided at Plymouth,NY, then when advanced in years went to live with his children in the Black River Country.
- Eunice   B-1783. Unmarried. D-May 14,1819 Plymouth, NY. Bur North Cem, Plymouth,NY.
- Miriam   M-Isaac **Sabin** (B-Sep 9,1781 in MA; Son of Ziba and Lydia [**Welch**] **Sabin**; M2-Sally _____ [B-1790 in NY]. D-May 7,1855 at Plymouth,NY; Bur North Cem,Plymouth,NY).
- Robert   B-1786 in MA. M-Polly _____ (B-1795; D-Mar 21,1842; Bur North Norwich Cem). D-Jan 28,1851. Both bur North Norwich Cem, North Norwich,NY.
- Hannah   B-1787. M-Chester **Allen** (B-Mar 3,1794; Son of Apollos and Deborah [**Pardee**] **Allen**; D-Oct 1,1877 at Smyrna,NY). D-Nov 21,1862 at Smyrna,NY. Both bur Stover Cem, Smyrna,NY.

David BLAIR   092   David BLAIR

Ralph Erskine B-1789. D-Nov 17,1818 at Plymouth,NY.
Bur North Cem, Plymouth,NY.
Theodosia B-1794. Unmarried. D-Jul 11,1857 at
Smyrna,NY.

OTHER INFORMATION: He had 100 acres of land in what is now Becket. He tilled his farm and worked at his trade of cooper, training his sons in both pursuits. Later he sold his farm and cooper's shop to his son Luther, and removed to Chenango County. New York State, where he settled on the Smyrna Road, one and one half miles northeast of the village of Plymouth.

Jedediah BLANCHARD   093   Jedediah BLANCHARD
          S. 14961   Private

RESIDENT DATE: - 1815
TOWN: Oxford
BIRTH DATE: Sep 29, 1762
BIRTH PLACE: Ashford, Connecticut (Windham County)
FATHER: Jedediah **Blanchard**
MOTHER: Martha
DEATH DATE: May 9, 1836
DEATH PLACE:
CEMETERY: Itaska
LOCATION: Barker, New York (Broome County)

TOMBSTONE INSCRIPTION: In   In memory of
                       Memory of   Abigail wife of
                       Jedediah Blanchard Jedediah Blanchard
                       Who died May   Who died May
                       9th 1836   22nd 1819
                       In the 75 year   In the 49th year
                       Of his age   Of her age

SERVICE: He enlisted as a private, at Windsor, Connecticut in the fall of 1779 for two months under Captain Granger in Colonel Doolittle's Connecticut Regiment and was stationed at New Haven where he served until he was discharged.

In April 1780 he enlisted for one year in Captain Bett's Company in Colonel Hoyt's Regiment at Nelson's Point, opposite West Point, New York. He was detached by Baron Steuben and transferred to Colonel Swift's Regiment under Captain Henry TenEyck. He marched from Nelson's Point to Peekskill, then to Verpank's Point, then to Fort Lee in New Jersey. He was then transferred to a Company of Rangers, and after scouting some time, rejoined his Company. Thence he

Jedediah BLANCHARD   093   Jedediah BLANCHARD

marched to Hackensack, New Bridge & to Toway. He then returned to Nelson's Point, where the army went into winter quarters in the highlands in November or December. He afterwards remained at Nelson's Point sixty days and then was returned to Captain Bett's Company in the Highlands until some time in February when he received permission to return home.

During the same month of February, 1781 he enlisted for one year in Captain Samuel Granger's Company of Connecticut State troops, Major Humphrey's Battalion and General Waterbury's Regiment.

Three days before this term had expired he enlisted for three years into Colonel Willet and McKinistry's New York State troops raised for the defense of the Mohawk country. He was ordered to Windsor, Connecticut in the recruiting service where he remained until June, 1782, thence marched to Nobletown, Columbia County, New York, the residence of Colonel McKinstry and while there news arrived that there was a suspension of hostilities and he was discharged.

FAMILY INFORMATION: He married Abigail _____. She was born in 1770. died May 22, 1819 and is buried with her husband.

Children:
Patty   B-1797. D-Apr 4,1839. Bur Itaska Cem,
         Whitney Point,NY.

OTHER INFORMATION: At the close of the war moved to Albany County, New York. In 1800 he moved to Franklin, Delaware County, New York, then to Oxford, Chenango County, New York, and then in 1815 to Lisle, Broome County, New York. He was listed in the 1810 census at Oxford, New York. He applied for a pension Aug 30, 1832, while a resident of Barker, Broome County, New York.

John BLANCHARD   094   John BLANCHARD
   -. 45291 drummer   DAR Patriot Index

RESIDENT DATE: - 1847
TOWN: Pitcher
BIRTH DATE: Mar 12, 1769
BIRTH PLACE: Sutton, Massachusetts
FATHER: *John Blanchard
MOTHER: Sarah Carroll
DEATH DATE: 1847

John BLANCHARD   094   John BLANCHARD

DEATH PLACE: Pitcher, New York
CEMETERY: Upper Cincinnatus
LOCATION: Cincinnatus, New York (Cortland County)
     *Captain in Revolutionary War. Pension #S 45290

TOMBSTONE INSCRIPTION: John Blanchard Jr
  (Plaque found in the   Drummer Mass Line
  Kellogg Library in   Revolutionary War
  Cincinnatus, New York-   1767   1847
  acquired for his grave)

SERVICE: At the age of twelve he was a drummer boy in Captain Hutchinson's Company, Colonel Davis' Regiment. Enlisted Jan 26, 1781 for three years. On his pension application # 45291 he stated that he enlisted in Sutton, Massachusetts, in February 1780 (wrong by year); that he joined the army at West Point, New York, in April or May following, and that he was discharged at Newburgh, New York, in 1783.

FAMILY INFORMATION: Married Sep 3, 1786 at Sutton, Worcester County, Massachusetts to Huldah **Carroll**, a daughter of Jonathan and Elizabeth **Carroll** and a niece of his mother. She was born Apr 5, 1767 at Sutton, Massachusetts, died Sep 11, 1820 at Cincinnatus, New York and is buried with her husband. He married second Sarah **Dixon**.

Children:
  John   B-1790. M-Diana _____ in Maine,NY.
  Sally   B-Aug 06,1794. M-Asa **Potter**. M2-Benjamin
           Davis in Honeoye,NY. (in War of 1812).
           D-Sep 17,1861 at Honeoye Falls,NY.
  Huldah   B-1796. M-Moses **Bennett**. M2-Nathan
           Slossom. D-Oct,1859.
  Lydia   B-Nov 28,1798 in Union,ME.
  Jonas   B-1801. D-1802 in Union,ME.
  Nancy   B-Jun 07,1803 in Union,ME. M-1829 to Eben
           Adams of Pitcher,NY.
  Isaac   B-1806. D-after 1827.
  Lovey   B-1810. M-Ebenezer (Ichabod) **Crittenden**
           in Pitcher,NY. (Son of Ebenezer
           Crittenden)

OTHER INFORMATION: On Apr 27, 1818 in the town of Cincinnatus, New York. Also on Jan 18, 1819. On Sep 12, 1820 he is listed as a farmer, now a day laborer at Cincinnatus, New York.

Elisha **BLOUNT**   095   Elisha **BLOUNT**
     W. 16850 Private

RESIDENT DATE: - 1820
TOWN: Lincklaen
BIRTH DATE: Jun 19, 1763
BIRTH PLACE: Preston, Connecticut (New London Co.)
FATHER: Ambrose **Blount**
MOTHER: Johanna **Clark**
DEATH DATE: Dec 26, 1835
DEATH PLACE:
CEMETERY:
LOCATION:

TOMBSTONE INSCRIPTION:

SERVICE: He enlisted, in the fall of 1778, for service as a substitute for Daniel Walton, of the town of Norwich, Connecticut, who had been drafted as a militia man. He went to New London, Connecticut, and from there to Black Point, west of New London and served as such substitute for the term of two months under Captain Moses Park and Lieutenant Mail; the regiment was under Adjutant Root. He then enlisted on board the privateer ship "Deponent" commanded by Captain Smedley for the term of six months in the spring of 1779. Immediately after his return, he enlisted into the Company of Captain Jabez Fitch of Norwich, Connecticut for the term of eight months and marched to New London, and from there to New Haven; discharged by Colonel Mott who commanded the Regiment; Joseph Winter was the Lieutenant. Entered the service again, for three months, in September 1780, as a substitute for Zephanah Bliss of Norwich, Connecticut, and went to New London; he along with twenty of his Company was detached and sent to Goshen Point in the town of Lyme for guard duty under Lieutenant David Bates.

FAMILY INFORMATION: Married Sep 10, 1782 at Preston, Connecticut to Sally _____. She was born in 1768 in the State of New York.

    Children:
      William   B-1789.
      Elias   B-1791.
      Elijah   B-1795.
      Walter   B-1797.
      Lemuel   B-1799.
      Pharoah   B-1801.
      Joseph   B-1803.
      Harry   B-1805.

| Elisha | BLOUNT | 095 | Elisha | BLOUNT |

Ezra	B-1807.
Dolly	B-1809. M-Eli D. **Catlin** (B-Sep 17,1784; Son of Elisha and Roxanna [**Dewey**] **Catlin**; D-1838; Bur Woodlawn Cem, Lincklaen,NY).
Mehitable	B-1811.
Sally	B-1813.

OTHER INFORMATION: He removed from Norwich, Connecticut to Greenbush, New York, and from thence to Oneida County, and then to Chenango County, New York, and then, about 1820, to the town of Basse, Orleans County, New York. He was granted a pension on his application filed from Genesse County, dated Oct 15, 1832, while a resident of Basse, Orleans County, New York. His widow was granted a pension on an application dated Sep 15, 1838, while a resident of Lincklaen, Chenango County, New York.

David F BONESTEEL   096   **David F BONESTEEL**
     R.   470 Private

RESIDENT DATE: 1848
TOWN: Smithville/German
BIRTH DATE: 1758
BIRTH PLACE: Claverack, New York
FATHER:
MOTHER:
DEATH DATE: Feb 20, 1848
DEATH PLACE: Smithville, New York
CEMETERY: Upper
LOCATION: Smithville, New York

TOMBSTONE INSCRIPTION: David F. Bonesteel
                                    Died
                               Feb. 20. 1849
                                Ae 96 yrs.

SERVICE: While residing in Claverack, New York he served with the New York Troops in May or June, 1775 for one week, no officers given, marched to Fort Stanwix to drive back the Indians, who had already gone back; from April, 1776, eight months and three days under Captain Henry Stupplebean, Colonel Hogoboom and General Van Rensselaer; and from April, 1777, six months and eight days under the same officers.

David F BONESTEEL			096		David F	BONESTEEL

FAMILY INFORMATION: Married to Susanna Meyers (Majerin).

Children:
  Geertruy Bp-Sep 21,1794 at Reformed Protestant
            Dutch Church, Wynantskill, Rensselaer
            Co,NY.
  Catharina Bp-Nov 23,1800 at Gilead Evangelical
            Lutheran Church, Center Brunswick,
            Rensselaer Co,NY.
  Frederich Bp-Oct 25,1805 at Gilead Evangelical
            Lutheran Church, Center Brunswick,
            Rensselaer Co,NY.

OTHER INFORMATION: Five or six years after the Revolution he moved to Troy and lived fifteen or sixteen years, then moved to Otsego County, where he lived twelve or fourteen years, and then in German, New York. He applied for pension Sep 21, 1832, at which time he was living in German, Chenango County, New York. His wife applied for a pension on March 27, 1854 through Cortland County, while a resident of German, Chenango County, New York.

Joshua BORDEN			097		Joshua BORDEN
        W. 16855 Private

RESIDENT DATE:			wife
TOWN:			Norwich
BIRTH DATE:		Apr 22, 1756
BIRTH PLACE:
FATHER:			John Borden
MOTHER:			Susannah Pearse
DEATH DATE:		Dec 29/30, 1825
DEATH PLACE:		Middletown, New York (Delaware County)
CEMETERY:
LOCATION:

TOMBSTONE INSCRIPTION:

SERVICE: While residing in Pomfret, Connecticut he enlisted Mar 1, 1778 and served as private in Captain Daniel Tyler's Company of artillery, marched to New London, where his Company was under Colonel Ledyard; in the summer of 1778, was in the battle of Rhode Island, at which time he was under Colonel Crane and General Sullivan, and was discharged about Mar 1, 1779; he again enlisted Mar 1, 1781, served as private in Captain James Dana's Company, Colonel Humphrey's

Joshua BORDEN   097   Joshua BORDEN

Connecticut Regiment, was in a skirmish at Throg's Point and was discharged after having served one year.

FAMILY INFORMATION: He married Mar 11, 1779 at Pomfret, Connecticut to Elizabeth (Betsey) **Pierce**, a daughter of Nathaniel and Priscilla **Pierce**. She was born May 14, 1756 at Pomfret, Windham County, Connecticut.

Children: all born Portsmouth, Newport, Rhode Island.
  Joseph H B-1781. M-Philura **Beckwith**
            (B-Apr 12,1788). D-Sep 14,1806.
  Richard   B-1783.
  John   B-1785.
  Sarah   B-1787. M-_____ **Kelley**.
  Susan   B-1790. M-George **Meade**.

OTHER INFORMATION: His widow applied for pension on an application dated Jul 17, 1837 while a resident of Norwich, Chenango County, New York.

Jabez **BOSS**   098   Jabez **BOSS**
        W. 16508 Private   DAR Patriot Index

RESIDENT DATE: 1818 - 1828
TOWN: Smyrna/Sherburne
BIRTH DATE: Mar 23, 1759
BIRTH PLACE: Rhode Island
FATHER:
MOTHER:
DEATH DATE: Jul 17, 1828
DEATH PLACE: Sherburne, New York
CEMETERY: Reynolds
LOCATION: Smyrna, New York

TOMBSTONE INSCRIPTION: A veteran of 1776
    (monument)   2nd R. I. Inft.
                             Jabes Boss.
                             1756 - 1832
                                 and
                                Sarah
                             1760 - 1843
                              His wife

SERVICE: In the battle of Trenton and Princeton, 1776; Captain James Tew; Colonel Lippett, Rhode Island line 12 months. June 1778 enlisted as private under Captain James Parker, Colonel Crary - fifteen months.

Jabez **BOSS** 098 Jabez **BOSS**

FAMILY INFORMATION: Married in 1779 or 1780 at South Kingston, Rhode Island to Sarah **Brayman**. She was born on Dec 28, 1757 and died Jan 18, 1842 at Smyrna, New York. She is buried with her husband.

Children:
Fannie   B-Mar 31,1786. D-1847 in Smyrna,NY.
           Bur Reynolds Cem, Smyrna,NY.
Soloman B B-Jul 25,1790. M-May 25,1813 to Catherine
           Knowles (B-1790;D-1834). D-Feb 27,1853.
           Both bur Reynolds Cem, Smyrna,NY.
Benjamin   B-Feb 18,1793.
Waity   B-Jun 29,1798. D-1875 in Smyrna,NY.
           Bur Reynolds Cem, Smyrna,NY.
Jessie   B-Jun 29,1798.
Jeremiah M B-Jul 07,1803.
David
Charles
Percy
Mary   M-Elnathan **Austin**.

OTHER INFORMATION: He was a pensioner in 1818. He moved to Sherburne in the Fall of 1827.

Timothy **BOSWORTH** 099 Timothy **BOSWORTH**
         W. 20738 Private   DAR Patriot Index

RESIDENT DATE: 1806 - 1837
TOWN: Pharsalia
BIRTH DATE: Feb 22, 1758
BIRTH PLACE: Bristol, Rhode Island
FATHER: William **Bosworth**
MOTHER: Mary **Fales**
DEATH DATE: Aug 17, 1837
DEATH PLACE: Pharsalia, New York
CEMETERY: Bosworth
LOCATION: East Pharsalia, New York

TOMBSTONE INSCRIPTION:
   (tilted back - has DAR marker)
                              Nancy Bosworth
      In   Died
   Memory of   Aug 3 1846
   Mr. Timothy   Aged 84 yrs.
    Bosworth   & 9 mo's
    Who died   Dust to its narrow house beneath
     Aug 17   Soul to its place on high
  1837 ae 79 y   They that have seen may with in death
  5 m and 27 d   No more may fear to die.

Timothy BOSWORTH   099   Timothy BOSWORTH

Should justice call us
  to the bar
  no man alive is
  guiltless there.

SERVICE: While he was a resident of Providence, Rhode Island, enlisted in April or May 1776, and served as a private in Captain Loring Peck's Company in a Rhode Island Regiment commanded first by Colonel Henry Babcock and then by Colonel Christopher Lippitt. He was in the battles of White Plains and Trenton and was discharged in October or November, 1777. He again enlisted in 1777 and served about one hundred days as a private engaged in guard duty, officers not stated. During Sullivan's Expedition he served fifteen days as a private under Captain Alter and was in a battle with the British. In September 1778 he again entered the service, at Boston, on board the sloop, "General Stark", under Captain Benjamin Pierce, and served until Dec 25, 1778. In January 1779 he entered the service at Providence, Rhode Island, on board the letter of Marque, "Star and Garter", under Captain Tredwell, was out about two months, when he was taken prisoner, placed on board the prison ship "Widbey", and confined one year. He was then placed on board a Tory brig, which was wrecked, enabling him to escape.

FAMILY INFORMATION: Married Jun 6, 1784 in Bristol, Rhode Island to Nancy **Monroe**, a daughter of William and Elizabeth **Monroe**. She was born Nov 12, 1761, died Aug 3, 1846 in Pharsalia, New York and is buried with her husband.

Children: (all except last 2 born at Bristol, RI.
  Allen   B-Apr 13,1785. M-Eunice **Brown**
           (B-Jan 22,1787; Dau of Rev War Vet
           Nathan and Eunice [**Brown**] **Brown**;
           D-Jun 1,1813; Bur Center Cem, Pharsalia,
           NY). M2-Almira **Coggeshall**
           (B-Aug 3,1793 Bristol,RI; Dau of Rev War
           Vet James and Martha [**Turner**]
           Coggeshall; D-Jul 16,1831; Bur
           Bosworth Cem, Pharsalia,NY). M3-Betsey
           (**Stanton**) **Gay** (B-1808; D-Sep 15,1892;
           Bur Mt Hope Cem, Norwich,NY).
           D-May 13,1861. Bur Bosworth Cem,
           Pharsalia,NY.
  William B-Mar 12,1787. D-Havana or Guadaloupe.

Timothy   BOSWORTH   099   Timothy   BOSWORTH

George   B-Sep 14,1789. M-Prudence **Brown** (Dau of
            Nehemiah and Barbara [**Stewart**] Brown;
            B-Nov 08,1792; D-Jun 17,1842; Bur
            Bosworth Cem, Pharsalia,NY). M2-Eunice
            (**Morgan**) **Coggeshall** (B-Apr 3,1795;
            Dau of Sanford and Sylvia [**Punderson**]
            Morgan; M1-Nicholas **Coggeshall**
            [B-Apr 13,1790 in Bristol,RI; Son of
            Rev War Vet James and Martha [**Turner**]
            Coggeshall; D-Mar 30,1830 Pharsalia,
            NY; Bur Northwest Corner Cem, Pharsalia,
            NY]. D-Oct 2,1881 at Willett,NY).
            D-Feb 25,1866 at East Pharsalia,NY.
Gardner   B-Feb 21,1792. M-Nancy **Frink**
            (B-Dec 20,1790; Dau of Rev War Vet
            Prentice and Prudence [**Frink**] **Frink**;
            D-Mar 31,1872 at McDonough, NY). In the
            War of 1812. D-Sep 16,1859 McDonough,NY.
            Both bur Union Cem, McDonough,NY.
Polly M   B-Sep 18,1794. M-Jonathan **Fargo** (B-1789;
            Son of Joshua and Sarah **Fargo**; In War
            of 1812; D-May 13,1845 at Pharsalia,NY).
            D-Jan 31,1854 at Pharsalia,NY. Both bur
            Northwest Corner Cem, Pharsalia,NY.
Timothy   B-Oct 20,1797.M-May 23,1819 Betsey **Pabody**
            (B-Mar 10,1800 Norwich,NY; D-Jul 4,1877
            Norwich,NY). D-Feb 11,1855 Norwich,NY.
Elizabeth   B-Nov 06,1799. M-1817 Gilbert **Fargo**
            (B-1799; Son of Joshua and Sarah **Fargo**;
            D-Apr 30,1879 at Pharsalia,NY).
            D-Nov 17,1880 at Pharsalia,NY. Both bur
            Northwest Corner Cem, Pharsalia,NY.
Ruth   B-Dec 03,1801. M-Joseph **Lord**
            (B-Aug 27,1796; Son of Rev War Vet
            Joseph and Caroline [**Sterling**] **Lord**;
            D-Apr 9,1854; Bur Ufford Cem, Pitcher,
            NY).
William   B-Sep 08,1804. M-Jan 15,1829 Betsey W
            Peck (Dau of Nathaniel and Mary
            [**Wilson**] **Peck**; B-Dec 31,1810 Amenia,
            NY; D-Nov 5,1857). D-Jan 30,1866.
Nancy Ann   B-Jul 25,1807. M-Jan 1,1827 Luther **Brooks**
            (B-1806; Son of Calvin and Betsey
            Brooks; D-Jan 9,1892 at Norwich,NY).
            D-Aug 17,1869 at Norwich,NY.
            Both are bur Mt Hope Cem, Norwich,NY.

Timothy BOSWORTH   099   Timothy BOSWORTH

OTHER INFORMATION: He came to Pharsalia, Chenango County, New York, from Bristol, Rhode Island and settled on lot #53 about a mile and a half north of East Pharsalia. He advanced in the State Militia to the rank of Second Major. He was allowed pension on his application executed Sep 29, 1832, while a resident of Pharsalia, New York.

John   BOWERS   100   John   BOWERS
       R.   1073 Private

RESIDENT DATE: 1805 - 1831
TOWN: Plymouth
BIRTH DATE: Nov 23, 1757
BIRTH PLACE: Dudley, Massachusetts (Worcester Co.)
FATHER: John Bowers
MOTHER: Rebecca Carpenter
DEATH DATE: Jan 08, 1831
DEATH PLACE: Norwich, New York
CEMETERY:
LOCATION:

TOMBSTONE INSCRIPTION:

SERVICE: Enlisted for the term of nine months about Apr 15, 1776 in the town of Thompson, Connecticut in the Company commanded by Captain Stephen Lyon in the Regiment commanded by Colonel John Chester in the Connecticut line. He continued to serve in the said Corps until about Feb 15, 1777, when he was discharged in Peekskill, New York. He was in the battle of Long Island.

FAMILY INFORMATION: Married on Mar 7, 1780 in Dudley, Massachusetts to Sarah Inman a daughter of Elisha Inman of Gloucester, Rhode Island. She was born in 1764 and died Aug 1, 1837 in Norwich, New York.

Children:
  Mary   B-Apr 12,1780 Dudley,MA. M-Palmer Edmonds
              (B-1785; D-Apr 21,1865). D-Mar 13,1843.
              Both bur Quarter Cem, Norwich,NY.
  Charles   B-Jan 12,1783 at Dudley,MA.
  Stephen   B-Nov 13,1784 at Thompson,CT. M-_____.
              D-1865 in Oxford,NY.
  Alpheus   B-Aug 13,1787 Thompson,CT. M-Esther _____
              (B-1780; D-Oct 5,1872; bur East Side
              Cem, Afton,NY).
  Huldah   B-Aug 24,1789 at Thompson,CT.

| John   BOWERS | 100 | John   BOWERS |

Sarah   B-Apr 03,1791 at Thompson,CT. M-Benjamin
           Jones. D-Jan 22,1867. Bur North Norwich
           Cem, North Norwich,NY.
John   B-Dec 20,1792 at Thompson,CT.
Rebecca   B-Nov 28,1795 Dudley,MA. M-___ Brookins.
Ephraim   B-May 08,1797 Dudley,MA. M-Dec 31,1817 to
           Esther Crandall (B-Jul 6,1798 Leyden,
           MA; Dau of Joseph and Esther [Crumb]
           Crandall. D-Sep 15,1866.)
Gilbert   B-Apr 10,1801 at Dudley,MA. M-Delilah
           Hancock (B-1800 in CT; Dau of Nathan
           and Phebe [Palmer] Hancock;
           D-Feb 3,1857; bur South Plymouth Cem,
           Plymouth,NY).
Lucy   B-Nov 10,1802 Dudley,MA. M-Orrin Belden.
Barnabus   B-Jan 26,1805 Dudley,MA. M-Patty Hancock
           (B-1805 in CT; Dau of Nathan and Phebe
           [Palmer] Hancock).

OTHER INFORMATION: On Feb 12, 1824, while a resident of Plymouth, Chenango County, New York he made an application for pension, which was rejected on the grounds that his service was rendered in a State Regiment and not on the Continental establishment.

| Jabez   BREED | 101 | Jabez   BREED |
| W. 19621 Private |

RESIDENT DATE: wife
TOWN: McDonough
BIRTH DATE: Feb 24, 1758
BIRTH PLACE: Stonington, Connecticut
FATHER: Allen Breed
MOTHER: Hannah Dewey
DEATH DATE: Oct, 1818
DEATH PLACE: North Stonington, Connecticut
CEMETERY:
LOCATION:

TOMBSTONE INSCRIPTION:

SERVICE: In 1776 he enlisted for a six-month period in Captain Latham Avery's Company, Colonel Oliver Smith's Regiment, Lieutenant Colonel Ely. He was at White Plains and other places. In 1777 he was at Groton and New London under Captain Elijah Avery for three months. In 1778 his service consisted of four months in Captain Benjamin Clark's Company at Groton Heights. In 1780 for five months and eleven months in Captain

Jabez BREED

William Richard's Company. In the fall of 1782 he spent two weeks at New London.

FAMILY INFORMATION: He married Jan 3, 1782 at Stonington, New London County, Connecticut to Sarah (Sally) **Chapman**, a daughter of Andrew and Hannah (**Smith**) **Chapman**. She was born Sep 4, 1766 at Stonington, Connecticut. She married second Hosea **Wheeler**, son of Jeremiah and Anna (**Pellet**) **Wheeler**. Hosea had married first on Feb 18, 1772 to Bridget **Grant**, a daughter of Oliver and Ann Borodel (**Billings**) **Grant**, born Sep 24, 1751 and died Sep 8, 1819. Hosea died Jul 13, 1829.

Children: (All born Stonington, Connecticut)
Sally	B-Mar 22,1783.
Hannah	B-Dec 18,1784.
Jabish	B-Sep 06,1786. M-Chloe **Eldridge**.
Polly	B-Apr 07,1788.
Andrew	B-Jan 25,1790.
Martha	B-Aug 19,1791.
Allyn	B-May 10.1793.
Gershom	B-Feb 10,1795.
Lucy	B-Mar 21,1797.
William	B-Jan 10,1799.
Anna	B-Jan 26,1801.
Abel	B-Oct 13,1805.
(female)	M-William P **Peabody**. Resided in McDonough,NY in 1840.

OTHER INFORMATION: He was sometime called Jabish. His widow filed a pension application dated Feb 12, 1840 while a resident of McDonough, Chenango County, New York. She was living with a son-in-law, William P Peabody. She filed for a BLW dated Mar 30, 1855 while a resident of Unadilla, New York.

Joseph BREED
W. 25282 Private   DAR Patriot Index

RESIDENT DATE: - 1850
TOWN: Lincklaen
BIRTH DATE: 1761
BIRTH PLACE: Charlestown, Massachusetts (Suffolk Co)
FATHER: Joseph **Breed**
MOTHER: Lydia **Bacon**
DEATH DATE: Jul 12, 1850
DEATH PLACE: Lincklaen, New York
CEMETERY: Woodlawn

| Joseph BREED | 102 | Joseph BREED |

LOCATION: Lincklaen, New York

TOMBSTONE INSCRIPTION: (Newer type stone)
Joseph
Breed
Pvt.
Poor's Regt.
Mass. Mil.
Rev. War
July 12, 1850

SERVICE: He enlisted at Hopkinton, Massachusetts where he resided in August or September 1777 in Captain Winch's Company, for three months, but continued for four months. Went to Vermont, thence to Ticonderoga then in possession of the enemy but soon taken by our troops. Reached Saratoga the night before General Burgoyne surrendered. To Albany, to Red Hook, to White Plains. Discharged in December. Enlisted in the summer of 1779 at Hopkinton under Lieutenant Claflin, Colonel Poor's Regiment. To West Point. Employed in common duty and in repairing and building forts. Discharged at West Point after six months. In the spring of 1780 he went to West Point and enlisted under Lieutenant Robert Muzzy of the continental army, Colonel Bedlow's Regiment. Served eight months. He was present at the taking of Ticongeroga and the surrender of Burgoyne.

FAMILY INFORMATION: Married Dec 12, 1786 at Hillsdale, Columbia County New York to Anna **Hutchinson**. She was born 1769 in Rhode Island.

Children:
William   B-1790 Hillsdale,NY.
Samuel   B-1794 Hillsdale,NY.
Obadiah   B-1795 Green River,NY.
Sylvia   B-1796. M-1821 to John **Pride** (B-1798; D-1874). D-1858.

OTHER INFORMATION: After the war he went to Green River, New York where he resided about 12 or 15 years. Then to Butternuts, New York where he resided perhaps 20 years. Then to Truxton, Cortland County, New York, where he resided for 15 years up to the point he applied for his pension on Sep 25, 1832. His widow was allowed pension on her application executed Nov 1, 1851, at which time she resided in Lincklaen, New York. In 1855, she was still residing in Lincklaen.

Joseph BREED

```
RESIDENT DATE:   1797 - 1828
TOWN:            Pharsalia
BIRTH DATE:      Feb 21, 1763
BIRTH PLACE:     Stonington, Connecticut
FATHER:          Allen Breed
MOTHER:          Hannah Dewey
DEATH DATE:      Sep 14, 1828
DEATH PLACE:     Pharsalia, New York
CEMETERY:        Center
LOCATION:        Pharsalia, New York
```

TOMBSTONE INSCRIPTION: In
Memory of
Joseph Breed
Who died
Sept 14 1828
Aged 66 years
7 months
& 6 days
But shall in silent accents he doth say,
prepare to mingle with your fellow clay.
In
Memory of
Rhody wife of
Joseph Breed
Who died Dec 9th
1827 aged
60 years
& 19
Days
She sleeps in Jesus and is blessed
how kind her slumbers are.

SERVICE: At the age of sixteen he enlisted and served in the militia.

FAMILY INFORMATION: Married in 1783 to Rhody Greene. She was born in 1767, died Dec 9, 1827 and is buried with her husband.

```
Children:
  Caleb      B-Jul 12,1785 in CT. M-Mar 1,1805 to Polly
             Dye (B-1784; D-Sep 24,1864).
             D-Jan 5,1857. Both bur Center Cem,
             Pharsalia,NY.
  Lucy       B-1787. M-Lewis Brown (B-1780; son of
             Nehemiah and Rebecca [Lewis] Brown;
             D-Mar 25,1818; Bur Center Cem,
             Pharsalia,NY).
```

| Joseph | BREED | 103 | Joseph BREED |

Rhoda B-Jul 1,1789 Westerly,RI. M-William **Lewis**
       (B-Oct 26,1782 in Westerly,RI; son of
       William and Hannah [**Thompson**] **Lewis**;
       D-Nov 1,1853). D-Nov 10,1878.
       Both bur Center Cem, Pharsalia,NY.
Joseph B-1790. M-Hannah **Sisson** (B-1792;
       D-May 15,1843). D-Jun 25,1844. Both bur
       Center Cem, Pharsalia,NY.
Hannah B-1793. M-Elem **Eldredge** (B-1794; D-1856).
       D-1864 at pitcher,NY. Both bur North
       Pitcher Church, Pitcher,NY.
Jabish B-1796. M-Chloe **Eldredge**. M-Louisa
       Eldridge (B-1798; D-Mar 22,1832; Bur
       Center Cem, Pharsalia,NY). D-1858.
Polly B-1800. M-Seth **Sabin**. D-1864 Spencer,NY.
Russel B-1803. M-Rebecca **Congdon**. D-1867. Both
       died at Chilton,WI.
Philura B-1805. M-Mar 8,1832 to Elisha **Gardner**
       (B-1806; son of Townsend and Thankful
       [**Geer**] **Gardner**). D-1864.
Clarissa B-1807. Unmarried. D-Apr 14,1825. Bur
       Center Cem, Pharsalia,NY.

OTHER INFORMATION: Migrated to Pharsalia, Chenango
County, New York in the early 1800's and settled in
the west part of the town.

Elisha BREWER   104   Elisha   BREWER
        W. 10454 Private

RESIDENT DATE: 1834
TOWN: Lincklaen
BIRTH DATE: Mar 23, 1766   (Stone must be wrong)
BIRTH PLACE: Tyringham, Massachusetts (Berkshire Co)
FATHER: Joseph **Brewer**
MOTHER: Jane
DEATH DATE: Feb 13, 1857
DEATH PLACE:
CEMETERY: City
LOCATION: Conneaut, Ohio   (Ashtabula County)

TOMBSTONE INSCRIPTION: (Four sided monument)
    Elisha Brewer   Amos Darling   P. M. Darling
    1757 - 1857   1790 - 1854   1822 - 1889
                         Fanny A   Adaline
    Leon Darling   His wife   His wife
    1858,   1787 - 1881   1832 - 1898
    G. W. Darling   DARLING
    1859 - 1909

Elisha BREWER   104   Elisha BREWER

SERVICE: While residing at Tyringham, Massachusetts he entered service in May 1782 serving as a private for one year in Captain Alden's Company, Colonel Ebenezer Sprout's Second Massachusetts Regiment. He marched to West Point and from West Point to Philadelphia, where he was involved in preventing a group of men from breaking open the bank to forcibly acquire their pay. Later at West Point he assisted in carrying the great chain from the river, helped get the cannon into the park, and helped dig a trench to set pickets.

FAMILY INFORMATION: He married Oct 18, 1788 in New Marlboro, Berkshire County, Massachusetts to Polly **Fitch**, a daughter of Joseph and Mary **Fitch**. She was born Aug 2, 1767 New Marlboro, Massachusetts. He married second Jul 21, 1841 at Ashtabula, Ohio to Chloe **Wellman**.

Children: ?

OTHER INFORMATION: After the war he lived at Tyringham, Massachusetts for a short time, then for a period of about eleven years at New Marlboro, Massachusetts; then removed to New Cannan, New York, where he lived for seven years. He then removed to Lincklaen, Chenango County, New York. A pension was granted on May 09, 1834 while a resident of Lincklaen, Chenango County, New York. He was listed in the census of pensioners from Virgil, Cortland County in 1840. His pension was transferred to Ashtabula, Ohio.

John BREWER   105   John BREWER
W. 01706 Private   DAR Patriot Index

RESIDENT DATE: 1808 - 1846
TOWN: Plymouth
BIRTH DATE: Aug 23, 1764
BIRTH PLACE: Colebrook, New York (Westchester County)
FATHER: Henry **Brewer**
MOTHER:
DEATH DATE: Nov 29, 1846
DEATH PLACE:
CEMETERY: Aldrich
LOCATION: Norwich, New York

John   BREWER

TOMBSTONE INSCRIPTION: John Brewer
                      Died
                      Nov 20, 1846
                      Aged 82 yrs.

John   BREWER

Mary
Wife of
John Brewer
Died
April 5, 1851,
Aged 84 years

SERVICE: While a resident of Stillwater, Saratoga County, New York, he served as a Private with the New York Troops as follows: From about the first of February, 1777, until the first of January, 1778, in Captain Silas Gray's Company in Colonel Van Vechten's Regiment, and was in the battle of Bemus Heights, in the siege of Saratoga and at the surrender of Burgoyne. From January, 1778 until 1781 he served various short tours during alarms, length of service not given, was under Captain's Ephraim Woodworth, Cornelius Baldwin, Peter Van Vort, Hezekiah Dunham, Washburn and Sherwood, and was in a skirmish near Fort George. From about March 1781, nine months in Captain's Holt Dunham's and Silas Gray's Companies in Colonel Marinus Willett's Regiment. Immediately after the expiration of the last noted service, he enlisted and served until May or June 1782, in Captain's Job Wright's and Peter B Tearce's Companies in Colonel Marinus Willet's Regiment.

He also served in the War of 1812 for three months as a Private under Lieutenant Colonel Thompson Mead in the 17th Regiment of New York militia and was in the battle of Queenstown.

FAMILY INFORMATION: Married in 1784 to Mary **Twist**. She was born on Jun 27, 1766, died Apr 5, 1851 and is buried with her husband.

Children:
  Jacob T   B-Sep 02,1784.
  Joseph D   B-Apr 24,1786.
  Henry   B-Dec 02,1788. M-Dec 2,1812 to Lucinda
             Johnson.
  David   B-Oct 20,1790.
  Joel F   B-Sep 07,1791. M-**Nancy Brewer** (B-1790;
             D-Feb 18,1878; Bur North Norwich Cem,
             North Norwich,NY).
  Nancy   B-Jun 16,1793.
  James W   B-Feb 19,1795.
  John   B-Feb 23,1797.
  Zara   B-Feb 19,1799. M-Clarissa _____ (B-1803;
             D-Jun 15,1888). D-Jun 23,1835. Both bur
             Mt Hope Cem, Norwich,N.Y.

John BREWER   105   John BREWER

Jesse F	B-Jan 19,1800. M-Rhoda **Aldrich** (B-Feb 15,1798 in RI; Dau of Joshua and Ruth [**Evans**] **Aldrich**; D-May 4,1884). D-May 22,1882. Both bur South Plymouth Cem, Plymouth,NY.
Peter P	B-Jun 13,1803.
Merit	B-Apr 06,1805.
Esther	B-Jun 18,1807. M-Ethan A. **Aldrich** (B-Apr 15,1801; Son of Gardner and Anne [**Colwell**] **Aldrich**; D-Jan 17,1885 at Addison,NY). D-Oct 26,1882 at Elmira,NY.
Polly	B-Oct 07,1808.
Olive	B-Nov 18,1811.

OTHER INFORMATION: He was allowed a pension on his application executed Aug 13, 1832 while a resident of Plymouth, New York.

Nathan   BREWSTER   106   Nathan   BREWSTER
         W. 5230 Private

RESIDENT DATE: 1811
TOWN: New Berlin
BIRTH DATE: Dec 24, 1758
BIRTH PLACE: New Windsor, New York (Ulster-now
FATHER: Orange County)
MOTHER:
DEATH DATE:
DEATH PLACE:
CEMETERY:
LOCATION:

TOMBSTONE INSCRIPTION:

SERVICE: He enlisted at New Windsor, Ulster County, New York in July, 1776 and served for ten days in Captain John Nichols' Company, under Lieutenant Colonel James McLanghery of the New York Line. Marched to Fort Constitution, then to Fort Montgomery on the Hudson River. In November, 1776 under General Clinton marched to New Jersey, then returned home the middle of January, 1777. In March, 1777 with the same Company and Regiment was called to put a chain across the Hudson River at Fort Montgomery where they detained about a week. April 1, 1777 he was drafted to garrison Fort Clinton and Montgomery for four months under Captain James Humphrey, Lieutenant Colonel Jas McLanghery, and Colonel Levi Paulding. Again called to Fort Montgomery for about a week due to some movement

Nathan BREWSTER   106   Nathan BREWSTER

of the British troops. Early in 1778 under Captain Christian VanDeusen in New Cornwall, Orange County, New York. Was in the Battle of Monmouth and helped build a fort at West Point called Fort Putnam involving two weeks. In June, 1779, under Captain Van Deusen, marched to Haverstraw near Stoney Point and camped, for two weeks, on Captain Hutchins' farm to watch the operation of the British at Stoney Point. Colonel Jesse Woodhull was commanding. He returned home when Wayne's army arrived. In October, 1779 was called to Fishkill, Dutchess County, New York for one month under Captain Van Deusen. In July, 1780 helped build fortress #3 at West Point with Zachariah DuBois commanding.

FAMILY INFORMATION: He married Jul 31, 1797 in Butternuts, New York to Hannah **Parker**, a daughter of Reuben and Hannah **Parker**. She was born in 1769.

Children:
Nathaniel B-Aug 25,1798. Resided in Augusta,OH.
Deborah   B-Apr 09,1800.
Martha   B-Jul 28,1802.
John C   B-Aug 19,1804. M-Aug 16,1830/1 to Eliza
           Watson.
Matilda   B-Aug 23,1806.
Maria   B-Aug 23,1806.
Nancy   B-Oct 09,1808.
Sarah Ann B-Jun 08,1811 in New Berlin,NY.
           M-Mar 17,1831 to John **Canning**.

OTHER INFORMATION: He applied for a pension on an application dated Oct 16, 1832, while a resident of Augusta Township, Columbiana County, Ohio. After the war he lived in Newburgh, New York until May, 1785; then moved to New York City, New York for two years; then moved back to Orange County, New York for one year; then moved to Saratoga, then a part of Albany County, New York; then to the town of Albany, New York; then to the town of Albany, New York; then to Salem, Washington County, New York for five years; then to Otsego County, New York for ten or eleven years; then to Chenango County for four years; then to Cortland County, New York until Jul 9, 1817; then moved to Columbiana County, Ohio for fourteen months; then to Marietta, Ohio for two years; then to Athens County, Ohio until Apr, 1830; and then to Augusta Township, Carrol County, Ohio. The 1840 pension census has him in Marion, Athens County Ohio at age 82. His widow applied for pension on an application dated Apr

Nathan BREWSTER   106   Nathan BREWSTER

18, 1855, while a resident of New Plymouth, Vinton County, Ohio. At that time Nathan was called "late of Morgan County, Ohio".

Orlando BRIDGEMAN   107   Orlando BRIDGEMAN
-. ----- Civil Service   DAR Patriot Index

RESIDENT DATE: 1790 - 1813
TOWN: Bainbridge
BIRTH DATE: 1743
BIRTH PLACE:
FATHER: Orlando **Bridgeman**
MOTHER: Martha **Belding**
DEATH DATE: Mar 14, 1813
DEATH PLACE: Bainbridge, New York
CEMETERY:
LOCATION:

TOMBSTONE INSCRIPTION:
        (Wife's stone not found)
    DAR reading--- Martha wife of Orlando D-Apr 5, 1823 ae 79 y.

SERVICE: In 1778 he was on the "Safety Committee" in Hinsdale, New Hampshire.

FAMILY INFORMATION: He married Martha **Wait**, a daughter of Simeon and Martha **Wait**. She was born Oct 5, 1744 in Whately, Franklin County, Massachusetts and died Apr 5, 1823. She is buried in the Guy cemetery in Afton, New York.

Children:
Reuben   B-Nov 29,1764. M-Feb 9,1786 Abigail **Town** (B-Apr 10,1767; Dau of Benjamin and Anna **Town** of Brattleboro,VT; D-killed instantly Jun 28,1798 by a falling well pole). M2-Mar 24,1799 to widow Anna **Goff** (B-Jul 30,1772 in Littlefield, CT; Dau of Isaac and Sarah [**Selkrigg**] **Foote**; D-Dec 29,1850). D-Jul 9,1834 Bainbridge, NY. All three are bur Guy Cem, Afton,NY.
Quartus   B-Jan 24,1769 in Brattleboro or Vernon,VT. M-1792 to Hannah Hitchcock (Dau of David and Hannah [**Merique**] **Hitchcock**; D-Nov 13,1835). D-Jan 9,1835 Syracuse,OH
Miriam   B-Apr 05,1773. M-Josiah **Stowell**. D-second person bur in the Smithboro,NY Cem.

Orlando BRIDGEMAN   107   Orlando BRIDGEMAN

Thomas   B-Jan 25,1777 Brattleboro,VT. M-Jan, 1810
          to Clarrisa **Wait** (B-Sep 14,1786 in
          Bainbridge,NY; Dau of Asa and Submit
          [**Smith**] **Wait**; D-Feb 25,1863 Addison,
          NY). D-Nov 2,1852 in Addison,NY.

OTHER INFORMATION: In 1784 his name appears on a petition to the authorities of the State of Vermont concerning "New York grant troubles". The bitter quarrel regarding the "Hampshire Grants" led to the settlement of Orlando and his sons in New York State. He received his grant July 11, 1786 and moved from Brattleboro within a few years. He settled his four children about him, one and one-half miles below Bettsburgh and died there.

George BRIGGS   108   George BRIGGS
           Ensign   DAR Patriot Index

RESIDENT DATE: 1796 - 1816
TOWN: Smyrna
BIRTH DATE: Apr 4, 1734
BIRTH PLACE: Portsmouth, Rhode Island (Newport Co)
FATHER: Job **Briggs**
MOTHER: Mary
DEATH DATE: 1816
DEATH PLACE: Smyrna, New York
CEMETERY:
LOCATION:

TOMBSTONE INSCRIPTION:

SERVICE: Served as an ensign from the state of Rhode Island in the Revolutionary War.

FAMILY INFORMATION: Married Mar 8, 1756 at Warwick, Rhode Island to Hannah **Wightman**. He married second Sarah **Wells**, a sister of John **Wells** of Goshen. He married third to Lydia _____ .

Children:
  Stephen   B-Nov 05,1756 Warwick,RI.
  John   B-Nov 04,1758 Warwick,RI.
  Giles   B-Feb 07,1761 Warwick,RI.
second wife
  George   B-Apr 29,1767 Warwick,RI. M-widow **Darrow**.
            Resided in Plymouth,NY. D-1835.
  Elizabeth B-Feb 13,1769 Warwick,RI.

George BRIGGS   108   George BRIGGS

    Arnold   B-Mar 23,1770 Warwick,RI. M-Olive **Morie**.
                Resided Smyrna,NY. D-1870.
    Isaac   B-Sep 20,1771 Warwick,RI. M-Sarah _____.
                D-1845.
    Sarah   B-Jan 20,1773. M-Benjamin **Reynolds**
                (B-1774; D-Jan 10,1854). D-Jan 20,1839.
                Both bur Reynolds Cem, Smyrna,NY.
    third wife
    Warren   B-Sep 17,1782. M-1807 to Tryphosa **Gardner**
                (B-Aug 26,1788; D-Aug 13,1841).
                D-Oct 14,1854 in Erie,PA.
    Rufus   M-_____. M2-Sally **Hopkins**. M3-_____.
                B-1783. D-1863.
    Mary   M-Stephen **Austin**. Moved west.

OTHER INFORMATION: Moved from Warwick, Rhode Island to
Albany County, New York in 1782, then to Easton,
Washington County, New York in 1794, thence to Smyrna,
Chenango County, New York in 1796.

Origen **BRIGHAM**   109   Origen **BRIGHAM**
  W. 5931 Surgeons Mate

RESIDENT DATE: wife
TOWN: Norwich
BIRTH DATE: Sep 10, 1757
BIRTH PLACE: New Marlboro, Massachusetts (Berkshire)
FATHER: Francis **Brigham**
MOTHER: Phebe **Ward**
DEATH DATE: Aug 6, 1816
DEATH PLACE: Schoharie, New York (Schoharie County)
CEMETERY: Old Stone Fort Church
LOCATION: Schoharie, New York

TOMBSTONE INSCRIPTION:
                            In
                        Memory of
                    Dr. Origin Brigham
                Who died August 6th 1816
                Aged 58 years 10 months
                        & 27 days
         A peaceful death is rich reward
   the joy of man the blessing of our Lord
      his spirits fled yet his honored name
      may shine in glory & immortal flame
       If honor shines & praises do redound
 he cannot ease the pain of those that feel the wound.

Origen BRIGHAM   109   Origen BRIGHAM

SERVICE: While a resident of New Marlboro, Massachusetts on Aug 1, 1777 he volunteered and served as a surgeons mate in Seth Warner's Regiment of the Massachusetts line. In the fall of 1780 the Regiment was in a battle, near Fort Edward, which nearly cut it to pieces, to the point it was disbanded. He went back to his father's home at that point and returned to the army on April 5, 1781, where he received a commission on Nov 5, 1782. He was discharged Jun 3, 1783.

FAMILY INFORMATION: He married Jan 14, 1784 to Eleanor Soul, a daughter of Moses and Eleanor (Williams) Soul. She was born Apr 18, 1764 in New Marlboro, Massachusetts and died Feb 11, 1852.

Children: ?

OTHER INFORMATION: He was a leading Physician and Surgeon in Schoharie County, New York. He was an original member of the Society of the Cincinnati. His widow applied for a pension on an application dated Nov 23, 1839 while a resident of Norwich, Chenango County, New York.

Hezekiah BROCKETT   110   Hezekiah BROCKETT
     W. 01001 Private

RESIDENT DATE: 1822 - 1851
TOWN: Oxford
BIRTH DATE: Oct 18, 1759
BIRTH PLACE: Wallingford, Connecticut (New Haven Co)
FATHER: Hezekiah Brockett
MOTHER: Hannah Ives
DEATH DATE: Apr 11, 1851
DEATH PLACE: Oxford, New York
CEMETERY: Riverview
LOCATION: Oxford, New York

TOMBSTONE INSCRIPTION:
    Hezekiah Brocket
    Revolutionary soldier
    Died
    Apr. 11, 1851
    Aged 91 years
    I have fought a good fight
    I have finished my _____
    I have kept the Faith

    Aseneth
    Wife of
    Hezekiah Brockett,
    Died
    July 27, 1861
    Aged 76 y'rs.

Hezekiah BROCKETT   110   Hezekiah BROCKETT

SERVICE: Served in the army from 1777 to 1783, first in the Company of Captain Elijah Humphreys, in the 4th Regiment commanded by Colonel Meigs, afterwards in the 3rd Regiment commanded by Colonel Samuel B Webb, in the Company of Captain Betts. He was at the siege of Yorktown, the taking of Stony Point, and the battle of White Plains.

FAMILY INFORMATION: Married first Dec 27, 1783 at Hamden, Connecticut to Ruth **Perkins**, a daughter of James and Margaret **Perkins**. She was born Jul 10, 1760 in Lynn, Connecticut. He married second 1825 at Wallingford, Connecticut (returned for marriage) to Aseneth **Clark**. She was born Sep 26, 1785, died Jul 27, 1861 and is buried in Riverview Cemetery, Oxford, New York.

Children:
  Ephraim   B-1787. D-1870. Bur Riverview Cem, Oxford, NY.
  Hezekiah B-1790. D-Sep 8,1854. Bur Riverview Cem, Oxford,NY.

OTHER INFORMATION: On Apr 3, 1818, he applied for a pension, which was granted Jun 12, 1818. By application dated Nov 11, 1822, his pension was transferred to Chenango County. The old veteran died in Oxford and was buried with military honors. The stars and strips, which in life he loved so well, shrouded his coffin; the booming cannon echoed from hill to hill as his bier passed along; military with glistening muskets and muffled drums formed a guard of honor to the Cemetery. Volleys of musketry were fired over his grave, as the old veteran was left to sleep peacefully, waiting the last great roll call. Mrs Brockett applied for a pension on Feb 19, 1853 which was granted on Jan 3, 1854. On Mar 24, 1855 she applied for a bounty land warrant. This too, was granted, and she obtained 60 acres of land.

Artemas BROOKINS   111   Artemas BROOKINS
    W. 20754 Private   DAR Patriot Index

RESIDENT DATE: wife
TOWN: Norwich
BIRTH DATE: 1757
BIRTH PLACE: Sheffield, Massachusetts
FATHER:
MOTHER:

Artemas BROOKINS   111   Artemas BROOKINS

DEATH DATE: Mar --, 1824 (as recalled)
DEATH PLACE: New York, New York
CEMETERY:
LOCATION:

TOMBSTONE INSCRIPTION:

SERVICE: He enlisted in January, 1777 and served in the Massachusetts line for six years. He served in different Companies under Colonel Joseph Royce. He was given the Badge of Merit for six years of faithful service. He was at the taking of General Burgoyne at Saratoga. Received a small wound in 1777. Was at the taking of Lord Cornwallis and was also in action at Rhode Island under Colonel Sprout. He was discharged June, 1783 in New Windsor, New York.

FAMILY INFORMATION: He married at Spencertown (now Hillsdale), Columbia County, New York in May, 1784 to Lois **Johnson**. She was born in 1762.

Children: (8)
  John   B-May,1791. M-Rebekah ___ (B-Oct 29,1797).
            Resided Norwich,NY. 4th child.
  Frederick   B-1802. Resided in Norwich,NY.
  Clarinda   B-1802.
  Sally   B-1805.

OTHER INFORMATION: He lived in Stockbridge, Massachusetts and then moved to Spencertown (now Hillsdale), Columbia County, New York. He was a Ships Carpenter until 1808 when he was affected by rheumatism. He applied for pension on an application dated Apr 17, 1818 while a resident of New York, New York. His widow applied Sep 16, 1841 while a resident of Norwich, Chenango County, New York.

Levi **BROOKS**   112   Levi **BROOKS**

RESIDENT DATE: 1829
TOWN: Norwich
BIRTH DATE: Jan 26, 1757
BIRTH PLACE:
FATHER:
MOTHER:
DEATH DATE: Feb 12, 1829
DEATH PLACE:
CEMETERY: Aldrich

Levi BROOKS   112   Levi BROOKS

LOCATION: Norwich, New York

TOMBSTONE INSCRIPTION:
    Levi Brooks   In
   A Revolutionary   Memory of Lydia
     Soldier   Consort of Levi Brooks
      Died   Who lived beloved & died
    Feb 12th 1829   Lamented July the 4th
   Aged 72 years   1806 in the 59
    & 16 days   Year of her age
                           Blest are the dead
                          Who die in the Lord

SERVICE: Described as a soldier on his tombstone.

FAMILY INFORMATION: He was married to Lydia _____.
She was born in 1747 and died Jul 4, 1806. She is
buried with her husband.

   Children: ?

OTHER INFORMATION:

Thomas BROOKS   113   Thomas BROOKS
    -. ----- Major

RESIDENT DATE: 1794 - 1822
TOWN: Plymouth
BIRTH DATE: 1761
BIRTH PLACE:
FATHER:
MOTHER:
DEATH DATE: Aug 30, 1822
DEATH PLACE:
CEMETERY: Stewarts Corners
LOCATION: Plymouth, New York

TOMBSTONE INSCRIPTION:

Blessed are the dead	who die in the Lord

                          In
                      Memory
                        of
               Thomas Brooks
      Who died August 30th
                    1822
           Aged 62 years
             and 11

Thomas BROOKS   113   Thomas BROOKS

                            Days
            Husband to Lucy & father to John,
            Clarisa, Elijah, Thomas, Roswell
            Electra, Socrates, Theseus, Clitus,
            & Caius _c, the best of father's
            how shall we discharge the grat-
                itude and duty we owe to him.
        For die to live is Christ & to die is gain.
                        B. H. King sculpt.
 (stone on ground and broken)   (stone leaning back)
                          In
                      Memory of
                         Lucy
                      Consort of
                     Thomas Brooks
                     Died Dec 31
                         1827:
                    Aged 71 years
                    _____ months
  My children dear come drop a tear
    on your kind mother's grave
    that _____
      your infant lives to save.

SERVICE: He is described as a soldier of the
Revolution in the DAR cemetery book. He is described
as a Revolutionary soldier, and having also
participated in Shay's rebellion, in the Chenango
County History by Smith.

FAMILY INFORMATION: Married Lucy _____. She was born
in 1756 and died Dec 31, 1827 at Plymouth, New York.
She is buried with her husband.

  Children:
    John   B-
    Clarissa   Unmarried school-teacher. D-at age 80,
                 in Plymouth,NY.
    Elijah   B-Nov 27,1781 Leyden,MA.
    Thomas   B-Dec 29,1783 Leyden,MA. D-Plymouth,NY.
    Roswell
    Electra
    Thesius
    Socrates   B-May 26,1788. M-_____. D-Aug 12,1841
                 Plymouth,NY. Bur South Plymouth Cem.
    Clitus   M-_____. D-locality of Ithaca,NY.
    Cassius   M-_____ **Mead** (Dau of Amos **Mead**).
                 D-Plymouth,NY.

Thomas BROOKS   113   Thomas BROOKS

OTHER INFORMATION: He came from the New England states (Massachusetts man) and settled on the west green in Norwich village, on which he built a log shanty. He removed at an early day to the southeast corner of the town of Plymouth, Chenango County, New York. He taught the first school in town located at Sherburne Four Corners. He was killed by the fall of a tree.

Adonajah BROWN   114   Adonajah BROWN
         W. 25287 Private

RESIDENT DATE: - 1847
TOWN: Guilford
BIRTH DATE: May 22, 1766
BIRTH PLACE: Bedford, New York
FATHER:
MOTHER:
DEATH DATE: Nov 9, 1847
DEATH PLACE: Guilford, New York
CEMETERY: Godfrey Corners
LOCATION: Guilford, New York

TOMBSTONE INSCRIPTION: Adonijah Brown
                                   Died
                              Nov 9, 1847.
                               Ae 83 y's
                      No mortal woes can reach the
              Ellen   peaceful sleeper here while
             Wife of Angels watch his soft repose.
          Adonigah Brown
               Died
         Dec. 26, 1855,
      Ae 90 y. 7 m. 20d.
   Yet again I hope to meet thee,
     when the day of life is fled.
 then in heaven with joy to greet thee
     where no farewell tear is shed.

SERVICE: He volunteered, while living with his father, in Bedford, Westchester County, New York, at the age of fourteen. He served from May, 1780 to October, 1782, as a private under Captain Samuel Lewis, Colonel Thadeus Crane's New York Regiment. He was stationed, with five others, at Pound Ridge, Westchester County, New York, about two miles from enemy lines, scouting during the day and standing guard at night. Captain Lewis would visit them about once per week. His group would often take a British soldier on the American

Adonajah BROWN   114   **Adonajah BROWN**

side of the line. His father kept the horses of Colonel Sheldon's Regiment during the winter of 1780. He saw the burning of Bedford. He was personally acquainted with Williams, and had seen Paulding, two persons who took Major Andre. He was also acquainted with General Thomas, Colonels. Miller, Sheldon, and Crane.

FAMILY INFORMATION: Married on Jan 27, 1789 to Eleanor _____ . She was born in 1767, died Dec 26, 1855 and is buried with her husband.

Children:
- Nancy   B-Jan 02,1790. Unmarried. D-Nov 15,1853 in Guilford,NY. Bur Godfrey Corners Cem, Guilford,NY.
- Edward M   B-Feb 13,1791.
- Nathaniel A B-Aug 27,1792.
- Alexander B-May 21,1796. M-Nancy _____ (B-1802; Jun 10,1873). D-Mar 12,1883. Both bur Morgan Cem, Guilford,NY.
- James L   B-Jan 21,1799. M-Phebe _____ (B-1801; D-Dec 18,1847; Bur Godfrey Corners Cem, Guilford,NY).
- Maria   B-Jul 24,1801. M-Samuel **Godfrey** (B-1803; D-Aug 14,1855). D-Sep 30,1882. Both bur Godfrey Corners Cem, Guilford,NY.
- Thadeus R B-Oct 16,1804.
- Eleanor   B-Jun 27,1806. M-Seth **Bowen** (B-1815; D-Dec 16,1879). D-Oct 18,1868. Both bur Godfrey Corners Cem, Guilford,NY.
- Sally Ann B-Sep 21,1808.

OTHER INFORMATION: After the war he resided in the counties of Ulster, Orange and Chenango. He applied for a pension on Jun 17, 1841, while a resident of Guilford, Chenango County, New York. His widow applied for a pension on Feb 18, 1853, while a resident of Guilford. A land warrant (BLWT 10303-160-55) was issued on Nov 20, 1855.

Barnabus BROWN   115   Barnabus   BROWN
         S. 29036 Private   DAR Patriot Index

RESIDENT DATE: 1793 - 1855
TOWN: New Berlin
BIRTH DATE: Jan 3, 1762
BIRTH PLACE: Rehoboth, Massachusetts
FATHER: Thomas **Brown**
MOTHER: Hannah **Jones**
DEATH DATE: Dec 6, 1855
DEATH PLACE: New Berlin, New York
CEMETERY: Fairview
LOCATION: New Berlin, New York

TOMBSTONE INSCRIPTION:
    Barnabus Brown   Nancy Medbury
    died Dec 6, 1855   wife of
         aged   Barnabus Brown
 93 yrs 11 mo & 3 days.   died March 6, 1846
                                      aged
                                69 yrs 5 mo 7 days

SERVICE: While a resident of Rehoboth, Massachusetts he enlisted Jun 20, 1773, and served as a private in Lieutenant Jabez Bullock's and Captain's Richardson's and Joseph Cole's Companies., Colonel Jacob's Massachusetts Regiment. The length of service was six months and twelve days.

FAMILY INFORMATION: Married Oct 13, 1795 to Nancy **Medbury**, a daughter of Nathaniel and Ruth (**Barnes**) **Medbury**. She was born Sep 29, 1776 and died Mar 6, 1846.

   Children:
   Sally Ann B-Oct 29,1796. M-Jan 11,1816 to Buel
                 Sherman. D-Aug 15,1826.
   Ruth   B-Apr 05,1799. M-Jan 26,1823 to Angell
                 Cleveland. D-Jan 9,1828.
   Nancy   B-Aug 18,1801. M-Sep 30,1827 to Buel
                 Sherman (D-Mar 27,1873). D-Mar 20,1873.
   Barnabus   B-Mar 20,1804. M-Sep 18,1829 Exeter,RI to
                 Eliza M **Cleveland** (B-Mar 20,1810;
                 D-Oct 26, 1861). D-Aug 13, 1857.
   Peleg   B-Dec 20,1806. D-Feb 21,1887. Was a
                 resident of Alabama
   Mary   B-May 11,1809. M-Oct 11,1840 to Charles L
                 Robinson (D-Apr 15,1890). D-Jul 8,1894.
   William   B-Aug 23,1811. M-Sep 9,1841 Maria **Medbury**
                 (D-Jul 7,1905). D-Mar 9,1856.

Barnabus BROWN   115   Barnabus   BROWN

Lewis   B-Nov 08,1814. M-Jan 14,1838 to Harriet E
            Monroe(B-May 12,1819; Dau of William
            and Sally [Barnes] Monroe;D-Jun 6,1886
            at New Berlin,NY). D-Sep 18,1905.
Lucretia   B-May 27,1817. M-Oct 19,1843 New Berlin,NY
            Jonathan M Lull (B-Mar 17,1808; Son of
            Nathan and Ruth [Moon] Lull;
            D-Mar 10,1877 at Morris,NY).
            D-Feb 15,1892 at Grand Rapids,MI.
Harvey   B-Sep 05,1820. D-Oct 29,1822.
Harry   B-Oct 29,1823. D-Mar 1,1824.

OTHER INFORMATION: He was allowed pension on his application executed Sep 7, 1832, at which time he was a resident of New Berlin, Chenango County, New York. On Mar 20, 1855, he applied for bounty land, at which time he was living in New Berlin, New York. He was allowed 160 acres on warrant #1902. In 1832, the soldier's sister Hannah Medbury, was of Chenango County, New York. She was born Jul 11, 1766, in Rehoboth, Massachusetts. The soldier served the town of New Berlin as a Justice of the Peace. He settled on a lot about a half mile west of New Berlin. He commenced housekeeping in a new log house erected for that purpose near where the old orchard stands, on the north side of the road running east and west through the farm. That orchard was among his first works after he commenced clearing up his farm. After a few years he built a more commodious house. It was a one story, steeple-roof building which was the residence of Judge Barnabus Brown, amidst his happy family of sons and daughters, through a long and useful life spent in private and public employment. He was commissioned Justice of the town of New Berlin by the Council of Appointment and served in that capacity several years. He was Supervisor for several years in succession. He was Judge in the Common Pleas Court in Clintonian times of State Politics.

Baron BROWN   116   Baron   BROWN
       S. 44658 Private

RESIDENT DATE: 1820 -
TOWN: Sherburne
BIRTH DATE: Sep 9, 1750
BIRTH PLACE: Ipswich, Massachusetts (Essex County)
FATHER: John Brown
MOTHER: Dorcus
DEATH DATE: Feb 27, 1829

Baron BROWN 116 **Baron BROWN**

DEATH PLACE:
CEMETERY:
LOCATION:

TOMBSTONE INSCRIPTION:

SERVICE: Served in Captain Bemis' Company, Colonel Whitney's Regiment of Massachusetts Militia eight months in 1775 in Cambridge, near Boston. Served five months in the same Regiment, different Company at Nantucket and Ticonderoga in 1776. In the early part of 1777 enlisted for three years in Captain Slayton's Company, Colonel Shepard's Regiment. Was discharged in 1783.

FAMILY INFORMATION: Married Feb 16, 1773 at Westminster, Worcester County, Massachusetts to Elizabeth **Snow**. She was born Feb 3, 1756 in Bridgewater, Plymouth County, Massachusetts and died on Jun 14, 1820.

Children:
Sarah   B-Jul 14,1773 at Westminster, MA.
Daniel A B-1775. M-Huldah **Wheeler**.

OTHER INFORMATION: Application for pension on Apr 18, 1818 with residence at Hamilton, New York. Took oath of residence, loyalty, and property at Sherburne, New York on Jun 14, 1820. On Nov 26, 1825 applied for and was granted 100 acres of land in Cayuga County New York for his service in the Revolution.

Christopher BROWN 117 **Christopher BROWN**
       W. 12339 Fifer   DAR Patriot Index

RESIDENT DATE: wife
TOWN: Norwich
BIRTH DATE: May 12, 1759
BIRTH PLACE: New London, Connecticut (New London Co)
FATHER: Jedidiah **Brown**
MOTHER: Sarah **Stubbins**
DEATH DATE: Sep 9, 1807
DEATH PLACE: Preston, Connecticut (New London Co)
CEMETERY:
LOCATION: North Stonington, Connecticut

TOMBSTONE INSCRIPTION: Eunice Brown
                            Died Oct 2, 1861,
                            Aged 75 y'rs.

Christopher BROWN   117   Christopher BROWN

SERVICE: In February, 1778 he enlisted; served for several years in the Connecticut Line, for Colonels Sherburne and Webb.

FAMILY INFORMATION: He married Aug 9, 1803 at Groton (now Ledyard) Connecticut to Eunice Lee, a daughter of Squire Lee. She was born in 1786, died Oct 2, 1861 and was buried in Mt Hope Cemetery, Norwich, New York.

Children:
  Coddington B-1804. M-Lucy __ (B-1804; D-Apr 7,1861).
        D-Aug 9,1864. Both bur Mt Hope Cem,
        Norwich,NY.

OTHER INFORMATION: His brothers included John, William, Gershom and Reuben. His widow applied for pension on an application dated Aug 27, 1853 while a resident of Norwich, Chenango County, New York. In 1853 a Jesse Brown, age 80, of Norwich, New York had married Abigail Lee a sister of the soldier's wife.
  NOTE: There was a Jesse Brown born Nov 14, 1773 in Stonington, Connecticut, a son of Jesse and Lydia Brown.

Elisha BROWN   118   Elisha BROWN
        S. 44654 Private

RESIDENT DATE: 1818
TOWN: Norwich
BIRTH DATE: 1758
BIRTH PLACE:
FATHER:
MOTHER:
DEATH DATE: Aug 22, 1832
DEATH PLACE:
CEMETERY:
LOCATION:

TOMBSTONE INSCRIPTION:

SERVICE: While a resident of Providence County, Rhode Island, he enlisted in January, 1776, and served one year as private in Captain Stephen Kimball's Company in Colonel Daniel Hitchcock's Rhode Island Regiment.

FAMILY INFORMATION: Married to _____. She was born in 1764.

Elisha BROWN   118   Elisha BROWN

Children:
  Leeman   B-1805
  Stephen   B-1808

OTHER INFORMATION: He was allowed pension on his application executed Apr 18, 1818, at which time he was living in Norwich, New York.

Elisha BROWN   119   Elisha BROWN
              -. ----- Private   DAR Patriot Index

RESIDENT DATE:
TOWN:
BIRTH DATE: 1731
BIRTH PLACE: Groton, Connecticut (New London County)
FATHER: Nathaniel Brown
MOTHER: Anna Haynes
DEATH DATE: Sep 18, 1813
DEATH PLACE:
CEMETERY:
LOCATION:

TOMBSTONE INSCRIPTION:

SERVICE: He was a private from the State of Connecticut.

FAMILY INFORMATION: Married to Content Leeds, a daughter of Thomas and Content (Williams) Leeds. She was born in 1733 in New London, Connecticut.

Children:
  Experience B-1756 Groton,CT.
  Jerusha   B-May 18,1764 Groton,CT.
  Elisha   B-1766 Groton,CT.
  Thomas   B-Mar 07,1769 Groton,CT.
  Elijah   B-May 17,1773 Stonington,CT.
  Deborah   B-1777 Groton,CT.
  Elizabeth B-1779 Groton,CT.
  Nathaniel M-Anna Johnson.
  Margery   B-May --,1786 MA. M-Owen Briggs

OTHER INFORMATION:

Jesse BROWN   120   Jesse BROWN
      -, ----- Private   DAR Patriot Index

RESIDENT DATE: 1797 - 1813
TOWN: Norwich
BIRTH DATE: Mar 19, 1739
BIRTH PLACE: Providence, Rhode Island
FATHER: Richard **Brown**
MOTHER: Mary
DEATH DATE: Apr 16, 1813
DEATH PLACE: Norwich, New York
CEMETERY: Mt Hope
LOCATION: Norwich, New York

TOMBSTONE INSCRIPTION: In
                                Memory of
                          Mary Consort of
                        Jesse Brown who died
                         Sept 17 1822 in the
                          74st year of her
                                  Age
                  To where this silent marble weeps
                    A friend a wife a mother sleeps
                    A heart within whose sacred call
                    The peacefull _____ lov'd to dare.
              Sacred
          To the memory of
            Jesse Brown
             Who died
          April 16th 1813
             In the
           75th year of
             His age
Ye mourning children as you pass by
        These monuments survey
Learn ere your solemn hour draws nigh
     To choose that better way

SERVICE: Served as a private in Captain George Peck's Company under command of Colonels Fry and Peck, Rhode Island line.

FAMILY INFORMATION: DAR has marriage to Nancy _____. Married to Mary **Brown**. She was born in 1748, died at Norwich on Sept. 14, 1822 and is buried next to her husband in the Mount Hope Cemetery.

  Children:
   Richard   D-at Plattsburg in the war of 1812.
                Unmarried.
   Nicholas   Removed to Michigan- not married.

Jesse BROWN   120   Jesse BROWN

Polly	M-Thomas **Steere** (B-May 3,1787; son of Stephen and Rizpah [**Smith**] **Steere**; D-Fentonville, MI).
Mercy	B-1774 in CT. M-Capt. Thomas **Lyon** (B-1762 Susquehannah Co, PA, D-Apr 1813- killed in the Battle of Little York). D-Oct 31,1862 in Guilford,NY. Bur Mt Hope Cem, Norwich,NY.
Hezekiah	B-Mar,1778 in RI. M-Sterling,CT. Elizabeth **Cole** (B-1783 Sterling,CT; Dau of Silas **Cole**; D-Feb 22,1866). D-Oct 24,1847. Both bur Mt Hope Cem, Norwich,NY.
Zerviah	B-Sep. 8,1780. M-William **Tiffany** (B-1781 in N. Adams,MA to Humphrey and Phebe [**Brown**] **Tiffany**, D-Oct 12,1866 at North Norwich,NY). D-Aug 6,1858 at North Norwich,NY. Both bur Kings Settlement Cem, North Norwich,NY.
Joseph	B-1783 in RI. M-Martha **Phillips** (B-1779; D-Dec 21,1850). D-Jan 30,1871 at N. Norwich,NY. Both bur Mt Hope Cem, Norwich,NY.
William	B-1789, RI. M-Mary W **Johnson** (B-1796; D-Mar 6,1827; Bur Mt Hope Cem, Norwich, NY). M2- Priscilla _____ (B-1799; D-Jun 30,1829; Bur Mt Hope Cem, Norwich, NY). M3-Lucretia_____ (B-1792 in CT; D-Feb 2,1860). D-Oct 13,1865 Plymouth, NY. He & 3rd wife bur South Side Cem, Plymouth,NY.
Susan	B-Jun 30,1794 CT. M-John **Holcomb** (B-1793 CT. Son of Abraham & Betsey [**Bosworth**] **Holcomb**; D-Nov 22,1855). D-Mar 12,1867 at Plymouth,NY. Both bur South Side Cem, Plymouth,NY.
Sally	M-Thomas **Cole**.
Elisha	(possible)

OTHER INFORMATION: Lived at Scituate, Rhode Island on land given him by his grandfather Richard **Brown** Sr. located on Mosquito Hawk Plain. He sold his farm in 1794 to Job **Steere** and in 1797 removed to Norwich, New York. Mount Hope Cemetery was part of the Brown homestead.

John   BROWN   121   John   BROWN
        S. 22660 Private

RESIDENT DATE: 1798 - 1815
TOWN: Norwich
BIRTH DATE: Aug 27, 1758
BIRTH PLACE: Canterbury, Connecticut (Windham Co)
FATHER: Benjamin **Brown**
MOTHER: Hannah **Benjamin**
DEATH DATE: May 28, 1847
DEATH PLACE:
CEMETERY: McLean
LOCATION: Groton, New York (Tompkins County)

TOMBSTONE INSCRIPTION: John Brown
                                   Died
                                May 28, 1847,
                                Aged 88 years
                                A soldier of the
                                  Revolution,
                                Lucy L. his wife
                                    Died
                                June 19, 1841,
                                Aged 81 years,
                                    BROWN

SERVICE: He enlisted at Canterbury, Windham County, Connecticut and served as a private in the Connecticut Line. At various times in 1775, totaling about six months, he was in Captain Benjamin Bacon's Company, part of the time under Colonel Halsey. In August, 1776 three months in Captain Benjamin Bacon's Company, Colonel Douglas' Regiment; from January, 1777, three months in Captain Benjamin Bacon's Company, Colonel Douglas' Regiment; from May, 1777 seven months in Captain Ebenezer Moseley's Company, Colonel John Ely's Regiment; from July, 1778, three months in Captain Cady's Company, was in the battle of Rhode Island; in 1779, two months, in 1780, one month, and in 1781, two months, no officers stated; in 1782, five months at Fort Trumbull, under Colonel McClellan.

FAMILY INFORMATION: He married Lucy L _____. She was born in 1760, died June 19, 1841 and is buried with her husband.

    Children:
    Lucy   B-Jun 11,1781 Canterbury,CT.
    John R   B-Dec 21,1782 Preston,CT. M-Elizabeth S
                _____ (B-1790; D-Aug 21,1865) In the
                War of 1812. D-Sep 2,1872. Both bur
                McLean Cem, Groton,NY.

John   BROWN   121   John   BROWN

Hutchinson B-Jul 17,1785 Preston,CT.
Molly Pemberton B-Feb 09,1789 Preston,CT
Benjamin   B-Aug 31, 1794 Preston,CT.

OTHER INFORMATION: He applied for a pension on an application dated Oct 8, 1832, while a resident of Dryden, Tompkins County, New York. After the war he moved to Preston, New London County, Connecticut for fourteen years; then to Norwich, Chenango County, New York for seventeen years; then to Dryden, Cayuga County (now Tompkins), New York. Soldier's brother Aruna **Brown** was aged 68 in 1834, a resident of Cherry Valley, Otsego County, New York. He had three other brothers in the war, to wit; Hutchinson (died during the war), Jedediah and Benjamin.

John   BROWN   122   John   BROWN
        W. 04562 Sergeant   DAR Patriot Index

RESIDENT DATE: - 1809
TOWN: Norwich
BIRTH DATE: Feb 19, 1755
BIRTH PLACE: Brimfield, Massachusetts (Hampden Co)
FATHER:
MOTHER:
DEATH DATE: Jun 6, 1809
DEATH PLACE: Norwich, New York
CEMETERY:
LOCATION:

TOMBSTONE INSCRIPTION:

SERVICE: While residing at Brimfield, Massachusetts, he enlisted in 1775 and served under Captain Parks, and at Saratoga under Captain John Carpenter, Colonel Ezra Wood. Original Connecticut as first sergeant Nov 15, 1778, under Captain Carpenter. He served in all about five years.

FAMILY INFORMATION: Married Dec 25, 1783 in Wilbraham, Massachusetts to Lovina **Lyon**. She was born in 1765. In 1811, at Norwich, New York, she married second Benjamin **Hovey** (Died 1817 near Erie Pennsylvania). In 1820 in Harbour Creek, Pennsylvania, she married third General Edward **Paine** (Died August 28, 1841 in Painesville, Ohio). She died Jan 9, 1846 in Norwalk, Ohio.

John BROWN   122   John   BROWN

Children:
  Orrel   Bp-Apr 28,1785 Brimfield,MA.
  Lorin   Bp-May --,1785 Brimfield,MA. Resided
                Battle Creek, Calhoun Co,MI.
  Statira   Bp-May 03,1789 Brimfield,MA. M-____ Clark.
                Resided Bellevue,Huron Co.MI.
  Almira   M-____ Turner. Resided Marshall,Calhoun
                Co,MI.
  Charles Pinckney B-Jan 29,1798 Union,CT. Resided
                Alabama, Genesee Co,NY.
  Amelia   M-____ Scott. Resided Toledo, Lucas Co,
                OH.
  Henry H   B-1802. Resided Norwalk, Huron Co,OH.

OTHER INFORMATION: Pension issued Jun 1, 1849 to
wife. Son, Lorin applied for the remainder of the
pension on behalf of the heirs.
   (TRY MADISON CENTRE, MADISON COUNTY--NO DATES GIVEN)

Jonathan BROWN   123   Jonathan   BROWN
     W. 5229 Private   DAR Patriot Index

RESIDENT DATE: - 1830
TOWN: Otselic
BIRTH DATE: Dec 20, 1757
BIRTH PLACE: Stonington, Connecticut (New London Co)
FATHER: James Brown
MOTHER: Abigail
DEATH DATE: Aug 11, 1830
DEATH PLACE: Otselic, New York
CEMETERY: Maple Grove
LOCATION: Otselic, New York

TOMBSTONE INSCRIPTION:
      In memory of
   Jonathan Brown Esq.
who departed this life Aug
11th 1830 in the 73 year of
         His age
A soldier of the Revolution
_____in
when you will _____ is gain   In
my pain is _____   Memory
my soul has reach'd the f__   of
                              Esther wife of
                              Jonathan Brown
                              Esqr. died March
                              23rd 1821, in

Jonathan BROWN 123 Jonathan BROWN

the 62 year
of her age
She in her youth the path of wisdom trod
and now her spirit has returned to God
here in this silent grave her body lies
till God her Saviour comes and bids it rise

SERVICE: On Apr 12, 1777, he as a resident of the town of Preston, Connecticut, enlisted as a private for three years. He was in Captain Belcher's Company, 1st Connecticut Regiment. He served until Apr 5, 1780, and was discharged at Springfield, New Jersey. He was in the battles of Stoney Point and Germantown. He enlisted again at Preston, Connecticut, for three months under Captain Halsey and went to Providence, Rhode Island. He was in the battle of the Mills, Long Island and battle of Harlem. In 1779 detached into the infantry under General Wayne and at storming of Stoney Point "In which he was in the forlorn hope in Captain Selden's Company".

FAMILY INFORMATION: Married Nov 30, 1780 in Preston, Connecticut, to Esther **Moon**. She was born Aug 13, 1759 in Rhode Island and died Mar 23, 1821. Married second Nov 11, 1827 in Norwich, N.Y. to Esther **Byington**, a daughter of Ashel and Mary **Byington**. She was born Oct 2, 1781 in Wallingford, New Haven, Connecticut. She moved to Ohio after the death of her husband.

Children:
Miner   B-1782 Stevenstown,NY. M-Clarrissa **Hayes** (B-1785; D-1869). D-1855 in Otselic, NY.
Esther   B-1789. M-Nicholis **Young**. D-Mar 13,1821. Bur Maple Grove Cem, Otselic,NY.
Olive   B-May 01,1798 Stevenstown,NY. M-Ransom **Smith**.
Jonathan   B-1800 Stevenstown,NY.
William M
Alonzo
Peleg
Sally   B-1804 Stevenstown,NY.M-Elisha **Burlingame**.
Esther   B-1806 Stevenstown,NY.
Abigail   B-1808 Stevenstown,NY. M-Joseph **Bourne**.
Exceen   B-1810 Stevenstown,NY. M-Justin **Burt**.
Cynthia   B-1812 Stevenstown,NY. M-Benjamin **Springer**.
Charlotte B-1814 Stevenstown,NY. M-Alexander **Webster**.

Jonathan BROWN   123   Jonathan BROWN

OTHER INFORMATION: He applied for a pension Jul 1, 1818. Residence at the time of application was Otselic, New York. Second wife Esther, a widow, applied for a pension Apr 19, 1853. Her residence was Elyria, Lorain County, Ohio, where she had lived for twenty years. Then, on Apr 19, 1855, still residing at Elyria, she applied for bounty land, which was granted for 160 acres of land on warrant #12826.

Jonathan BROWN   124   Jonathan BROWN
    S. 3058 Private   DAR Patriot Index

RESIDENT DATE: 1832
TOWN: Sherburne
BIRTH DATE: Jun 13, 1748
BIRTH PLACE: Norwalk, Connecticut (Fairfield County)
FATHER:
MOTHER:
DEATH DATE: May 15, 1841
DEATH PLACE: Norwalk, Ohio (Huron County)
CEMETERY:
LOCATION:

TOMBSTONE INSCRIPTION:

SERVICE: While residing in Norwalk, Connecticut he enlisted for two years, ten months and fifteen days served as a private in the company of Captain Stephen Betts, Colonel Samuel B Webb's Connecticut Regiment. He saw General Washington and General Knox at West Point.

FAMILY INFORMATION: Married _____.

Children:
  Jonathan   M-Jan 8,1807 in Chenango Co.,NY to Phebe
             Tiffany (B-North Adams,MA; Dau of
             Humphrey and Phebe [**Brown**] **Tiffany**).
             D-Apr 28,1839 at Milan,OH.
  Lewis

OTHER INFORMATION: Since the war he resided at Norwalk, Connecticut, Walton and Franklin, Delaware County, New York. He applied for a pension on Oct 16, 1832, while a resident of Sherburne, Chenango County, New York. On Mar. 4, 1836 he applied for a pension transfer while a resident of Warren County, Pennsylvania. Then on Oct 18, 1837 he applied for a pension transfer to Pittsburgh, Huron County, Ohio.

Josiah BROWN   125   Josiah   BROWN
-. ----- Captain

RESIDENT DATE: 1796 -
TOWN: Norwich
BIRTH DATE: Aug 8, 1748
BIRTH PLACE:
FATHER:
MOTHER:
DEATH DATE:
DEATH PLACE:
CEMETERY:
LOCATION:

TOMBSTONE INSCRIPTION: NOTE: A Josiah Brown is buried in town of Hamilton cemetery (D-Aug 12, 1826 Ae 72-Rev war vet. Death 1820 or age 78 would match. Son Joseph resided in Hamilton.
                    In
                Memory of
            Lucy; wife of
          Josiah Brown who
          Died Feb 19, 1813
                Aged 64
                  Years
Grate mystries that's ben long conseald
    Now unto hir will be reveald
  No more she views as through glass
    But sees her Jesus face to face.

SERVICE: At the outbreak of the war, Captain Brown resided in one of the fertile Connecticut valleys, where he owned a large farm of 300 acres, all well stocked, and had by his thriftiness accumulated funds so that he had much money out in interest. At the first sign of hostilities, he enlisted a company of men and went to the front with them as their leader, fighting under the great commander-in-chief, General George Washington, during the entire war. He and his men were with the troops that spent the hard winter at Valley Forge. The poorly-clad men, many of them barefooted, appealed so to the sympathies of Captain Brown that he called in the money which he had loaned out at interest and purchased clothing and shoes for his freezing troops. When the food supplies ran short, the captain took 300 bushels of potatoes from his cellar and killed his two yoke of cattle, using the supplies thus obtained to feed his Company. Later on he slaughtered his herd of cattle and his sheep and finally mortgaged his farm, all of which was for the cause of independence. At the end of the war, independence was achieved but Captain Brown came out

Josiah   BROWN   125   Josiah   BROWN

of the struggle an old man and poor in pocket because
of the sacrifices he had made. The government was
impoverished by the long struggle and had no money
with which to reimburse those whose unselfishness had
made success possible.

FAMILY INFORMATION: Married 1766 in Colchester, New
London County, Connecticut to Lucy **Skinner**, a
daughter of Joseph and Elizabeth **Skinner**. She was
born Jun 8, 1749 in Colchester and died Feb 19, 1813,
being buried in the Heady's Corners cemetery at
Plymouth, New York.

Children:
- Josiah   B-Oct 28,1767. M-Nov 14,1788 Sophia **Graves** (Dau of Matthew and Hannah [**Morton**] **Graves**).
- Lucy   B-Nov 02,1769. M-Jun 9,1788 at Whately,MA Charles **Graves** (Dau of Matthew and Hannah [**Morton**] **Graves**; M2-**Crosby**; D-1842 at Saybrook,OH). D-1802.
- Elizabeth B-Oct 30,1771.
- Hannah   B-Nov 11,1773. M-William **Ransford** (B-1769 at Voluntown,CT; son of William and Abigail [**Hascall**] **Ransford**; D-Oct 26,1826 at Norwich,NY; Bur Mt Hope Cem, Norwich,NY). D-Norwich,NY.
- William   B-Aug 08,1776.
- Dorothy   B-Mar 05,1779. D-Mar 1,1783.
- Anna   B-Apr 25,1781. M-William **Wait** (B-Sep 18,1779; Son of John and Mary [**Frary**] **Wait**; D-Aug 9,1825). D-Dec 11,1857. Both bur Woods Corners Cem, Norwich,NY.
- Joseph   B-Mar 17,1783. M-Clara **Heady**.
- Dorothy   B-Mar 21,1785. M-Doctor **Wales**.
- Mary   B-Jun 21,1787. M-Daniel **Heady** (B-1783; Son of Rev War Vet Daniel **Heady**; D-Feb 12,1864). D-Feb 26,1864. Both bur Heady's Corners Cem, Plymouth,NY.
- Edward   B-Dec 19,1790.
- Reuben   B-Mar 22,1792. D-Sep 15,1792.

OTHER INFORMATION: The war's hardships did not daunt
the captain so he took his family, and bravely made
his way to the west to begin life anew. He came to
Norwich and in 1796 settled at what was later to be
called Woods Corners.

Nathan BROWN 126 Nathan BROWN
-. ----- Private

RESIDENT DATE: 1808 - 1847
TOWN: Pharsalia
BIRTH DATE: Jun 18, 1765
BIRTH PLACE: Stonington, Connecticut
FATHER: Nathan **Brown**
MOTHER: Lydia **Dewey**
DEATH DATE: Jun 02, 1847
DEATH PLACE: Pharsalia, New York
CEMETERY: Center
LOCATION: Pharsalia, New York

TOMBSTONE INSCRIPTION:
```
    Nathan Brown              Sacred
        Died                  To the
    June 2 1847              Memory of
   Aged 82 years              Eunice
   11 m & 15 ds            Wife of Capt.
                            Nathan Brown
                             Who died
                           Sept 28 1826
                            In her 60
                               Year
```
And I heard a voice from heaven
saying unto me write blessed are
the dead, which die in the Lord from
henceforth yea saith the spirit
that they may rest from their labour
and their works do follow them.

SERVICE: Has a DAR marker placed on the grave site.
Entered the service as a substitute for his father.

FAMILY INFORMATION: Married Mar 29, 1786 at Stonington, Connecticut to Eunice **Brown** a daughter of Ichabod and Thankful (**Baldwin**) **Brown**. She was born on Feb 15, 1767 at Stonington, Connecticut and died Sep 28, 1826 at Pharsalia, New York. She is buried with her husband.

Children:
  Nathan   B-Sep 22,1786. M-Oct 8,1809 Polly **Weaver**
            (B-Sep 2,1790; Dau of Lodowick and Polly
            [**Brown**] **Weaver**; D-Feb 21,1853)
            . D-Jan 15,1854. Both bur Center Cem,
            Pharsalia,NY.

Nathan BROWN 126 Nathan BROWN

Eunice B-Jan 22,1787. M-Allen **Bosworth**
(B-Apr 13,1785; Son of Rev War Vet
Timothy and Nancy [**Monroe**] Bosworth;
M2-Almira **Coggeshall** [B-Aug 3,1793 in
Bristol,RI; Dau of James and Martha
[**Turner**] Coggeshall; D-Jul 16,1831;
Bur Bosworth Cem, Pharsalia,NY];
M3-Betsey [**Stanton**] Gay [B-1808;
D-Sep 15,1892; Bur Mt Hope Cem, Norwich,
NY] D-May 13,1861; Bur Bosworth Cem,
Pharsalia,NY). D-Jun 3,1813. Bur Center
Cem, Pharsalia,NY.

Patty B-Feb 17,1791. M-Lodowick **Weaver**
(B-Apr 5,1788; Son of Lodowick and Polly
[**Brown**] Weaver; M2-Matilda Weaver
(first cousin). D-Mar 12,1815. Bur Center
Cem, Pharsalia,NY.

Sally B-Mar 27,1793.

Alfred B-Jan 22,1796. In the War of 1812.
M-Phallie **Breed** (B-1794; D-Feb 7,1873).
D-May 28,1861. Both bur North Pitcher
Cem, Pitcher,NY.

Charles B-Jun 21,1798 at Stonington,CT. M-Perlina
Brown (B-1802; Dau of Jabish & Katurah
Brown; D-Mar 25,1859). D-Jan 20,1873 at
Pharsalia,NY. Both bur Center Cem,
Pharsalia,NY.

Ephraim P B-Nov 13,1800 Stonington,CT. M-Apr 29,1827
Orilla **Hakes** (B-May 23,1808; Dau of
Perez & Deborah [**Starkweather**] Hakes;
D-Mar 3,1886 at Rochester,NY).
D-Jan 21,1885 at Pharsalia,NY.
Both bur Center Cem, Pharsalia,NY.

Betsey A B-Apr 14,1802. M-Amos **Breed**.D-Sep 8,1831.
Bur Center Cem, Pharsalia,NY.

Roxana B-Jun 29,1804. D- 7,1852.

Almira B-Aug 07,1806. M-Fayette **Mace**.
D-Oct 19,1856.

OTHER INFORMATION: Came to Pharsalia from Belchertown, Massachusetts in February 1808 with his family consisting of his wife, 10 children and a black servant named Henry. He settled on lot #33 in the west part of Pharsalia, on the line of the town of Pitcher. It consisted of 100 acres, which later was owned by his son Ephraim. He served as town clerk for ten years as well as other offices.

Reuben BROWN   127   Reuben   BROWN
         W. 20775 drummer

RESIDENT DATE: wife
TOWN: Oxford
BIRTH DATE: May 28, 1748
BIRTH PLACE: Sudbury, Massachusetts (Middlesex Co)
FATHER: Jotham **Brown**
MOTHER: Hepzibah
DEATH DATE: Mar 5, 1830
DEATH PLACE: Wallingford, Connecticut
CEMETERY: (2 DAR burials)
LOCATION: (one Preston Plains Ct.)

TOMBSTONE INSCRIPTION:

SERVICE: He enlisted in January, 1777 at Durham, Connecticut and served as a drummer in Captain Samuel Barker's Company, Colonels William B Douglas and Return Meigs Regiments in the Connecticut Line. He was discharged on Jan 5, 1780 at Morristown, New Jersey.

FAMILY INFORMATION: He married in October, 1783 at Durham, Massachusetts to Matilda **Higgins**. She was born in 1767 and died Mar 4, 1846 in Oxford, New York.

Children:
   Amos   B-Nov --,1785. D-infant.
   Charles   B-Jul --,1787. D-1789.
   Henry   B-Dec 03,1789. D-by 1840.
   Seth   B-Sep --,1792. D-prior to 1840 in the West Indies.
   Nathaniel B-Mar --,1794. D-by 1840.
   Elijah   B-Jun --,1797. D-by 1840.
   Dennis   B-Oct 03,1799. Resided in Stamford,NY
   David   B-Aug 10,1802. Resided in Oxford,NY in 1840 along with his mother
   Betsey   B-Jun 23,1805. M-___ **Andrews**. D-May,1839 at Oxford,NY.

OTHER INFORMATION: His occupation was that of a shoemaker. He applied for pension on an application dated Mar 31, 1818 in Middlesex County, Massachusetts, while a resident of Durham, Massachusetts. He had lost his eyesight. His widow applied Sep 25, 1839 while a resident of Oxford, Chenango County, New York.

Samuel BROWN   128   Samuel   BROWN
-. ------ Private   DAR Patriot Index

RESIDENT DATE: wife
TOWN: New Berlin
BIRTH DATE: Dec 6, 1737
BIRTH PLACE:
FATHER: Richard Brown
MOTHER: Mary
DEATH DATE: c1812
DEATH PLACE: Scituate, Rhode Island
CEMETERY:
LOCATION:

TOMBSTONE INSCRIPTION: In
                               Memory of
                              Ruth wife of
                              Samuel Brown
                                Who died
                              Jul 19. 1834
                           Ae 85 yrs & 2 mo.
                  The glass has run my work is done
                  my hours are at rest, no mourning
                  friends shall shed a tear, my God has
                           thought it best

SERVICE: Served as a private from Rhode Island.

FAMILY INFORMATION: Married Dec 26, 1765 in Scituate, Rhode Island to Ruth **Wheeler**. She was born in 1749 and died Jul 19, 1834. She is buried in the Coon Cemetery in New Berlin, New York.

Children: All born in Scituate, Rhode Island
  Mary*   M-Benejah **Dyer**.
  Malachy   B-1770. D-Dec 29,1788.
  Amy   B-1770. M-Squire **Smith** (B-Oct 18,1768 Smithfield,RI; Son of Noah and Keziah [**Man**] **Smith**; Rev War Vet; M2-Lydia [**Benson**] **Cook** [Widow of Joseph **Cook** [B-1745; D-Feb 8,1863 Ira Twp, Cayuga Co, NY]. D-Sep,1824 RI). D-Dec 3,1814 South New Berlin,NY. Bur Quarter Cem, Norwich, NY.
  Rebecca   B-1773. M-William **Shepard** (B-1768; D-Oct 28,1849). D-Sep 22,1855. Both bur Fenner Cem, New Berlin,NY.
  Avis   B-May 23,1776. M-Philip **Peck** (B-Jun,1776; D-Feb 17,1856). D-Aug 8,1862. Both bur Dyer Cem, New Berlin,NY.
  James

Samuel BROWN   128   Samuel BROWN

Jeremiah B-1786. M-Susannah _____ (B-1786;
          D-Jul 4,1869). D-Dec 29,1876. Both bur
          Foster Cem, Norwich,NY.

OTHER INFORMATION:

*NOTE: May be the Mary buried in Coon Cemetery as 3rd
wife of Asa **Williams**. Stone reads "Mary 3 wife of/Asa
Williams/Died Aug 13 1834/Ae 65 yrs". (Asa has 4
wives buried here)

Thomas   BROWN   129   Thomas   BROWN
  -. ----- Sergeant   DAR Patriot Index

RESIDENT DATE: 1797 - 1814
TOWN: New Berlin
BIRTH DATE: Apr 16, 1733
BIRTH PLACE: Rehoboth, Massachusetts (Bristol Co)
FATHER: Isaac **Brown**
MOTHER: Esther **Bowen**
DEATH DATE: Mar 11, 1814
DEATH PLACE:
CEMETERY: Medbury
LOCATION: New Berlin, New York

TOMBSTONE INSCRIPTION:
                                              In
                     In   Memory
                   Memory   of
                     Of   Hannah wife of
                Thomas Brown   Thomas Brown
                  Who died   Who died
                March 11th 1811   Oct 7th 1799
                In the 82d year   In the 62d year
                    Of his   Of her
                     Age.   Age.
              The dust unto the dust returnes
              and tears bedew the lonely way
              the corps lies in the silent grave
              beneath the cold and damping day
              why should we starte and fear to die
              what timorous worms we mortals are
                death is the gate of endless day
              and yet we dread to enter their.

SERVICE: Served as a sergeant from Massachusetts.

FAMILY INFORMATION: Married first to Ruth _____.
She was born in 1737 and died Feb 8, 1759. Married
second Oct 15, 1761 In Dighton, Bristol County,

Thomas **BROWN** 129 Thomas **BROWN**

Massachusetts to Hannah **Jones**, a daughter of Honor **Cary**. She was born in 1737, died Oct 7, 1799 and is buried with her husband.

Children:
- James   B-Jan 28,1759. D-Nov 30,1776 by drowning.

second wife
- Isaac   M-Adah **Mudge**.
- Barnabus   B-Jan 03,1762 Rehoboth,MA. M-Oct 13,1795 Nancy Medbury (B-Sep 29,1776; dau of Nathaniel and Ruth [**Barnes**] Medbury; D-Mar 6,1846). D-Dec 6,1855 New Berlin, NY. Both bur Fairview cem,New Berlin,NY.
- Ruth   B-Nov 11,1763. M-_____ **Jacobs**. M-Capt. James **Cate**. D-before Nov 12,1813.
- Hannah   B-Jul 11,1766. M-Joseph **Medbury** (B-May 10,1758 Scituate,RI; son of Isaac and Dorothy [**Brown**] Medbury; D-Feb 12,1839). D-Oct 10,1837. Both bur Medbury Cem, New Berlin,NY.
- Esther   B-Jun 09,1768. M-George **Wightman**.
- Sabra   B-Mar 26,1773. M-Thomas **Medbury** (B-Jun 16,1774 at Scituate,RI; son of Nathaniel and Ruth [**Barnes**] Medbury; D-Aug 27,1834 at Erieville,NY). D-Feb 28,1826.
- Ebenezer   B-Jul 11,1775. D-Nov,1776.
- James W   B-Oct 30,1777. M-Hannah _____ (B-1780; D-Jul 25,1801). M2-Lydia **Medbury** (B-1778; dau of Nathaniel and Ruth [**Barnes**] Medbury; D-Apr 2, 1832). D-Dec 6,1813. All 3 bur Medbury Cem, New Berlin,NY.
- Thomas   B-May 01,1779. M-Mar 29,1801 to Nancy **Frink** (B-Oct 7,1785; D-Dec 2,1852 in New Berlin,NY. D-May 28,1854 in Farmington, WI.
- Honnour   B-Mar 25,1781. M-Israel **Angell**. M2-Nathan **Stewart**.

OTHER INFORMATION: He came with his family and effects from Rhode Island, the land of his nativity to New Berlin, Chenango County, New York. One or two years previous James and Barnabus, his sons had been sent to explore the new country and prepare a dwelling place for the family. They came by ox team, bringing some necessary articles for the occasion, and fixed the future home of the family on a lot situated on Great Brook.

Martin BRUNDAGE   130   **Martin BRUNDAGE**
W. 45309 Private   DAR PATRIOT INDEX

```
RESIDENT DATE:       - 1832
TOWN:             Pitcher
BIRTH DATE:              1763
BIRTH PLACE:             New Hampshire
FATHER:
MOTHER:
DEATH DATE:              1832
DEATH PLACE:    Pitcher, New York
CEMETERY:
LOCATION:
```

TOMBSTONE INSCRIPTION:

SERVICE: Was a private in Captain Purdy's Company, Colonel Thomas' Regiment, Westchester County, New York Militia.

FAMILY INFORMATION: Married 1784 to Rachel **Golden**.

Children:
Adelia   B-Mar 30,1785 Resided in Jones,IA.
Betsey   M-Elisha **Ackerman** in Pitcher,NY.

OTHER INFORMATION:

William BRUSH   131   **William BRUSH**
-. ----- Lieutenant   DAR Patriot Index

```
RESIDENT DATE:       - 1830
TOWN:             Norwich
BIRTH DATE:       May 12, 1750
BIRTH PLACE:      Huntington, New York (Suffolk County)
FATHER:           Reuben Brush
MOTHER:           Ruth Wood
DEATH DATE:       May 18, 1830
DEATH PLACE:      Norwich, New York
CEMETERY:         Mt Hope
LOCATION:         Norwich, New York
```

TOMBSTONE INSCRIPTION: (Stones laying flat on ground)
        Sarah   In
       Consort of   Memory of
     Wm Brush Esq   William Brush
        Died   Esqr. who died
      Oct. 1819.   May 18th 1830
In the 63 year of her age   Aged 80 years
         and beloved mother

William BRUSH 131 William BRUSH

SERVICE: Served as a lieutenant in the Vermont Militia in Captain Samuel Herrick's Company, in 1780, and under Captain Isaac Tichinor, in 1781.

FAMILY INFORMATION: Married Nov 28, 1775 at Bennington, Vermont, to Sarah **Thompson**. She was born at Nine Corners, Rensselaer County, New York in 1756, died Oct 19, 1819 and was buried in Webster Street Cemetery at Malone, New York.

Children:
  (male)   B-1776 Amenia,NY.
  (male)   B-1778 Amenia,NY.
  (female)   B-1780 Vergennes,VT.
  Sarah Thompson   B-1783 Vergennes,VT. M-Feb 16,1808 at Terrisburgh,VT to Joseph Seneca **Fenton** (B-Jan 21,1781 at Worthington, MA); D-Nov 14,1851 Flint,MI.
  (female)   B-1785 Vergennes,VT.
  (female)   B-1787 Vergennes,VT.
  (female)   B-1789 Vergennes,VT.
  Fanny   B-May 07,1790 Vergennes,VT.

OTHER INFORMATION: He died at the home of his daughter Sarah in Norwich, New York.

Thomas BUCK 132 Thomas BUCK
   S. 1463 Private

RESIDENT DATE:
TOWN: Greene
BIRTH DATE: Sep 7, 1763
BIRTH PLACE: Somers, Connecticut (Tolland County)
FATHER: Thomas **Buck**
MOTHER: Anna
DEATH DATE: Jan 6, 1841
DEATH PLACE:
CEMETERY: Old Brockport   AKA- High Street
LOCATION: Sweden, New York (Monroe County)

TOMBSTONE INSCRIPTION:
In
Memory of
Thomas Buck
Who died Jan 6, 1841
Aged 79 years

Thomas BUCK   132   **Thomas BUCK**

SERVICE: He enlisted at Shaftsbury, Bennington County, Vermont in July, 1776 and served under Captain Daniel Galucia in the Vermont Line for short periods of time totaling more than one month.

In the month of April, 1777 he volunteered at Bennington and marched to Castleton, where he stayed about three weeks. A few days after returning home he marched to Ticonderoga under the command of Captain Huntington and Colonel Robison. He was at the Fort when it was taken. He retreated with the army to Bennington and was engaged there for one week as a Teamster in drawing provisions for the army. He then left with his Company and marched to Saratoga and was stationed at Schuylers Mills during the battle there. He returned home shortly after the battle having been absent about eight months.

In 1778, 79, 80, and 81 was called out at various times and served as a minute man for a couple weeks three or four times a year. This service is estimated to be a total of six months.

FAMILY INFORMATION: He married May 22, 1785 at Woodstock, Windham County, Connecticut Abigail **Carpenter**, a daughter of Daniel and Anna **Carpenter**. She was born Nov 20, 1766 at Rehoboth, Bristol County, Massachusetts.

Children:
  Cyril   B-Oct 19, 1785 Bath, NH.
  Nancy   B-Jan 01, 1788 Bath, NH.
  Mary   B-1792 South Dansville, Steuben Co, NY.

OTHER INFORMATION: He applied for a pension on an application dated Oct 15, 1832, while a resident of Howard, Steuben County, New York. After the war he lived at Sidney, Otsego County, New York; then at Greene, Chenango County, New York; then to Howard, Steuben County, New York.

Reuben BUCKINGHAM   133   **Reuben BUCKINGHAM**
    S. 44708 Private

RESIDENT DATE:
TOWN: Otselic
BIRTH DATE: Aug 29, 1745
BIRTH PLACE: Saybrook, Connecticut (Middlesex Co)
FATHER: Gideon **Buckingham**
MOTHER: Jemima **Pelton**
DEATH DATE: Feb 4, 1828

Reuben   BUCKINGHAM   133   Reuben   BUCKINGHAM

DEATH PLACE: Georgetown, New York (Madison County)
CEMETERY:
LOCATION:

TOMBSTONE INSCRIPTION:

SERVICE: Sometime in February or March, 1775 he enlisted, served seven months as private in Captain David Smith's Company, Colonel Elmore's Connecticut Regiment; enlisted in February or March 1776, served nine months as private in Captain David Smith's Company, Colonel Elmore's Connecticut Regiment; enlisted Feb 7, 1777, served seven months as private in Captain David Smith's Company, Colonel Chandler's Connecticut Regiment.

FAMILY INFORMATION: Married first to Mabel **Ball** of New Haven, Connecticut. Married second in 1809 in Chenango County, New York to Philena **Chapin**, a daughter of William and Martha **Chapin**. She was born in 1772 in Springfield, Massachusetts.

Children:
  Lucinda   B-1780. M-Benjamin **Upham**.
  Jedediah   B-Sep 16,1786. M-Olive **Follet**.
  Reuben   B-Aug 5,1787. M-Katie **Cook** (B-1791;
              D-Oct 20,1879; D-Jan 14,1859 Otselic,NY.
              Both bur Maple Grove Cem, Otselic,NY.
  James   M-Lucy **Lampson**.
  Charlotte M-Calvin **Hollis**.
second wife
  Herman Chapin B-Mar 15,1812 Chenango Co.

OTHER INFORMATION: Was allowed pension on his application executed Feb 15, 1819, as a resident of Georgetown, Madison County, New York.

George   BUGBEE   134   George   BUGBEE
         S. 16666 Private

RESIDENT DATE: 1808 -
TOWN: Columbus
BIRTH DATE: 1762
BIRTH PLACE: Little Nine Partners, New York
FATHER:
MOTHER:
DEATH DATE:
DEATH PLACE:
CEMETERY:

George **BUGBEE** 134 George **BUGBEE**

LOCATION:

TOMBSTONE INSCRIPTION:

SERVICE: While residing at Saratoga, New York, he volunteered in May, 1777, served six weeks as a private in Captain Jones' New York Company, was employed in scouting against the Indians and was in several skirmishes with them; in the summer of 1777, he moved to Nine Partners, New York, volunteered there in July or August, 1777, served six weeks as a private in Captain Elijah Herrick's Company, Colonel Herrick's New York Regiment; was stationed at Peekskill, where he kept guard and repaired the works at that place; he again volunteered in June 1778, and served four months as a private in Captain Hartwell's Company, Colonel Vandeburg's New York Regiment; was again engaged as a guard and in working on the fort at West Point.

FAMILY INFORMATION: Married ?

Children: ?

OTHER INFORMATION: After the war, he lived in Little Nine Partners, New York and in Middletown, Delaware County, New York. He was allowed pension on his application executed Nov 15, 1832 while residing in Columbus, New York. He was in Newstead Township, Erie County, New York during the 1840 census.

Caleb **BURDICK** 135 Caleb **BURDICK**
X. 42671 Private DAR Patriot Index

RESIDENT DATE: 1799 - 1822
TOWN: Guilford - McDonough
BIRTH DATE: 1753
BIRTH PLACE: Westerly, Rhode Island (Washington Co)
FATHER: Hubbard **Burdick**
MOTHER: Avis **Lewis**
DEATH DATE: Jul 9, 1822
DEATH PLACE: McDonough, New York
CEMETERY: Union
LOCATION: McDonough, New York

Caleb BURDICK   135   Caleb BURDICK

TOMBSTONE INSCRIPTION: Caleb Burdick
                                 1753 - 1822
(on monument with others)
(Small stone nearby with   Huldah
    DAR marker)   His wife
                                 1759 - 1831

SERVICE: Served in Captain Joel Mead's Company, Colonel Henry Ludington's Regiment of Dutchess Company Militia.

FAMILY INFORMATION: Married about 1778 in Washington County, Rhode Island to Huldah _____. She was born in 1759, died in 1831 and is buried with her husband.

Children:
- Amos B   B-1792. M-Dec,1827 Polly (Mary) **Kenyon** (B-1798 McDonough,NY; Dau of Benjamin and Isabel [**Ketcham**] Kenyon; D-May 10,1882 Howell,MI). D-1876 Leslie,MI.
- Joshua   B-1795 Dutchess Co. Unmarried. D-1837 at McDonough,NY. Bur Union Cem, McDonough, NY.
- Lewis L   B-1797 Dutchess Co. M-Melissa **Andrews** of Preston NY (B-1807, D-Apr 9,1867). D-Feb 27,1868. Both bur Union Cem, McDonough,NY.
- Anna   M-Orin **Fuller** (Son of Rev War Vet Israel Fuller). Resided Gerry,Chautauqua Co, NY.
- Caleb   M-Martha **Clark**. D-Silver Creek, Chautauqua Co,NY.
- Polly   M-Jesse **Everett**. Resided in German, NY.
- Jane   M-_____ **Burdick**.
- Enoch   M-Ch_____. Resided Embro,Canada.

OTHER INFORMATION: Went from Rhode Island to Dutchess County, New York. Came to Guilford, New York and was there in 1799. Shortly after he removed to McDonough, New York.

Elijah BURDICK   136   Elijah BURDICK
     -. ----- Private   DAR Patriot Index

RESIDENT DATE: - 1833
TOWN: Pharsalia
BIRTH DATE: 1758
BIRTH PLACE: Hopkinton, Rhode Island
FATHER: Daniel **Burdick**

Elijah BURDICK   136   Elijah BURDICK

MOTHER: Martha **Wilcox**
DEATH DATE: Dec 17, 1833
DEATH PLACE: Pharsalia, New York
CEMETERY: Burdick
LOCATION: Pharsalia, New York

TOMBSTONE INSCRIPTION: (Cemetery farmed over)
                         (Stone found in a field border area)
                         Elijah Burdick
                         Died
                         Dec 17, 1833,
                         Aged 75 y'rs.

                         Avis,
                         His wife
                         Died
                         Feb. 18, 1836
                         Aged 75 y'rs.

SERVICE: A Private from Connecticut.

FAMILY INFORMATION: Married to Avis **Robinson**, daughter of William and Avis (**Burdick**) **Robinson** of Hopkinton, Rhode Island. She was born Jul 12, 1759 at Hopkinton, Rhode Island and died Feb 18, 1836 at Pharsalia, New York. She was buried with her husband.

Children:
Avis   B-May 17,____. no issue.
Ezra   B-Jul 04,1782. M-Martha **Fish**
           (B-Nov 16,1785; D-Apr 11,1827 Pharsalia,
           NY). M2-Mary **Hart** (B-Jan 19,1789;
           D-May 17,1858). D-Jul 3,1859 McDonough,
           NY. All 3 bur Burdick Cem, Pharsalia,NY
           (on fathers monument).
Daniel   B-Dec 21,1785. M-Dec 22,1808 Nancy **Lewis**
           (B-New London,CT; Dau of Jesse and Mary
           [**Potter**] **Lewis**). M2-Betsey **Bentley**.
Martha   B-Feb 02,1790. M-Lot **Crandall**. D-Otselic,
           NY.
Elizabeth B-Apr 07,1792. M-Rev. Jonathan **Crandall**
           (Jan 18,1789; Son of Carey and Mary
           [**Slocum**] **Crandall**; D-Nov 23,1836 at
           Alfred, NY). D-Oct 15,1866 Andover,NY.
Hannah   B-Jan 08,1794. M-_____ **Stanton**.
Eunice   B-Mar 28,1797. M-Nov 19,1815 Nathan **Frink**
           (B-Apr 18,1792; son of Nathan and Olive
           Frink of Stonington,CT; D-Nov 24,1850).
           D-Dec 1,1874. Both bur East Pharsalia
           Cem, Pharsalia,NY.

Elijah BURDICK 136 Elijah BURDICK

Sarah   B-Mar 03,1804. M-Jefferson Green.
         D-Otselic,NY.

OTHER INFORMATION:

Gideon BURDICK   137   Gideon BURDICK
       S. 3107 Private   DAR Patriot Index

RESIDENT DATE:
TOWN:
BIRTH DATE: Nov 6, 1762
BIRTH PLACE: Hopkinton, Rhode Island
FATHER: Thomas Burdick
MOTHER: Abigail Allen
DEATH DATE: Apr 5, 1846
DEATH PLACE: Quincy, Illinois
CEMETERY:
LOCATION:

TOMBSTONE INSCRIPTION:

SERVICE: He enlisted in 1780 at Catskill, Greene County, New York and served in the New York Line. He was a Private in Colonel Dubois' Regiment of New York Levies and served three weeks. From Jul 25, 1780, he served three months as Private in Captain Jacob Wright's 6th Company of Colonel Philip Van Cortlandt's Second Regiment, New York Line and was discharged Oct 25, 1780. He also served in Captain Daniel Delevan's Company of Colonel William Malcom's Regiment New York Levies, and in 1782 in Colonel Marinus Willet's Regiment.

FAMILY INFORMATION: He married Catherine Robertson. She was born in 1775 in New York and died Nov 27, 1806 in Irving, Township of Hanover, Chautauqua County, New York. He married second in 1814 to Jane Ripley, a widow of Samuel Brown. She was born in 1773 in New York and died in 1848.

Children:
Abigail   B-Feb 07,1793. D-Nov,1872.
Thomas   B-Nov 17,1795 in Canajoharie,NY.
           M-Mar 18,1828 Jamestown,NY Anna Higley
           (B-Nov 29,1806 in Marlboro,Vt; Dau of
           Oliver and Lucretia Higley).Resided in
           Los Angeles, CA.

Gideon   BURDICK   137   Gideon   BURDICK

    Rebecca   B-Dec 16,1801 in Cayuga,NY. M-1824 Hiram
                 Winters (B-Apr 5,1805 in Westfield,NY;
                 Son of Andrew & Hannah [**Wood**] Winters;
                 M2-Sophia **Tucker**; D-Oct 21,1889).
                 D-Aug 15,1852 in Scotts Bluff,NE. while
                 on a long trek across the plains to
                 Utah. Buried on the trail.
    Elias   B-May 01,1804. Unmarried. D-May 3,1876 in
                 Pleasant Grove, UT.
    Alden   B-Sep 12,1806. M-1825 to Jerusha **Parks**
                 (B-NY; Dau (prob) of Benjamin and Lucy
                 [**Wilkenson** or **Clark**] parks).
                 D-Aug 20,1845 in Nauvoo,IL.
second wife
    Lucinda   B-Dec 11,1815. M-John Benjamin **Baldwin**
                 (B-May 4,1806 in Windham,NY; Son of
                 Benjamin and Abigail [**Osborn**] **Baldwin**;
                 D-Dec 4,1895 Alexandria,Mo) D-Dec 8,1895
                 in St. Francisville,MO.
    Lois Maria B-___ ___,1818. M-Aug 9,1842 in Ohio to
                 John **Finkle** (B-1818). D-Nov 9,1891.
    Osmer   B-Jun ___,1820. D-Oct ___,1827.
    Mary   B-Apr 10,1823. M-___ **Davis**. D-1859.
    Jonathan   B-___ ___,1826. D-1828.

OTHER INFORMATION: He applied for a pension on an application dated Oct 12, 1832, while a resident of Busti, Chautauqua County, New York. He resided in Catskill, New York for several years after the war; then at Canajoharie, Montgomery County, New York; then moved to Chenango County, New York; then to Batavia, Genesee County, New York; then to Athens County, Ohio; then to Ellery, Chautauqua County, New York; then to Busti, New York in 1836; then to Geauga County, Ohio. His widow was living in Quincy, Illinois in 1847.

    One story told of him concerned one day he went into the field to labor, and hung his coat upon a fence post. By night time he found a little bird had built its nest in the sleeve. Rather than disturb the nest he left the coat there until the young were hatched and able to leave.

    At the birth of his first child, the life of his young wife was hanging in the balance. He went out alone and prayed that God would spare her life, and covenanted that if she lived he would always keep that day in the year for fasting. She was spared, and every year on Feb 7th he would go out into the woods and spend the day alone, keeping tryst with his God.

    He became a Latter Day Saint and moved westward with the body of the church. His last days were spent

Gideon **BURDICK**   137   Gideon **BURDICK**

in Quincy, Illinois, and his descendants were prominent members of that religious body. He died firm in the faith, requesting his children to do the work for him in the temple that he could not live to do himself.

Hazard **BURDICK**   138   Hazard **BURDICK**
   S. 9296 Private   DAR Patriot Index

```
RESIDENT DATE:      - 1841
TOWN:               Preston - Norwich
BIRTH DATE:         Jan 25, 1759
BIRTH PLACE:        South Kingston, Rhode Island
FATHER:             Oliver Burdick
MOTHER:             Lydia Elderton
DEATH DATE:         Jan 25, 1841
DEATH PLACE:        Norwich, New York
CEMETERY:           Burlingame
LOCATION:           Norwich, New York
```

TOMBSTONE INSCRIPTION:
        Hazard Burdick   Esther Burdick
            Died   Died
        Jan 25 1841   August 28, 1847
        Ae 82 yrs.   Ae 95 yrs.

SERVICE: While a resident of Westerly, Rhode Island, he enlisted in December 1776, serving nearly three years. Fifteen months in Captain Thomas Thompson's Company, Colonel Barton's Regiment; from sometime in May 1778, six months in Captain Nathan Pembleton's Company, Colonel Babcock's Regiment; from sometime in 1780, six months in Captain Peckham's Company, and later one month in Captain Pembleton's Company. He was in no battles but in several skirmishes.

FAMILY INFORMATION: Married 178- to Esther **Shirley**, a daughter of Denison **Shirley**. She was born in 1752, died Aug 28, 1847 in Norwich, New York and is buried with her husband.

   Children:
Hazard   B-1784. M-Martha _____. D-Nov 31,1873.
           Bur Mt Hope Cem, Norwich,NY.

| Hazard BURDICK | 138 | Hazard BURDICK |

Susannah B-1785. M-first David **Goodrich** (B-1778;
            D-Oct 2,1849; Bur Burlingame Cem,
            Norwich,NY). M2-Col. Zodack **Adams**
            (B-Feb 15,1780; Son of Ebenezer and Mary
            [**Morse**] **Adams**; In War of 1812;
            M1-Content **Train** (B-May 15,1781;
            D-Sep 6,1848). D-Sep 22,1856; Bur South
            Plymouth Cem, Plymouth,NY).
Samuel   B-Aug 26,1788. M-first Lora **Brown**,
            M2-Polly M **Beal** (B-1805; D-1880 Norwich,
            NY). D-1854 at Norwich,NY. He & 2nd wife
            bur Burlingame Cem, Norwich,NY.
Bridget (Polly) B-1790. M-David **Eccleston**
            (B-Sep 15, 1785; Son of Rev War Vet
            David and Catherine [**Fanning**]
            Eccleston; M2-Susan **Harvey**
            [B-May 6,1799; Dau of Rev War Vet John
            and Polly **Harvey**; D-May 4, 1871].
            D-Aug 30,1872 Norwich,NY).
            D-May 20,1847. All 3 Bur Mt Hope Cem,
            Norwich,NY.
Rowland   B-May 11,1793. M-first Alvira **Webb**,
            M2-Eunice **Talbot**, M3-Mary **Grigsby**.
Lurana   B-1795. M-Christian **Bort**.
John   B-Apr 17,1797. M-Pharma **Brown**.
Rev Lorenzo Dow B-Aug 17,1799. M-Cynthia **Dyer**
            (B-1799; D-Jul 12,1885). D-Feb 22,1882.
            Both bur Mt Hope Cem, Norwich,NY.
William Dennison B-Dec 19,1801. M-Clarrissa **Parks**.

OTHER INFORMATION: Resided in South Kingston and Westerly, Rhode Island, Plainfield, Richfield, Butternuts, Preston, and Norwich, New York. He was allowed pension on his application executed Aug 16, 1832, while a resident of Butternuts, Otsego County, New York. He was a Free Will Baptist minister.

| Luke BURDICK | 139 | Luke BURDICK |
| -. ----- Private | | DAR Patriot Index |

RESIDENT DATE: - 1825
TOWN: Lincklaen
BIRTH DATE: Apr 25, 1749
BIRTH PLACE: Hopkinton, Rhode Island
FATHER: William **Burdick**
MOTHER: Sarah **Edwards**
DEATH DATE: Jan 5, 1825
DEATH PLACE: Chenango County, New York
CEMETERY:

Luke BURDICK   139   Luke BURDICK

LOCATION:

TOMBSTONE INSCRIPTION:

SERVICE: Lucas Burdick of Hopkinton enlisted Oct 11, 1781 in Captain Allen's Company, Colonel Christopher Smith's Regiment, Rhode Island Troops, Revolutionary War.

FAMILY INFORMATION: Married Nov 8, 1772 at Norwich, Connecticut, to Sarah **Haskell**, a daughter of Elijah and Sarah (**Read**) **Haskell**. She was born Nov 14, 1750 at Norwich, New London County, Connecticut.

Children:
Luke   M-Lucy B **Burdick**
Jason   B-1783 at Hopkinton,RI. M-May 1,1809 at
                Hopkinton,RI to Susannah **Peckham**
                (B-Jul 4,1780 at South Kingston,RI; dau
                of Capt. Samuel and Hannah [**Stanton**]
                Peckham). D-Nov 10,1866 Hopkinton,RI.
James Reed   B-Apr 10,1776 Hopkinton,RI. M-Sep 8,1796
                to Martha **Coon** (B-Feb 27,1776; dau of
                Joshua and Margaret [**Burdick**] **Coon**;
                D-Mar 20,1847 Truxton,NY). D-Jul 4,1851
                at Truxton,NY.
Benjamin   B-May 05,1780. M-Nov 18,1803 to Anna
                Cardner (B-Aug 29,1780 in RI;
                D-Mar 4,1875 DeRuyter,NY). D-Nov 26,1840
                at DeRuyter,NY.
Sarah   B-1789 at Hopkinton,RI. M-1803 to Elias
                Irish (B-1781 at Hopkinton,RI; son of
                Benjamin **Irish**). D-1817 at Truxton,NY.
Kenyon (?)

OTHER INFORMATION: His will was probated at Hopkinton, Rhode Island on Jan 31, 1825.

Nathan BURLINGAME   140   **Nathan   BURLINGAME**
        S. 8118 Private   DAR Patriot Index

RESIDENT DATE: 1833
TOWN: Bainbridge
BIRTH DATE: Feb 24, 1762
BIRTH PLACE: Scituate, Rhode Island (Providence Co)
FATHER: Thomas **Burlingame**
MOTHER: Jane **Sheldon**
DEATH DATE: Aug. 7, 1856
DEATH PLACE: Windsor, New York

Nathan BURLINGAME   140   Nathan BURLINGAME

CEMETERY: Mountain View/Lester
LOCATION: Windsor, New York (Broome County)

TOMBSTONE INSCRIPTION: Nathan Burlingame
                               A Soldier of the Revolution
       Sarah   died
       Wife of   Aug 3, 1857
    Nathan Burlingame   Aged 95 y'rs
        Died   5 M's & 10 D's
     May 4, 1836,   This Wearisome head is at rest
    Aged 73 years.   its thinking and achings are not
                                this quiet unmovable breast
                              is heared by affliction no more

SERVICE: While residing in Gloucester, Rhode Island, he was enrolled at the age of sixteen as a member of a Militia Company of that town, and served as a Private as follows: from Aug 3, 1778, one month in Captain Benajah Whipple's Company, Colonel Chad Brown's Regiment; from August 1779, four months and one week in Captain Stephen Olney's Company; from August 1780, two months in Captain Stephen Olney's Company; from July 1781, two months in Stephen Olney's Company, was in a skirmish at Butts Hill; from July 1782, one month in Captain Stephen Olney's Company. In the service in 1778, Lieutenant Benjamin Burlingame was in Captain Benajah Whipple's Company.

FAMILY INFORMATION: Married May 13, 1782 in Gloucester, Providence County, Rhode Island to Sarah **Bartlett**, a daughter of Richard and Keziah (**Fuller**) Bartlett. She was born May 8, 1763 in Gloucester, Rhode Island, died May 4, 1836 and is buried with her husband.

    Children:
      Thomas   B-Jul 28,1787 Ashford,CT. M-Zuba
                    Kirkland.
      Richard   B-Oct 6, 1790 Providence,RI. M-1810 to
                    Sally **Landers** (B-1790; Dau of Isaiah
                    and Therza [**Phelps**] **Landers**;
                    D-Sep 17,1843). D-Feb 23,1873. Both bur
                    East Side Cem, Afton,NY.
      Nehemiah   B-1793 Gloucester,RI.
      Amasa
      Celinda   B-1805. M-James **Rockell**.

Nathan BURLINGAME   140   Nathan BURLINGAME

OTHER INFORMATION: He lived, after the Revolution, in Ashford, in Killingly, Connecticut, in Foster, Rhode Island, in Sturbridge, Massachusetts, in Londonderry, Pennsylvania, and in Colesville, New York. He was allowed pension on his application executed Feb 12, 1833, then a resident of Bainbridge, New York. He was living in Windsor, New York in 1855.

Silas BURLINGAME   141   Silas BURLINGAME
 -. ----- Private   DAR Patriot Index

RESIDENT DATE: 1793 - 1829
TOWN: New Berlin
BIRTH DATE: May 20, 1739
BIRTH PLACE: Cranston, Rhode Island
FATHER: Moses **Burlingame**
MOTHER: Lydia **Baker**
DEATH DATE: Nov 5, 1829
DEATH PLACE: New Berlin, New York
CEMETERY:
LOCATION:

TOMBSTONE INSCRIPTION:

SERVICE: Served as a Sergeant in Captain Wall's Company of the Rhode Island Line, Aug 17, 1778, moving a short time later to New York State. He then served as Private in Captain Winne's Company, Colonel Cornelius Van Vehggten's Regiment of Albany County New York Militia.

FAMILY INFORMATION: Married in Cranston, Rhode Island, Nov 11, 1764 to Mehitable **Fisk**, a daughter of Samuel and Mehitable (**Wheaton**) **Fisk**.

   Children:
   Josiah   B-Aug 19,1769 Coventry,RI. M-Apr 11,1788
              at Greenfield,NY Martha **Brewster**
              (B-Nov 29,1766 in Greenfield,NY;
              D-Apr 1805). M2-May 1807 New Berlin,NY
              Betsey **Allen** (B-Mar 11,1790 Bowerstown,
              Otsego Co,NY; D-Branch,MI.).
              D-Mar 8,1837 at Branch,MI.
   Caleb   M-Matilda **Salisbury**.
   Lydia   M-Joel **Bancroft**.

Nathan BURLINGAME   140   Nathan BURLINGAME

Daniel (Rev) B-May 11,1773. In RI. M-1799 Elizabeth
            Ludlow **Holmes** (B-Mar 25,1782; Dau of
            Jedediah and __ **Holmes**; D-Sep 19,1865).
            D-May 10,1824. Bur Holmesville Cem,
            New Berlin,NY.

OTHER INFORMATION: He left home at the age of fifteen and followed the seas for fifteen years. About 1793 he removed from Providence, Rhode Island to Ambler Settlement, a hamlet of New Berlin, Chenango County, New York and settled on lots #76 & #77. He was among the first settlers there.

Jeremiah BURLINGHAM   142   Jeremiah BURLINGHAM
- ----- Private   DAR Patriot Index

RESIDENT DATE: 1826
TOWN: Norwich
BIRTH DATE: Feb 19, 1753
BIRTH PLACE:
FATHER:
MOTHER:
DEATH DATE: Sep 15, 1826
DEATH PLACE:
CEMETERY: Evergreen (White Store)
LOCATION: Norwich, New York

TOMBSTONE INSCRIPTION:
            Jeremiah Bur-   Mrs Leah
            ligham died Sept   wife of Jeremiah
            15th 1826 AE   Burlingham died
            73 years 6m &   Nov 5th 1817 in the
            26 days   68th year of
far beyond the pregnant sky   her age
there the hopes of masons lye
masons happy choice above
masons blury blesing prove
friendship harmony & love

SERVICE: A Private from Connecticut.

FAMILY INFORMATION: Married Leah **Ide**, a daughter of Nicholas and Rachel (**Day**) **Ide**. She was born Mar 14, 1748 in Attleboro, Bristol County, Massachusetts and died Nov 5, 1817. She is buried with her husband.
    Children: ?

OTHER INFORMATION:

Blackleach   BURRITT   143   Blackleach   BURRITT
- ----- preacher   DAR Patriot Index

RESIDENT DATE:
TOWN: Sherburne
BIRTH DATE: 1740
BIRTH PLACE: Stratford, Connecticut (Fairfield Co)
FATHER: Peleg **Burritt** Jr
MOTHER: Elizabeth **Blackleach**
DEATH DATE: Aug 27, 1794
DEATH PLACE: Winhall, Vermont
CEMETERY: secluded spot on the eastern slope of
LOCATION: the Green Mountains in an unmarked grave.

TOMBSTONE INSCRIPTION:

SERVICE: He was the noted patriot preacher, who suffered imprisonment in the notorious Sugar House at New York, as the penalty for his zeal, ability and courage during the perilous days of the Revolution. He was nursed by the father of Washington Irving.

FAMILY INFORMATION: Married 1765 to Martha **Welles** of Stratford, Connecticut, a daughter of Gideon **Welles**. She died in 1786. He married second Deborah **Wells**.

Children:
  Eunice   B-1766. M-_____ Golden. M2____ Hopkins.
  Melissa   B-Feb 26,1768. M-James **Raymond**.
  Martha (Patsy) B-Oct,1770. M-Elisha **Gray**
             (B-Sep 24,1765 at Dover,NY; son of
             Nathaniel and Deborah [**Lathrop**] **Gray**;
             D-1823 at Talmadge, Summit Co, OH).
             D-Jun,1851 at Madison, OH.
  Sarah   B-Jan 29,1772. M-Gurdon **Wells** (B-1757 at
             Stratford, Ct; D-Dec 27,1827 Lincklaen,
             NY). D-Oct 31,1831 at Lincklaen,NY. Bur
             Woodlawn Cem, Lincklaen,NY.
  Eli   B-Mar 12,1773. M-Mabel **Stratton**.
  Gideon   B-Sep 15,1774. D-killed over aged 80.
  Diantha   B-Jan 09,1776. M-May 26,1793 Winhall,VT to
             John **Gray** Jr. (B-Dec 15,1769 in Cannan,
             NY; Son of Rev War Vet John and Betsey
             [**Skeel**] **Gray**; D-Apr 24,1859 at
             Forestville,NY). Both bur Sheridan
             Center Cem, Sheridan,NY.
  Rufus   B-1777.
  Blackleach B-Oct 27,1779 Upper White Hills,CT.
             M-Nov 1,1802 Upper White Hills, CT to
             Sarah **Hubbell** (B-1779; Dau of John and
             Sarah [**Curtis**] **Hubbell**; D-Oct 1,1870).
             D-Oct 1,1830 Clifford,PA.

Blackleach BURRITT   143   Blackleach BURRITT

Prudence   B-Nov 02,1782. M-James Welles (B-1781,
            D-1848). D-1852.
Samuel   B-Mar --,1784.
Susannah   B-Mar 05,1785. M-first ___ Fowler.
            M2-___ Adams.
second wife
Selah   B-1792. D-Nov 19,1810 at Sherburne,NY. Bur
            Quarter Cem, Sherburne,NY.
Deborah   M-Milo **Hatch** (B-Mar 25,1794 Sherburne,NY;
            Son of Joel and Ruth [**Gray**] **Hatch**;
            D-Aug 5,1830 Baltimore,MD). D-Oct,1854.

OTHER INFORMATION: Preached the first sermon at Mad Brook Mill, Sherburne, New York. He had been the pastor of the little flock while they tarried at Duanesburg, had come on to view the land, and to see how his neighbors and kindred (three of his daughters married three of the pioneers) were prospering in their new homes. He was a graduate of Yale.

Hubbard **BURROWS**   144   Hubbard **BURROWS**
    W. 25316 Private

RESIDENT DATE:
TOWN: Coventry
BIRTH DATE: Mar 24, 1763
BIRTH PLACE: Groton, Connecticut
FATHER: Hubbard **Burrows** (killed in the battle
MOTHER: Priscilla **Baldwin**   at Fort Griswold)
DEATH DATE: Aug 13, 1832
DEATH PLACE: Erie County, Pennsylvania
CEMETERY: Erie City
LOCATION: Erie, Pennsylvania (Erie County)

TOMBSTONE INSCRIPTION: (Office at Erie City Cemetery checked. They did not have a record of his burial)-----
                    Mary
                   Wife of
               Hubbard Burrows
                Hero of 1776.
                    Died
                Feb. 6, 1833,
               Aged 83 y'rs.
              6 mo's. & 3 da.

Hubbard BURROWS   144   Hubbard BURROWS

SERVICE: He enlisted in March or April, 1781, at New London, Connecticut for a term of three years. He was in the Fourth Company of Captain Joseph Williams, Colonel Samuel B Webb's Third Regiment of the Connecticut Line, and was discharged in New York City on Jan 4, 1784.

FAMILY INFORMATION: He married Feb 25, 1790 at Guilford, Vermont to Mary **Wilkins**. She was born Aug 3, 1769, died Feb 6, 1853 and is buried in the Oakwood cemetery, Stilesville, Delaware County, New York. Second wife Rebecca _____. She was born in 1789.

Children:
- Sarah   B-Sep 06,1790 at Guilford,Vt. M-Daniel **Stiles** (B-Apr 11,1787; Son of Aaron and Catherine [**Conklin**] **Stiles**; D-Apr 12,1848 Delaware Co,NY). D-Jul 9,1865 at Deposit, Delaware Co,NY.
- Hubbard   B-1791 in Guilford,Vt.. M-Hannah **Briggs** (B-1796; Dau of Randall and Lydia [--] **Briggs**; D-Dec 16,1873). D-Feb 22,1845 Stilesville,NY. Both bur Oakwood Cem, Stilesville,NY.
- Priscilla S B-Apr 26,1796 Greene,NY. M-Jun,1811 to Ashbel **Stiles** (B-Sep 6,1792 Newark,NJ; Son of Aaron and Catherine [**Conklin**] **Stiles**; D-Nov 6,1852 at Athens, Calhoun Co,Mi).
- John B   B-Oct 14,1800 in Tompkins, Delaware Co,NY. M-Hannah **Cook** (B-Oct 20,1805 New York; D-Jan 16,1874). D-Jul 6,1858. Both bur Oakwood Cem, Stilesville,NY.
- Henry   B-Feb 04, 1808 in Deposit, NY. M-Cynthia **Smith** (B-Apr 20,1811 Cortland Co,NY; Dau of James **Smith**; D-Mar 6,1877). D-Feb 5,1890. Both bur Pine Grove Cem, Deposit,NY.

second wife
- Oliver H   B-1814.
- Percilla S B-1818.

OTHER INFORMATION: He moved from Guilford, Vermont to Coventry, New York; then to Tompkins, New York. About 1809 he moved to Athens, New York, then went to Erie County, Pennsylvania and never returned to his family. He applied for pension on an application dated Feb 10, 1820 while a resident of Mill Creek Township, Erie County, Pennsylvania. His widow applied Feb 21, 1849 while residing in Tompkins, New York.

Nathan BURROWS   145   **Nathan BURROWS**
-. ----- Private   DAR Patriot Index

RESIDENT DATE:	- 1808
TOWN:	Coventry
BIRTH DATE:	May 17, 1744
BIRTH PLACE:	Groton, Connecticut
FATHER:	John **Burrows**
MOTHER:	Desire **Packer**
DEATH DATE:	Aug 18, 1808
DEATH PLACE:	
CEMETERY:	Wylie
LOCATION:	Coventry, New York

TOMBSTONE INSCRIPTION: Here lies Nathan Burrows died Aug 19th 1808 ae 64

SERVICE: Served in the Connecticut troops.

FAMILY INFORMATION: Married first Jun 2, 1765 in New London Connecticut to Amy **Williams**, a daughter of Nathaniel and Amie (**Hewitt**) **Williams**. She was born Jan 14, 1746 in Stonington, Connecticut. Married second in 1788 to Sarah Williams. She died on May 1, 1820.

Children:
Joseph	B-Jul 18,1765 Stonington,CT. M-3 times. D-Nov 28,1850.
Waity	B-1767. M-Lathan **Fitch** (D-1808). D-1863.
George	B-1769. M-Sarah **Fitch**.
Betsey	B-1771. M-Benjamin **Ashley** (maybe **Ashby**).
Amy	B-1773. M-Warren **Parker**.
Abigail	B-1775. M-Samuel **Rathborn**.
James	B-1777. M-Polly **Brown**. D-Dec 25,1811.
Nancy	B-1779. M-Beriah **Grant**.
Experience	B-1781. M-Jan 1,1806 John **Woodward**.
Lydia	B-1783.
Desire	B-1787. D-Feb 19,1808. Bur Wylie Cem, Coventry,NY.
second wife	
Benjamin	B-Oct 20,1789. D-Mar 27,1876.
Jesse	B-1791. M-Nancy _____. M-Mariett _____ B-1803; D-Apr 21,1852. Bur Upper Page Brook Cem, Greene,NY.
Nathan	B-1793.
Betsey	B-1795.

| Nathan BURROWS | 145 | Nathan BURROWS |

Simeon   B-1798 Groton,NY. M-Nancy Ann **Elliott**
         (B-Jan 13,1800 Greene,NY; Dau of Joab
         and Nancy [**Kendrick**] Elliott;
         D-Oct 27,1884 Greene,NY).D-May 2,1873.
         Both Bur Upper Page Brook Cem, Greene,
         NY.
Edward   B-Jun,1806.

OTHER INFORMATION:

| Charles BURZETT | 146 | Charles BURZETT |
S. 44356 Private

RESIDENT DATE: 1818
TOWN: German
BIRTH DATE: 1762
BIRTH PLACE:
FATHER:
MOTHER:
DEATH DATE:
DEATH PLACE:
CEMETERY:
LOCATION:

TOMBSTONE INSCRIPTION:

SERVICE: He enlisted in the summer of 1775 at a fort on the Kennebeck River in the "Province of Maine" and served as Private in Captain Dearborn's Company, was taken prisoner in the Battle of Quebec, later exchanged, joined his Company and was in the Battle of Saratoga; he then enlisted in Danbury, Connecticut and served as Private in Captain John Webb's and Elijah Wadsworth's Companies, Colonel Elisha Sheldon's Second Continental Dragoons to the close of the war, was in the battles of Poundridge, King's Bridge and Tarrytown.

FAMILY INFORMATION: Married to Eunice _____. She was born in 1757.

   Children: ?

OTHER INFORMATION: Was allowed pension which was issued Apr 15, 1819. In 1818 he lived in German, Chenango County, New York.

Abial BUSH   147   Abial BUSH

RESIDENT DATE: 1806/09
TOWN: Oxford
BIRTH DATE: Aug 27, 1739
BIRTH PLACE: Enfield, Connecticut (Hartford County)
FATHER: Joshua **Bush**
MOTHER: Experience **French**
DEATH DATE:
DEATH PLACE:
CEMETERY:
LOCATION:

TOMBSTONE INSCRIPTION:

SERVICE: Served in the war of the Revolution from 1775 to 1779.

FAMILY INFORMATION: Married Patience _____ .

Children:
  Abial   B-1775 in CT. M-Roxilena _____ (B-1778;
            D-Feb 10,1839). D-Jun 18,1855. Both bur
            Ives Settlement Cem., Guilford,NY.
  Ozias   B-Feb 06,1780 Enfield,CT. M-Clarissa **Ives**
            (B-1780; D-1842). D-1870. Both bur Ives
            Settlement Cem, Guilford,NY.

OTHER INFORMATION:

Charles BUSH   148   Charles BUSH

RESIDENT DATE: 1784 - 1810
TOWN: Bainbridge
BIRTH DATE: BP-Nov 7, 1766
BIRTH PLACE: Sheffield, Massachusetts (Berkshire Co)
FATHER: Elnathan **Bush**
MOTHER: Vashti **Stebbins**
DEATH DATE: 1812 +
DEATH PLACE: Batavia, New York (Genesee County)
CEMETERY:
LOCATION:

TOMBSTONE INSCRIPTION:

SERVICE: The History of Chenango County describes Charles as having served during the entire period of the Revolutionary War's continuance.

Charles BUSH   148   Charles BUSH

FAMILY INFORMATION: Married in 1794 to Joan Brown **Harrington**, a daughter of Mary **Harrington**. She was born Nov 16, 1771 in Canterbury, Windham County, Connecticut. This was the first marriage contracted in the town.

Children: ?

OTHER INFORMATION: He came to Afton with his father and family in 1784. He lived with his mother on the homestead until his removal, about 1810, to Vincennes, Indiana. He died at Batavia while on his way to Bainbridge on a visit, soon after the close of the War of 1812.

Elnathan BUSH   149   Elnathan BUSH
-. ----- patriotic Service

RESIDENT DATE: 1784 - 1791
TOWN: Bainbridge
BIRTH DATE: 1728 (BP-Mar 8, 1730)
BIRTH PLACE: Westfield, Massachusetts (Hampden Co)
FATHER: Jophet **Bush**
MOTHER: Orphah
DEATH DATE: *May 15, 1791
DEATH PLACE: Bainbridge, New York
CEMETERY: Bush
LOCATION: Bainbridge, New York
               *First death in the town.

TOMBSTONE INSCRIPTION:
              In   In
         Memory of   Memory of
       Elnathan Bush   Vashti
         Who died   Wife of
       May 15th 1791   Elnathan Bush
      Aged 63 years   Who died
 (with Rev War plaque + flag)   Nov 8th 1813
                                           Aged 81 years

SERVICE:

FAMILY INFORMATION: Married May 18, 1760 at Springfield, Hampden, Massachusetts to Vashti **Stebbins** a daughter of Benjamin and Mary (**Day**) **Stebbins**. She was baptized Aug 13, 1732 in Springfield, Massachusetts, died Nov 8, 1813 and is buried with her husband.

| Elnathan | BUSH | 149 | Elnathan BUSH |

Children:
- Charles   BP-Nov 07,1766 Sheffield,MA. M-1794 (first in the town) to Joan **Harrington**. D-Batavia,NY, while traveling from his home in Vincennes,IN.
- Japhet   BP-Dec 02,1761 Sheffield,MA. M-_____. D-Vincennes,IN.
- Joseph   BP-Feb 03,1769 Sheffield,MA. M-1795 to Susan **Weeks** (B-1775; D-Dec 29,1797). M2-Apr 5,1799 to Betsey **Strong** (B-1780; Dau of Jabin **Strong**; D-Feb 5,1853). D-Sep 23,1851. Both bur Bush Cem, Bainbridge,NY.
- Polly   M-Gideon **Freeborn**. D-at Caneadea,NY.

OTHER INFORMATION: The first settlement upon the tract granted to the Vermont sufferers, and, so far as the information extends, in the original County of Chenango, was made near Bettsburgh, in the present town of Afton, 1784, by Elnathan Bush, who came from Sheffield, Mass., where for eighteen years, he held under the King the office of sheriff, which, his sympathies being with the Americans, he resigned at the opening of the Revolutionary War, in which his son Charles served during the whole period of its continuance. They came as far as Cooperstown on horseback, and thence by canoe down the Susquehanna, leaving Cooperstown on the second of May. After visiting the locality with a view to settlement before the Revolutionary War, he first settled on the west side of the river, opposite Stowel's Island, about two miles below Afton.

| Jonathan | BUSH | 150 | Jonathan BUSH |

-. ------ Sergeant   DAR Patriot Index

RESIDENT DATE: - 1816
TOWN: Oxford - Guilford
BIRTH DATE: Mar 2, 1747
BIRTH PLACE: Enfield , Connecticut
FATHER: Joshua **Bush**
MOTHER: Experience **French**
DEATH DATE: Feb 23, 1816
DEATH PLACE: Guilford, New York
CEMETERY: Ives Settlement
LOCATION: Guilford, New York

Jonathan BUSH   150   Jonathan BUSH

TOMBSTONE INSCRIPTION:
Jonathan Bush
Died
Feb 23, 1816,
Aged 69 yrs

Patience
Wife of
Jonathan Bush
Died
Jan 12 1828,
Aged 77 yrs.

SERVICE: Served as a Sergeant in Connecticut under Captain Thomas Abbe in the attachment of Minute Men which left Enfield to fight at Concord Bridge.

FAMILY INFORMATION: Married 1768 to Patience **Killum**, a daughter of Lot and Jemima **Killum**. She was born in 1751 and died Jan 12, 1828. She is buried with her husband.

Children:
Ruth   B-1769. M-Thomas **Abbe** (Son of Capt. Thomas **Abbe**).
Edith   B-1771.
Jonathan   B-1773.
Ozias   B-Feb 6,1780 in Enfield,CT. M-Fanny **Trask** (B-1782; Widow of Simon **Trask**; D-Jul 4,1865).
Tabitha   B-1782. D-Sep 30,1805. Bur Ives Settlement Cem, Guilford,NY.
Luther   B-1784.
William   B-1787.
Joshua   B-Dec 9,1789. M-1812 to Louisa **Ingersoll** (B-Jun 6, 1792; Dau of Oliver and Hannah [**Burghardt**] **Ingersoll**; D-Mar 17,1869). D-Sep 12,1883 at Columbus,PA.

OTHER INFORMATION: Was an innkeeper. He lived on Merchant street and owned considerable land in the village. Washington Park was once a cornfield owned by his son.

Allen BUTLER   151   Allen BUTLER
        S. 12398 Private   DAR Patriot Index

RESIDENT DATE: - 1819
TOWN: Greene
BIRTH DATE: Apr 14, 1754
BIRTH PLACE: Westerly, Rhode Island
FATHER:
MOTHER:
DEATH DATE: Feb, 1839
DEATH PLACE: Bath, New York   (Steuben County)

Allen BUTLER   151   Allen BUTLER

CEMETERY:
LOCATION:

TOMBSTONE INSCRIPTION:

SERVICE: While living with his parents he enlisted at Wilbraham, Massachusetts in the fall of 1776 and served three months as a Private in Captain Daniel Caldwell's Company, Colonel Shepard's Massachusetts Regiment. He enlisted in the fall of 1780, served three months in Captain Abel Keep's Company, Colonel Moseley's Massachusetts Regiment. Marched to Schoharie under Sir John Johnson and Colonel Butlero to check the ravages of the Indians.

FAMILY INFORMATION: He married Nov 5, 1774 at Wilbraham, Hampden County, Massachusetts to Elizabeth **Dunham**. Was still living in 1832.

Children:
(female)   B-
Allen   B-May 18,1785 Sandisfield,MA. Resided in
            Steuben Co,NY in 1851.
Ira   B-Aug 30,1787 Sandisfield,MA.
Asa   B-Jan 30,1790 Sandisfield,MA.

OTHER INFORMATION: At age five moved to Stafford, Connecticut and at age twelve moved to Monson, Massachusetts for a short while; then to Wilbraham, Massachusetts and lived there seven to eight years after his service; then moved to Sandisfield, Massachusetts; then to Greene, Chenango County, New York; then to Bath, Steuben County, New York. He applied for pension on an application dated Oct 16, 1833 while a resident of Bath, Steuben County, New York. He was elected assessor in the first Greene town meeting in 1798.

Elias BUTTON   152   Elias BUTTON
     S. 44711 Sergeant   DAR Patriot Index

RESIDENT DATE: 1802 -
TOWN: Pharsalia
BIRTH DATE: May 18, 1748
BIRTH PLACE:
FATHER: Daniel **Button**
MOTHER: Elizabeth **Palmeter**
DEATH DATE: 1830
DEATH PLACE:

Elias BUTTON   152   Elias BUTTON

OTHER INFORMATION: He was allowed a pension on his application executed May 15, 1818, at which time he was residing in Chenango County, New York. In 1821 he was residing in Pharsalia, New York.

Joseph BUTTON   153   Joseph BUTTON
       S. 9638 Private

RESIDENT DATE: 1823
TOWN: Columbus
BIRTH DATE: 1760
BIRTH PLACE: Hopkinton, Rhode Island
FATHER: Daniel **Button**
MOTHER: Elizabeth **Palmeter**
DEATH DATE: 1845
DEATH PLACE:
CEMETERY:
LOCATION:

TOMBSTONE INSCRIPTION:

SERVICE: belonged to the Company commanded by Captain Benjamin West or Welsh in the Regiment commanded by Colonel John Topham's Regiment of Rhode Island troops.

FAMILY INFORMATION: Married 1789 in Hopkinton, Washington County, Rhode Island to Eunice **Louise**.

Children:
- Henry   B-Sep 2,1790 at Hopkinton,RI. M-Oct 1,1811 at Franklin Co,MA to Sally **Fletcher** (B-Apr 17,1794 at Franklin Co,MA; dau of John and Silence [**Curtice**] **Fletcher**; D-Dec 24,1836 at Columbus,NY; Bur Welch Cem, Columbus,NY). M2-Oct 1,1837 at Columbus,NY to Rachel **Fletcher** (B-Apr 10,1804 at Franklin Co,MA; dau of John and Silence [**Curtice**] **Fletcher**; D-Aug 27,1885 at Brooklyn,NY). D-Jun 9,1848 at Springfield,PA.
- Loesa   B-1792 Hopkinton,RI. M-_____.
- James   B-1794 Hopkinton,RI. M-Polly **Burdick**.

OTHER INFORMATION: He lost a leg in the service. He belonged to the Shaker-Quaker denomination and often danced to show his religious zeal. On Oct 15, 1823 he applied for pension while a resident of Columbus,

Elias **BUTTON**   152   Elias **BUTTON**

CEMETERY:
LOCATION:

TOMBSTONE INSCRIPTION: (Wife stone not found)

SERVICE: Enlisted at Enfield, Connecticut, about May 1, 1775, served eight months as Private in Captain Hezekiah Parsons' Company, Colonel Pitkin's Connecticut Regiment, was in the battle of Bunker Hill and in several skirmishes in that vicinity; he enlisted in Springfield, Massachusetts, in March, 1776, served as a Private in Captain Enoch Chapin's Company, Colonel Elisha Porter's Massachusetts Regiment, marched to Quebec and was in several skirmishes there and in Montreal, returning to the United States, was in the battle of Springfield, New Jersey and was discharged in that state. In November 1777, he was appointed Sergeant over the guard at Enfield, Connecticut, also had charge of General Prescott's Guard and served over five months. He also served on a number of short tours, at various places, dates and names of officers not given.

FAMILY INFORMATION: Married on Nov 25, 1777 to Sarah **Bleuet** at Enfield, Hartford County, Connecticut. She was born on Feb 1, 1763 a daughter of Guinnet **Bleuet** and Abigail **Prior** and died Mar 17, 1834 at Pharsalia, New York. She is buried in the East Pharsalia cemetery, Pharsalia, New York.

Children:
  Elias   B-Dec 04,1778 Enfield,CT.
  Bleuet   B-Mar 02,1781 Enfield,CT. M-Betsey _____
            (B-1805, D-Jun 11,1888).
  Gwinnett B-Oct 14,1783 Enfield,CT. M-Nancy **Baker**
            (B-1789 in CT). D-Nov 1,1854.
  Sally   B-Jun 26,1786 Enfield,CT.
  Roswell   B-1792 Enfield,CT. M-1818 to Abigail **Buck**.
            D-1859.
  Orrin   B-Jul 05,1795 Enfield,CT. M-_____.
  Alva   B-1796 Enfield,CT.
  Charles   B-1798 Enfield,CT.
  Grace   B-1801 Enfield,CT.
  Nancy   B-1807 Enfield,CT.
  Julius   B-May 17,1816 Enfield,CT.
      (one daughter married George **Champlin** - other
            Gideon **Thornton**)

Revolutionary War Vets Chenango County-NY 197

Joseph **BUTTON** 153 Joseph **BUTTON**

Chenango County, New York. On Apr 29, 1839 he had removed to Springville, Susquehanna County, Pennsylvania to reside with his sons and son-in-law. In the 1840 census he is shown in Springville, Pennsylvania with Abner Burdick.

Zebulon **BUTTON** 154 Zebulon **BUTTON**

RESIDENT DATE: 1810
TOWN: Coventry
BIRTH DATE: Apr 28, 1753
BIRTH PLACE: Stonington, Connecticut (New London Co)
FATHER: Zebulon **Button**
MOTHER: Sybil **Walbridge**
DEATH DATE:
DEATH PLACE:
CEMETERY:
LOCATION:

TOMBSTONE INSCRIPTION:

SERVICE: He served May 5, 1775 to Sep 21, 1775 and from Feb 27, 1776 to Jul 4, 1776 according to family genealogy.

FAMILY INFORMATION: Married _____.

  Children:
  John   B-1776 Stonington,CT. M-Sally **Sou**; Resided LaFayette,NY.
  Zebulon   B-1782 Stonington,CT. M-1806 Preston,CT. Olive **Cheney** (B-Dec 20,1786; Dau of Benjamin and Eunice [**Hubbard**] **Cheney**; D-Feb 25,1868 at Sangerfield,NY). D-May 17,1836 at Otisco,NY.
  (female) B-1785 Stonington,CT.
  William   B-1787.
  Charles   B-Jul 13,1789 at Susquehannah,NY. M-Mar 3,1812 at Chittenango,NY to Cynthia **Watson** (B-Nov, 26,1795).
  (female) B-1792 New London,CT.
  William   B-1802 New London,CT.

OTHER INFORMATION: He was in Coventry, Chenango County, New York at the 1810 census.

www.ingramcontent.com/pod-product-compliance
Lightning Source LLC
Chambersburg PA
CBHW060115170426
43198CB00010B/897